Social Policy from the Grassroots

Published in cooperation with
the United Nations Children's Fund
and the Center for Social Policy
and Planning in Developing Countries,
Columbia University

Social Policy from the Grassroots

Nongovernmental Organizations in Chile

EDITED BY
Charles Downs, Giorgio Solimano,
Carlos Vergara, and Luis Zúñiga
TRANSLATED BY
Paula Orr

Routledge
Taylor & Francis Group
LONDON AND NEW YORK

First published 1989 by Westview Press, Inc.

Published 2019 by Routledge
52 Vanderbilt Avenue, New York, NY 10017
2 Park Square, Milton Park, Abingdon, Oxon OX14 4RN

Routledge is an imprint of the Taylor & Francis Group, an informa business

Library of Congress Cataloging-in-Publication Data
Del macetero al potrero. English.
Social policy from the grassroots : nongovernmental organizations in Chile / edited by Charles Downs . . . [et al.].
p. cm.—(Westview special studies in social, political, and economic development)
Translation of: Del macetero al potrero.
ISBN 0-8133-7776-5
1. Chile—Social policy. 2. Non-governmental organizations—Chile. 3. Human services—Chile. I. Downs, Charles, 1950- . II. Title. III. Series.
HN297.D45 1989
361.6'1'0983—dc20

89-33742
CIP

ISBN 13: 978-0-367-28757-3 (hbk)

ISBN 13: 978-0-367-30303-7 (pbk)

Contents

Foreword

The United Nations Children's Fund (UNICEF) has traditionally maintained very fruitful relationships with non-governmental organizations. What we want to emphasize here is the significant role that these institutions play in designing and implementing programs to promote the development of children and women. This book is an analysis of non-governmental organizations and how they relate to social policies. The articles included here provide very important data that UNICEF will undoubtedly need to take into account in setting policies, particularly for Chile, where there has been a significant change in the context in which social policies operate, and the conditions found today are not the same as in the past.

Of the institutions of civil society—non-governmental organizations—in existence today, some are grassroots organizations with methods of operation based on the principles of workers' self-management, whereas others are institutions that provide scientific and technical skills as a means of increasing the social welfare of sectors of the population living in conditions of extreme poverty. The staff of these organizations at both the management and technical levels are generally people with academic training who are either already well-known for their achievements in universities or public service, or come from younger generations of professionals and intellectuals working in fields concerned with development problems. The volume of technical resources these organizations work with is as great as the tremendous moral commitment of their staffs and the solidarity they show with the worst-off sectors and those who are most vulnerable to the negative effects of the economic crisis.

What can these institutions of civil society offer in terms of social policies for children? The answer is, clearly, a great deal. We would argue moreover that the full scope of their potential is much greater than can be appreciated today, in the present situation of social fragmentation.

These institutions have, for example, drawn up proposals on how pre-school care could be extended in areas of critical poverty by involving mothers and young people, and on how to get local communities involved in primary health care; designed and trained local people to build low-cost, odorless latrines that prevent the spread of infectious diseases; found ways of making significant savings in the consumption of energy during food preparation; and they have in-depth knowledge of the practical problems involved in organizing income-generating projects within an economy of poverty.

There is no need to give further examples. We believe that in many cases these institutions are the starting point in a search for low-cost, effective solutions, based on participation and innovative methods, to the severe problems associated with poverty and in meeting the challenges presented by a social policy that has been adapted to the characteristics of today's situation.

This nascent civil society, which is seeking a role in social policy-making, represents a social capital of incalculable value. This capital must not be ignored in assessing the resources available for designing and carrying out social policies to benefit children. For this reason, the UNICEF Area Office for Argentina, Chile, and Uruguay has dedicated considerable efforts to supporting the present line of work.

The state, however, plays and will continue to play a central role in social policy; it has responsibilities that it cannot evade. The real problem is how to forge a link, particularly at the local level, between the work and contributions of non-governmental organizations and the state apparatus.

There is a great deal to do. This book seeks to make a contribution to the collective task by presenting a series of theoretical discussions and concrete experiences that share the perspective described—a perspective that must continue to underlie the United Nations Children's Fund's work.

I would also like to say how valuable an experience it has been for the UNICEF Office to work on this publication with the Center for Social Policy and Planning in Developing Countries at Columbia University in New York. Given that so little research has been done in this field, it is important that prestigious institutions and individuals who want to put themselves at the service of child survival and development in these countries should unite their efforts.

Within the framework and in the spirit of the United Nations Children's Fund's fortieth anniversary, we see this book as a very meaningful first step and are encouraged to continue our efforts to achieve a better quality of life for all children.

Paolo Basurto
UNICEF Representative for
Argentina, Chile, and Uruguay

Preface

The publication of this book coincides with the first anniversary of the creation of the Center for Social Policy and Planning in Developing Countries, which is part of the School of International and Public Affairs at Columbia University in New York.

The Center, which has both academic staff and students from diverse fields of study, was created for the purpose of contributing to the analysis of economic and social conditions of low-income sectors of the population in developing countries and to the responses that governments have made to the present situation of crisis. At the same time, the Center seeks to learn from projects being carried out at local and at national levels and to participate in defining feasible and innovative social policy approaches that not only take economic factors into account but also look at the cultural and political conditions of the communities in which these policies are to be introduced.

At present, the priority areas of concern for the Center are health and nutrition, and urban and regional development. We collaborate on these subjects with academic, non-governmental, governmental, and international institutions, making analyses of programs and policies, jointly carrying out applied research, arranging exchanges of students and academic staff, and holding seminars and conferences. We are also creating an information and documentation unit on social policies at Columbia University. This unit collects bibliographical materials and publications from different countries.

The aim of this book is to provide conceptual principles and empirical data for the analysis of and search for feasible and appropriate solutions to the many serious problems affecting children from the poorest sectors throughout the Americas. With this end in view, we have chosen to present a series of accounts of projects carried out by non-governmental organizations in Chile, whose work has taken place in the difficult and changing conditions of the past decade.

To a great extent, the same concern that led us to propose and produce this book was also the motivating influence in the creation of the Center and in our collaboration with national and international institutions working in the field of social policy in developing countries.

We refer here to the need to identify, understand in detail, and evaluate the new approaches found in the Americas. These approaches respond to present-day economic, social, and, in certain countries, political restrictions, as well as to the wealth of initiatives being generated within civil society that need to be coordinated with public agencies.

These initiatives involve at least three actors: the urban and rural communities, which are organizing in order to participate and find solutions to basic problems of survival; the intermediate organizations, which generally provide support and technical assistance and work directly with members of the community and grassroots organizations; and the state, an actor whose behavior is complex and variable and that generates social policies and programs. In the state we find a growing trend towards decentralization as a means of increasing efficiency, reducing bureaucracy, and bringing down costs. Thus local government becomes the focus of the debate on social policies.

Among the challenges implicit in this book are, first, the question of how and in what conditions these three actors can coordinate their work; second, what are the possibilities or limitations of the projects and programs being carried out by non-governmental organizations, and will these limitations affect the ability of non-governmental organizations to broaden their spheres of action; and third, the need to define the conceptual principles and methods of work that would enable these programs to make significant contributions in designing social policies in the region. Finally, a number of questions and hypotheses are put forward on which further research needs to be done; the Center for Social Policy and Planning in Developing Countries is ready to make an examination of these issues in conjunction with the United Nations Children's Fund and non-governmental organizations as soon as possible.

We publish this book convinced that taking non-governmental organizations' work "from micro to macro" will make a major contribution toward assuring that the children of our countries will have the opportunity to develop side by side in equality and in nations that offer them welfare and freedom.

Giorgio Solimano
Professor of Public Health and Director,
Center for Social Policy and Planning
in Developing Countries,
Columbia University, New York

1

The New Context of Social Policy in Chile and the Space for Non-Governmental Organizations

Carlos Vergara

United Nations Children's Fund (UNICEF)

This article examines one main question: why do we need to introduce the subject of non-governmental organizations into the discussion of social policies?

Traditionally, the subject of social policy has referred almost exclusively to the state's potential sphere of action. Latin American literature on this subject, particularly in the 1960s, abounds in analyses of the relationship between economic development and social development and the way that this is translated into practical measures by state action in the sphere of economic and social policy. As a result, the different social actors' strategies for producing and distributing wealth are concerned only with the problem of how to control the state apparatus.

This idea of the exclusive responsibility of the state for social policies is deeply rooted in the history of Latin America in this century, particularly in the second half of the century. Indeed, after the great crisis of 1929, the state began to play a progressively more important role in formulating and implementing social policies, and also in providing certain minimum levels of welfare for the population.

Getulio Vargas' regime in Brazil, the reforms introduced by Cárdenas in Mexico, and the election of the Popular Front in Chile are clear examples of the need to provide some protection for salaried workers, whose numbers and importance have been increasing. The idea that the state is the body responsible for social welfare has come to be increasingly widely accepted, especially in countries where the process of urbanization occured early on. The characteristics of the type of state responsible for providing social services emerged clearly in Chile, where programs with very broad coverage were implemented in the fields of public health, education, housing, and the social services in general.

Favorable external conditions, both economic and political, coinciding with periods of internal economic boom based on the success of import-substitution industrialization policies and on the high prices obtained for raw materials on the world markets, made it possible to finance costly social policies providing broad coverage. In turn, these policies generated complex technical and bureaucratic organizational structures within the state.

Thus, in Chile at least, this form of state, so often acclaimed as "developmentalist," became the main field of political struggle in a democracy where social pressures and political debate focused mainly on distributive policies. Chile had, therefore, a highly centralized state apparatus whose size increased continually. This state made all technical and political decisions on the distribution of products, was organized into complex technical bureaucracies based on a formal rationality, and was increasingly unable to respond to the particular needs and characteristics of regional, local, or neighborhood conditions.

In this sense, the tremendous social progress made by the state in the provision of services was not paralleled by the quality of the services offered, a result quite simply of the distance separating the common citizen from the levels of the state apparatus where decisions were made.

Changes of Context

As described briefly above, three fundamental features characterize the kind of state which provides social services: (1) adequate public revenues to finance costly social policies; (2) a democratic environment in which the political struggle over distributive policies is the main subject of debate and where efforts are focused principally on controlling the main state apparatus; and (3) the social distance between this centralized state and the common citizen. All this, of course, is in the context of a sustained policy designed to provide increasing satisfaction of the basic social needs of the population.

Towards the end of the 1960s, however, and particularly in the second half of the 1970s, the situation for setting social policies underwent a radical change, with the result that the reality of today is completely different.

Impoverishment

The benefits of the import-substitution model, in terms of its ability to maintain constant high growth rates, seemed to be exhausted by the end of the 1960s; at the same time, there was a progressive decline in terms of trade. The petroleum crisis set off a succession of economic crises which have continued up to the present, and which have hit the developing countries particularly hard, with negative effects on the living standards of major sectors of the population.

In the case of Chile, a few indicators serve to demonstrate the process of impoverishment which has affected all the countries of Latin America in different ways and to different degrees. Using guidelines for measuring poverty established by the United Nations Economic Commission for Latin America (ECLA), around 1970 roughly 15% of families were below the poverty line.[1] In 1983, about 30% of families were below the poverty line.[2] The rate of unemployment which had historically stood at about 6-8% reached a level of 30% in 1982, and has remained at a chronic level of about 20% throughout the past decade.[3] If 1970 is taken as the base 100, in 1984 the real salary index was 81.[4] Taking 1978 as the base 100, the minimum salary in 1984 was 65.

It is not our intention to burden this study with endless statistics. Our concern is rather to underline one idea: the economic crisis has brought a significant deterioration in the living standards of the population, affecting the poor most severely. Furthermore, it does not seem possible that the economy can recover sufficiently to restore indicators for employment, salaries and welfare to their former levels in the short term, regardless of the prevailing macro-economic policies, political systems, and ideologies. In other words, we are talking about a structural crisis with short-, medium-, and long-term effects, and not just a momentary crisis with only temporary or transient effects.

In social terms, therefore, the fundamental problems are employment and income, which raise the question of how to develop survival strategies for considerable sectors of the population. It should also be said that these problems exist in a situation where the mass of the population has access to social services provided by the state, particularly education and health services, which have brought significant improvements in the indicators of infant mortality and nutrition and ensured that universal coverage of education is maintained in the first grades of the school system.

The process of impoverishment is also being felt in state institutions. The low growth rates when the crisis was most acute, the fall in national income, the low prices paid on international markets for raw materials, and in particular the heavy burden of the need to service the foreign debt (approximately US$1,800 per capita), have severely restricted the state's freedom to make investments or use resources to finance social policies in a context in which there are growing social demands. Indeed, the state's tremendous efforts to maintain the level of social investment are being increasingly threatened by restrictions on the budget.

Administrative Decentralization in the Management of Social Policies

Over the past decade Chile has experienced a process of decentralization of the state's functions. The basic characteristic of this decentralization has been the transfer of certain traditionally centralized duties to local level management by the municipal councils. This reform in the administration of the state apparatus has of course caused polemics and controversy, which in turn have had repercussions on the wider political scene. We want to emphasize here, however, that social functions have in effect been passed down to the municipal council level, without discussion of specific aspects of the transferral.

Indeed, virtually the entire management of the school system, a significant proportion of pre-school care and primary health care, selection of beneficiaries to receive food subsidies and social benefits in general, investments in infrastructure, urbanization, environmental sanitation, and a whole range of activities associated with the quality of life, have now been incorporated into a municipal-level decision-making structure. Thus many of the demands on the central level of an anonymous, distant, and increasingly inaccessible state can now logically be directed to closer, more accessible, and familiar levels. The municipal councils have for their part had to create technical teams and decision-making structures, increased their budgets, and are taking day-to-day decisions on education, health, sanitation, etc., from positions much closer to the beneficiaries.

The Challenges of the New Context of Social Policy

In this context of spreading and deepening poverty, increasingly severe restrictions on the finances available for social investment, and locally-based decision-making structures, the mathematics of social policy used in the 1960s cannot offer satisfactory solutions. The problem of the cost of policies to be implemented thus becomes an issue of particular importance. It is clear, for example, that the provision of pre-school care cannot be significantly increased using the same elements as in the past; the ability to keep the numbers of people assisted by complementary food programs at the same level as a decade ago is coming increasingly under risk, and similar problems are emerging in virtually every sphere associated with the quality of life. As a result, in the face of growing demands, restrictions on the budget represent a serious threat to both the coverage and the quality of the services provided.

The first major challenge, therefore, is to find, through social policies which are inexpensive and at least as effective, if not more so, than traditional approaches, ways of ensuring increased coverage and improved attention. This will involve putting a great deal of scientific and technical know-how to work, carrying out serious and coordinated experimental activities, and making rigorous evaluations of these experiments.

In part for reasons of cost, but also and more importantly because of the level of social development of the grassroots organizations, community participation in managing social policy has become a crucial issue today. The main guarantee that social behavior which fosters child survival and development will be maintained is each family's own conviction that these measures are useful, along with the active involvement of the community in defending and developing all its abilities.

The design, elaboration, and dissemination of socially appropriate technologies which are also easy for poor families to use as strategies for survival is, moreover, a fundamentally important social need. These include technologies for generating income, oriented in particular towards women; technologies intended to bring about a significant reduction in the energy used to prepare food; technologies concerned with the design and creation of kitchen gardens to allow each family to cover its own dietary needs; technologies designed to recover land which is undergoing a process of rapid desertification and on which large numbers of families are living; technologies which will ultimately help to improve the quality of family life, in the context of severe restrictions on family budgets and unemployment that represent a serious threat to children's survival and development.

The search for simple measures, accessible to both families and communities, which are low-cost and have proven to be highly effective, is an essential task under the existing social conditions.

The Response of Non-Governmental Organizations

In the past ten or 15 years, Chilean society has seen the birth and development of a large number of private, non-governmental institutions whose work is based on the principles of development. There are considerable differences between these organizations in terms of size, issues of concern, levels of coverage provided, and geographical areas covered. They do, however, share a number of very important characteristics: (1) they work with groups of people living in conditions of critical poverty; (2) they use innovative methods of social work which emphasize community participation and the development of the beneficiaries' ability to resolve their problems autonomously; (3) many of their programs have proved to be very effective.

The technical and managerial positions in these institutions are fundamentally occupied by former academics, along with a new generation of professionals from fields associated with development. These employees have a moral commitment to improving the lot of the poorest sectors, particularly children, which is expressed by direct involvement with grassroots organizations and the application of scientific and technical knowledge to resolve the real problems that people living in poverty confront every day.

The institutions which concern us here are, characteristically, run by their own employees, who either seek to uncover and develop existing capabilities in those they serve in order to help them solve their own problems, or who have particular scientific and technical skills and whose main concern is to use these skills in overcoming the real problems of poor people. Presently, over a hundred institutions of this kind are engaged in designing and implementing social development policies. New institutions are continually being set up, and many new projects carried out.

Due to the characteristics of these institutions, however, their programs necessarily provide coverage on only a small scale. Along with their small scale of operations, these projects are often not properly evaluated, nor are their technical and operational contributions sufficiently publicized. Thus some non-governmental institutions are not aware of relevant and important achievements made by others, and these programs cannot be taken into account in developing further programs in the public sector.

These institutions form a fragmented set with little intercommunication, and without the necessary mechanisms for co-ordinating activities or for a satisfactory relationship with the public sector. The tremendous potential of these institutions to contribute to improving the welfare and quality of life of the poorest groups cannot be fully realized, since the transfer of activities onto a larger scale would only be possible through the state apparatus.

Furthermore, in the traditional setting of public policy, the state is not in a position to absorb the achievements and innovations introduced and validated by non-governmental institutions, when it implements its own social programs. When the decision-making functions of the state apparatus have been decentralized and local technical teams established, however, an ideal climate exists for relations between non-governmental development institutions and public sector bodies to flourish.

Indeed, given that these private institutions are characterized by their direct contact with people's real needs, their work on small-scale programs, and their ability to mobilize social resources within the community, either the municipal level or the sphere of local government would be an ideal arena in which to transfer technological achievements and broaden their scale of operations.

Mention has already been made of the advantages of non-governmental institutions in the technical fields, advantages which allow them more successfully to explore low-cost, highly effective measures in a wide variety of areas. Indeed, these institutions have considerably more experience than the public sector with making technical innovations in the sphere of low-cost social action, using appropriate technology, and encouraging the active participation of the community.

Finally, the existence of a variety of non-governmental institutions working in the field of social development makes it possible to talk of effective pluralism in the technical sphere, in social work, and in putting programs into action. Equally important is the fact that their presence opens up a broad area for the discussion of forms and styles of economic and social development, and ways of dealing with the problem of poverty.

The creation of intermediate institutions between citizens and state, the mobilization of local resources in the design and implementation of social policies, the decentralization of public policies, community participation, technical contributions made by non-governmental organizations to social programs, and the extention of scales of operation, are among the more important elements in the field of social policy today.

A fruitful relationship between grassroots communities, non-governmental institutions, and public sector organisms (fundamentally at the local level) demands that all these sectors go through a process of social education in order to learn how to respond adequately, each within its own sphere of action, to the challenges involved in overcoming poverty in Chile.

Notes

1. This is a reference to what has been termed "income poverty" as opposed to "capital resources poverty," and which is measured by variables other than that of occupation-income.

2. J. Rodriguez, "Magnitud de la Pobreza," *Distribución del Ingreso o Impacto del Gasto Social en Chile.* ILADES, September 1985.

3. Includes the minimum employment program (PEM) and the employment program for heads of household (POJH). Calculated using official figures.

4. Official statistics taken from the National Institute of Statistics.

2

Experiments in Community Education and Some Thoughts on How to Extend It on a Mass Scale

Patricio Cariola, S.J., and Alfredo Rojas

Center for Research and Development in Education (CIDE)

This chapter describes three experiments in community education carried out by the Center for Research and Development in Education (CIDE) in Chile, and then goes on to discuss the way that alternative social policies are designed and put into practice. We will identify those elements common to all three experiments, in order to indicate some of the conditions necessary to extend this methodological model, which has been developed out of local experiences, and incorporate it into a social policy. Given that these experiments cannot be extended without state policies to provide funding and create adequate administrative arrangements, also included are some thoughts on direct or indirect state action in the sphere of community education, and the policies that would be needed to implement a broad public model similar to the one proposed.

In addition, and given that one of the essential characteristics of these programs—apart from their involvement in resolving one or more of the problems found in low-income areas—is development and social organization in the search for and construction of an identity and autonomy for low-income groups as political actors, it is vital to give some thought to the relationship between these three experimental programs and the state.

This study is based on the work of a center for research and educational action which, having started virtually from scratch, has managed over the past 15 years to produce some 15 different programs now being used with varying degrees of success in several areas of the country. The results of this experience are reflected in the development of a particular approach to community education, strategies for introducing programs, and in the systematic production of descriptions, analyses, and investigations. The issue raised by this book has also been important in our discussions, and we have referred to it familiarly in the terms used in the title: how can we move from micro to macro, from flowerpot to field, or from the local to the national level?

What follows is, in part, a first attempt to respond to these questions. These initial answers, however, raise new questions, which can only really be answered once the move has been made effectively. Despite this, as we shall see throughout this chapter and in the conclusions, these experiences may serve to enrich the development of individuals, communities, and nations along the way from micro to macro, from flowerpot to field.

Three Programs in Community Education

First Program: "We're Living Together . . . What Now?"

This educational program focuses on family life.[1] Its objective is to increase and improve communication between couples in low-income areas, and to encourage more co-operative and equal relationships. The premise of this program is that problems of communication between husband and wife and the undervaluation of the woman's role causes a gradual and progressive deterioration in relationships and in family life. Through an active and participatory educational process involving groups of couples (in which there are moments of intense communication), situations are discussed, perceptions and ways of understanding are compared. Thus the partners learn to communicate better. With increased communication, changes in the relationship occur, and the atmosphere in the family improves.

The program brings together young couples from low-income areas who meet in small groups (local groups). With guidance from a monitor, the groups discuss particular problems in their families. The program continues for two periods (known as workshops) of six or seven sessions each. In each session, a climate for communication is created, so that the couples can begin to explore their problems using a methodology based on "starter subjects." There are manuals and guidelines for the monitors, along with simulation games and other materials to support the work. The monitors are couples, from the same socio-economic background as the participants, who have either been involved in a local group in the past, or in the pilot stages of the program.

This project was started in 1981. The first years were spent designing a program (content, methods, and materials) which was later tested in pilot projects. Once its definitive form was developed, the program was applied on a mass scale in four areas of Santiago, and subsequently in five provinces of the country. So far 311 workshops attended by 1,588 couples have been held; 187 couples have become monitors. More than 90% of the participants are under 30 years old and live in areas of poverty or extreme poverty.

The preparation and training of the monitors involve a further educational process, which becomes the central element in the strategy for disseminating the program. One of the first requirements for the program was that it should be easy to replicate and transfer to the community. For this reason, the monitors must be couples who have participated in one or more Workshops and who come from the same social background as the other participants. This training, which concentrates on communicating an active, participatory view of education and on the use of supplementary materials, enables the couples to go back into their communities and lead other workshops. This activity is unpaid; the monitors receive only enough money to cover transportation and any necessary materials. Some local monitors, who have sufficient free time and interest in the program, have gained enough experience to play a more important role, such as coordinating the work of CIDE's central technical team with the local monitors. This activity is paid.

The program's operational costs are relatively low. At present, the cost of training a couple as monitors is US$10, which begins to be repaid when the couple applies what they have learned to their work with other couples.

The rate at which the program has spread, the requests from other parishes for workshops, the number of couples involved as participants and monitors, and, most importantly, the opinions of the people who have participated in the workshops show that the program has undoubtedly had a growing impact and relevance in low-income sectors.

"We're living together . . . what now?" has made it possible to meet an extremely important need found in low-income sectors, that of communication between husband and wife. In the communications initiated by the program, one of the key issues that arises is that of sexual problems, which, according to the participants themselves, are often discussed for the first time in these meetings.

The workers who designed and introduced this program participated, up to 1980, in the Parents and Children Program (PCP).[2] Experience there suggested that many of the problems which children have at school could be dealt with much more easily if low-income families could discuss their problems "from the very moment that the family comes into existence, when the man and woman decide to live together as a couple."[3]

Second Program:
"Training for Unemployed Young People"

This training program is aimed at young people in low-income urban areas who, when they finish or leave school, cannot find work. For three months, the young people spend three hours a day, four days a week, being taught a trade by a skilled worker who lives in the community and comes from the same socio-economic background. The fifth day is spent discussing issues related to the young people's personal and social lives.

A fundamental aim of this program is to provide training for young people who would have difficulties in obtaining such training through the formal education system.[4] Another goal is the development of an alternative methodology for work with young people of this kind by creating flexible, low-cost training workshops which take advantage of resources available in the community (instructors and existing meeting places or workshops). The program is oriented to the demands of either the formal or informal sector of the economy and develops a methodology for training which combines learning technical skills with a process of personal and social growth.

As in the first program, the foundation of this work is monitors, in this case the skilled workers who are members of the community and who are trained by the project's central team. These instructors are paid and receive support, teaching materials, and advice on technical and educational issues. In order to start its work in low-income areas, the program established agreements with several institutions already engaged in support work in these sectors. These institutions—Fundación Obispo E. Chávez, Fundación Missio, Vicaría Zona Sur—are part of, or have links with, the Catholic and Evangelical Churches.

The program was started in 1980, immediately after a study of employment training revealed a lack of formal training institutions in urban, low-income areas. What courses did exist were inappropriate to the informal urban job market. This market normally holds the only possibility of work for young people from low-income areas.

Once the programs had been designed, the first stage was a pilot project involving five workshops. Then came a consolidation stage in which thirteen workshops were run in five different skills. This made it possible to define a working method and resolve the main methodological problems by 1981.

At present, about twenty-five workshops in fourteen different skills are held each month in Santiago and eight other cities; 2,349 young people of both sexes (an average of 20 participants in each workshop) have been involved in these, with 71.5% successfully completing their training. The average age of the participants has never been more than 24 years old; their per capita income has averaged less than 1,262 Chilean pesos per month (about US$6, in 1986). The cost of the whole training for each of the young people is approximately US$60.

A follow-up survey of the students who completed the course showed that, although the results were not spectacular, a significant proportion did obtain jobs or become self-employed workers. While only 2.8% were working before the course, when the follow-up survey was made 9.4% were working. Before the course 5% were self-employed workers; after it the level rose to 14.4%.[5]

The social aspect of this training was organized according to the participants' interests and using methods of community education. The follow-up showed that 44.2% of those completing the course became participants in some kind of social organization. Of the men, for example, 31% were members of sports clubs.

This second program has expanded rapidly, thus demonstrating a positive response from the target population. The program responds to a real need by offering unemployed young people the chance to learn a trade. That the trade is learned by "working" under the guidance of a skilled craftsman, who has also learned through practical experience, adds to the attraction of the program. The young people therefore have a real feeling of learning. Although the complementary social training uses other methods, the young people likewise express themselves and participate actively. In contrast to the frequent failures and frustrations which most young people experience in school, social relations, and often in their families as well, in the workshops they can rebuild their own identities and obtain some skills with which to find work.

Third Program: "Peasant Education"

This program is being carried out in 20 peasant communities in Osorno, in the south of Chile. The communities are made up of 30 to 60 families who live in extreme poverty. This poverty is due to a lack of land, and a scarcity of jobs.[6]

There are two main aims of this program. First, to carry out educational work associated with rural life and a local agricultural economy, in order to improve aspects of production (kitchen gardens, animal rearing, fruit trees, etc.) and thus assist the peasants to cope more effectively with economic difficulties. Second, to promote peasant organization. In the short range, this means encouraging concrete social activities in order to activate a sense of community which can be a resource that benefits all.

Coordinators, similar to monitors in the other programs, are trained to carry out the educational processes. Support materials have also been developed for use in back-up activities. The peasants are encouraged to participate in the activities of the radio station, "La Voz de la Costa," which belongs to the FREDER foundation and is linked to the Catholic Church.

The program is divided into seven subject units: (1) better organization for the community; (2) health in winter; (3) family and diet; (4) family and kitchen gardens; (5) trees; (6) animals and poultry; and (7) children and ourselves. These subjects are discussed in meetings held periodically in buildings used for community activities. To encourage the participants (men and women) to communicate and express their ideas, support materials—games or other activities designed to enable the group to talk about their experiences—are used.

Community activities are planned at the meetings, e.g. raising funds for the community medicine store or the children's Christmas party, and arrangements to participate in "La Voz de la Costa" are made. Practical activities for individual members of the community are also planned, e.g. explanations of how to make an organic kitchen garden (using "hot beds" or "raised beds"), how to start a plant nursery, or how to vaccinate animals.

A central team in Osorno has overall responsibility for the program. The activities, however, are organized by coordinators from the peasant communities. The aim is for the local coordinators to run the activities and become, along with the whole community, increasingly autonomous.

The coordinators are young (the average age is 24), and are usually unmarried men or women who have had between five and eight years of schooling. Despite their youth, they are generally respected by the peasants who participate in the meetings. As in the program for couples, this work is usually voluntary; the co-ordinators receive payment only for transportation and the materials they use.

Training the coordinators is a very important part of the program. It involves eight monthly workshops lasting three days each. During the training, topics in education, such as the use of active and participative methodologies, are examined; the subject areas and relevant materials are reviewed; working sessions in the community are dramatized; and the purpose of this work and experiences in carrying it out are discussed.

The peasant communities' initial acceptance of this program can be explained by the fact that the idea, the format, and the original team of workers developed out of a previous community program, the Parents and Children Program. The coordinators are, however, the principal reason why the program has taken root. On average, 16.2 people from each community participate in the program; in no case are less than 25% of the members of the community involved. In 1984, regular monthly meetings were held in 20 communities. Their accomplishments included training peasant leaders, recording programs for "La Voz de la Costa," fund-raising for various purposes, and improving family vegetable gardens.

Experience with a Methodology and Some Thoughts on How to Extend Its Use

Before putting forward any ideas on social policy for community education, we feel that we need to bring out some of the common elements found in this methodology, and the problems which might arise if it were introduced on a mass scale. The common elements are research activities, close contact with the community, links with support institutions, the problem of costs, role of the monitors, training of the monitors, program contents, and variety of objectives. We will discuss these issues individually.

Research Activities

Two of the three programs described, for couples and for peasant education, were designed to meet needs detected while carrying out the Parents and Children Program, itself based on national and international research on child development. The third program, training for unemployed young people, arose from a number of studies on this issue. The members of the team which initially drew up this program had had experience in carrying out programs in low-income areas, and shared an institutional outlook sensitive to the needs of these sectors.

In all these cases, research and the experiences of working in low-income areas are interrelated.[7] This relationship is due to the particular characteristics of CIDE as an institution where staff who have done post-graduate research (in Chile or abroad) meet and discuss issues with staff working in the field, so that they can work together to find solutions to problems arising in the course of different community education programs. This exchange also allows a cross-pollination between programs with roots in very varied educational approaches (e.g., Piaget, Rogers, Freire, "educational technology") and results in a methodological style that varies according to subject, type of people participating, and the particular approach of each team.

Thus, the first common characteristic of these programs is that each was both preceded and accompanied by a considerable period of research and discussion. Underlying these studies were a number of more or less explicit basic hypotheses related to the program's content and methodology, and to the results to be achieved at the personal and social levels. These hypotheses were tested and adapted according to the results obtained in the field, and to the theoretical and methodological ideas arising from discussions among members of the central team.

Essential to the institutional conditions needed to successfully introduce community education programs is a minimum space for research, where different academic disciplines can be brought together, guidelines set out, written accounts can be systematized and produced, and questions arising from practical work can be raised and answered. Experience has shown that the development and implementation of community education programs demands a basic level of research as well as an institutional environment not only of close collaboration but also flexible enough to adapt itself to the rhythm of the participants. These conditions are not normally found in public administration, where there is political pressure to produce immediate measures. Rather, a "cultural pace" is needed, to allow for the full cycle of discussion-action-discussion.

Another characteristic of all three programs is that the technical team works with the grassroots groups—who are represented by a monitor—only during the design phase. Once the program has been designed, it is repeated, adapted, or selected parts of it are used, depending on the interests of the group. There is no permanent contact between a professional and a particular group. The crucial "hand-over" to the groups is accomplished not by the professionals, but by the monitors.

Close Contact with the Community

In our experiences, we have not found any programs arising directly out of a spontaneous demand from the grassroots. The programs are rather a process in which the community is invited to participate, an idea which has to be "sold," an experience discussed in conversations, visits, demonstrations, and local celebrations. When the aim is to interest other institutions, the programs are explained in articles, documents, national or international meetings, and videos. These other institutions are basically local development agencies, trade union organizations, co-operatives, and funding agencies.

Cases have arisen, however, in which a grassroots organization seeks financial support on its own account and requests only occasional support from CIDE. This can be seen more clearly in rural areas where the community has already had some experience of community education, and contact with support institutions. This implies the presence of a team or "external agent" whose role in and relationship with the community gives rise to a theoretical and methodological debate which is beyond the scope of this article, but is fundamental in this process and in the situation of atomization and social fragmentation seen in Chile today.

A Colombian educator once said that "projects are not invented, they are discovered,"[8] suggesting by this that a project comes out of the correct identification of a need felt by the grassroots of society. In order to identify these needs, a very close involvement with poor sectors of the population is necessary. A central planning office can use indicators and indexes to identify the need, for example, to improve the diet of poor families, but to go from the identification of this need to drawing up a precise program to meet it (organizing and educating the community to improve dietary standards permanently and autonomously), requires a great deal more than a "macro" outlook and quantitative information. It is here that the external agents, who act as links between the needs of the community and the other resources available in society, assume their full importance.

Links with Local Community Support Institutions

A project is a proposal for action, and a community can accept or reject it, attend or stay away from meetings, respond to the invitation or not. Only an in-depth, qualitative understanding of and familiarity with the neighborhood will allow programs to be drawn up which take into account the diverse aspects of the situation, the range of motives and incentives required for community involvement, and other conditions necessary for a project to be successfully introduced. In our experience, social engineering is not sufficient to guarantee that the programs will succeed.

If the identification of a need demands familiarity with the area, this familiarity is still more important when it comes to introducing a program in the community. As our three experiences demonstrate, there is always someone, either an individual or an institution, in the area or community who acts as an intermediary, a bridge. Members of a technical team cannot just arrive at a house, propose an activity, and hope to get an enthusiastic response; an introduction must somehow first be made. This may come about through the Parents and Children Program, in areas where it has been working for several years; or through the parish priest; the organization "Fundación Missio;" the radio station "La Voz de la Costa;" or a community leader. The introduction must be by someone who can be relied on, and who in turn trusts the people who will carry out the program, knows that their work is good, that they are reliable, and, in the participants' own words, "they're not here for party political reasons."

The initial introduction of a program, when it is still in the experimental phase, requires constant communication between the team and the participants. A variety of contents and activities must be proposed, and reactions to them tested, until the program responds appropriately to the culture and interests of the participants. This implies the existence of a set of conditions for generalized social actions or community education programs. They must be highly decentralized, carried out from a position as close as possible to the community for which they are intended, and at the "cultural pace" necessary for working with individuals and institutions already established in the community.

A further condition derives from the fact that these programs must be adapted to the particular situation in each area. Those who create and carry out the programs should have sufficient freedom for ongoing consultations with the future beneficiaries in order to best adapt the design of an individual program or community education project to the needs of the community where it is to be implemented. Any attempt to extend programs on a broad scale should involve the participation of support institutions at the local level. This is a vital means of ensuring that there is an organic link with grassroots communities.

Many local institutions which provide support to low-income neighborhoods have incorporated community education methods. These institutions have developed an independent capacity for making diagnoses, programming, designing materials, and making evaluations. Albeit on a smaller scale, these support institutions are beginning to do almost the same work that CIDE is doing on a wider scale, by encouraging active, participative discussions within their teams of workers. These developments depend on the degree to which different institutions are colored by changes in their leadership, interests, and resources, as well as on whether or not educational activities are central to the institution's work. This ability to change, to make use of available capacities, may be very important in the attempt to extend a program on a broad scale while maintaining the same methodology.

Problems of Cost

In the programs for couples and for peasants, the majority of the monitors work on a voluntary basis, with only a few coordinators receiving wages. In general the monitors are young people who see these programs not as a kind of employment but rather as an opportunity to use their free time creatively, and to meet other people from their own and other communities. The unit costs of operation for community education programs tend to be lower than those of formal education.

This can be explained by the fact that these programs activate social forces which would otherwise remain dormant, or would operate only in strictly domestic or individual spheres. The programs appeal to solidarity, and they offer services. The forces which they activate have little exchange value in the marketplace, in the "modern" sectors of the economy, or in a world of buying, selling, and profits. These social forces, however, have use value, especially in terms of the practical and the symbolic knowledge (culture) without which communities could not have come into being.

Taking Howard Richards' approach,[9] it may be argued that the activation of these community resources is one of the most important benefits of the programs. The young monitors represent a human and cultural potential for which there is no outlet in the labor market. Because of the present economic crisis, as well as the model of industrialization which has been introduced in recent years, these young people have been marginalized. By working in these programs, however, they are able to express their creative capacities and talents.

The appeal to solidarity in the use of human resources and the infrastructure of the community is acceptable when it is made by organizations and institutions which have their roots in the community itself. But it is likely that this same appeal, if made by state agencies—which are generally more distant and impersonal—will meet with difficulties. For example, can the state, or any other public institution, train and use voluntary monitors? In principle the answer is yes; it has been possible in certain circumstances and through an appeal to deeply held social or political beliefs (for example, with voluntary literacy workers).

It is evident, however, that in other circumstances the state's use of unpaid teachers may be simply another means to avoid spending more resources on traditionally marginalized sectors, as well as a way to weaken the teachers' union, as in the case of the instructors used to give the Community Courses in Mexico. While this is a complex problem which has given rise to considerable debate, we believe that the degree to which the government gets involved or maintains its distance in poor communities, and the degree to which it puts the welfare of these communities before that of other social groups, is what will allow us to say where the employment of community resources is or is not legitimate. Of course, the communities' own decision on whether or not to participate in these programs is the ultimate determination of legitimacy.

Returning to the main subject of this discussion, the job training program is a different situation, since here the skilled workers who give the courses do receive payment. This allows for the socialization of trade skills which normally are either commercialized at a price well beyond what unemployed young people could pay, or taught in a skilled craftsperson-apprentice situation to which these young people do not have access. Thus, at a relatively low cost and through the use of community resources—the skilled craftspeople—marginalized young people can learn skills which would otherwise be beyond their reach.

One example of the activation of dormant social resources is the meeting places used for the community education programs. Buildings belonging to the parish or community are used, and only a small amount must be paid to cover rent and/or cleaning. Community education programs do not require great investments in infrastructure, or big budgets to cover the maintenance of premises. The programs use what is available, not only to reduce costs but also, very importantly, because this kind of education is generated by the community rather than passively received, as is the case in formal education.

Although operating costs are low, there are major initial expenses during the experimental stages of the programs. These kind of expenses can also arise during the implementation of the program, for reformulation, evaluation, and if the experience is to be described and shared with other researchers and/or centers. If these programs are not accompanied by some sort of ongoing input and exchange, they soon become sterile texts. For the programs to function people have to believe in them, and not only in their technical, economic, and administrative viability, but also in their content and social relevance.

The costs may be low in relation to the scale on which the programs are carried out, but program size depends not only on the funds available but also on the program's image and the interest it arouses among potential organizers and participants. These programs cannot be sold as uniform packages, nor can they be publicized using conventional commercial mechanisms.

From the perspective of most non-governmental organizations, the initial cost of designing, testing, and publicizing the program is part of the institutions' running costs. The major part of this cost is salaries. The unit value is set by the market, according to levels of qualification; a researcher working in an NGO will therefore not cost more than a researcher employed by a university or by the state. The specific characteristics of these institutions, and in particular their small size, which greatly reduces administrative costs, and their close contact with the community, allow research, design, and dissemination of programs to be directly transferred to poor areas, with little additional cost to them.

Because of their social position and very low incomes, as well as the present conditions of economic crisis, the beneficiaries of and participants in these programs can make virtually no material contribution to them. This means that such activities cannot be self-financing and that the NGOs working in community education need to seek external funding to maintain them. When it comes to extending them on a mass scale, however, part of the cost could be absorbed by the state. In this case the state, through its government and planning agencies at central, regional, or local levels, could define the subjects and geographic areas to be covered, resources to be invested, and minimum goals to be attained. Interested NGOs could make use of these resources, committing themselves to achieve the minimum goals, but at the same time reserving the right to use the methodologies best adapted to the conditions found in the community and add the organization's own institutional objectives.

Another method of funding could come from the organs of local power themselves, and their departments of social action and community education. In this case, it would be important for these agencies to coordinate their work with community institutions: churches, unions, parents' associations, neighborhood organizations, and others. A third approach might be to subsidize educational activities which are of interest to the state but carried out by community organizations. The state might, for example, support educational activities organized by unions, women's workshops run by women's organizations, or civic and political education provided by the political parties.

Any of these methods, alone or in combination, would ensure that the institutions involved were in close contact with low-income groups, would not raise administrative costs unnecessarily, and would avoid bureaucracy. In a situation with an improving economy and political freedom, the participants themselves would ideally be able to finance these activities themselves. Although these activities are on a "micro" scale, they are nevertheless of great cultural importance.

Role of the Monitors

The three programs described here have transformed members of the community into educators, organizers, and communicators. The monitors represent the link between the team which started the activity and the community which carries it on and takes control of it. The monitors are the key element in this transfer, and no one else makes such good use of the programs. Monitors are a resource and a potential that remains in the communities.

The supplementary materials are the vehicle for introducing the active-participative methodology, and the instrument that makes using it possible. Using supplementary materials allows the monitors to concentrate all their efforts on bringing the group to life. The process to be used is indicated in a "guide," and the materials are available to stimulate discussion.

In principle, a central team of experienced professionals first carry out research and identify a need. They then define certain basic contents, organize and design materials, outline support activities, and establish profiles and strategies for recruiting and training monitors. This preliminary work is perfected during the pilot stage, but the real change in the project comes when the monitors are incorporated into it.

The point when the latent social forces begin to be deployed—which Fals Borda has compared with the potential unleashed at the moment when the nucleus of an atom is split[10]—comes when the monitors start work. The most important task of both the monitors (volunteer) and the coordinators (who receive a small payment) is to organize the groups. It is here that their skills in facilitating participation are put to the test. The monitors become the project's educators, communicators, and organizers within the community or neighborhood. Their training, therefore, is extremely important.

Monitors' Training

The monitors represent the key to the success and extension of these programs, and their training is the central team's most important responsibility.

This training may take a variety of forms in terms of length and intensity, the way in which it is given, and the point in the program at which it occurs. What remains constant, however, is emphasis on experimentation, the dramatization of situations which are likely to arise, and the use of the same active-participative methodology as the monitors themselves will later use. This is in marked contrast with formal education, where future teachers are urged to use an active form of education while they themselves are kept in a passive position, and taught an educational theory which they have no opportunity to put into practice. We have found, moreover, that it is easier to teach a virtually illiterate peasant to use this methodology than it is to teach it to a professional teacher, who tends to repeat the same models used in his/her own training.

It has become increasingly clear that community education programs are useful tools for training. One of the most valuable aspects of the training is that it develops the human resources of the community, particularly women and young people, who are given the experience of effectively leading a group in a process of learning, becoming more organized, and communicating with other groups. Some monitors may later make contact with other institutions and get support to organize and train other monitors.

CIDE's programs have gradually evolved from training monitors to run specific programs to a broader training for community educators in order to help them deal with the different problems arising in their communities. The idea is to train people to respond to the challenges arising in daily life and in the production process. Members of the community are encouraged to participate, which transforms them into social actors who can identify and tackle the causes of their problems.

This experience has also led us to organize workshops on community education at different levels for social workers and other professionals. This is another way of sharing the new methodological approaches we have developed. The project on Systematization of Experiences in Community Education contributes to these workshops, providing information on experiences and ideas which have been developed, as well as very valuable subject matter for the training itself.[11]

Program Contents

These three programs have in common a sequence of processes and contents that have been crystallized in printed materials. This material is defined during the pilot or elaboration stage and produced in the relevant amounts when the program is extended. This means that the programs are in a sense "packaged," which would seem to contradict the methodological principles we have outlined. Our experience, however, has shown that it is impossible to respond individually to each group's rhythm of needs and interests.

What can be done is to offer various alternative programs, based on discussions with similar groups and presented as thematic units. In fact, the same topics tend to be requested, although the sequence in which they are done may vary. This can be seen clearly in the Peasant Education Program and in the social training units of the Program for Unemployed Young People. In the Program for Couples, the sequence is more important, and the program is therefore given as a whole.

The development of new programs and units obviously increases the opportunities for choice. One of the objectives of the Peasant Training Program is to create a "library of programs." The radio station announces the programs that are available, and the communities can request whichever is relevant to the problems they are facing at the time.

A similar role is played by CIDE's Central Materials Bank. Materials produced by CIDE and other centers are available there. Advice is given on which program, or what activities or materials would be best suited to the interests of the group.

The flexibility of the materials themselves is vital. They must be designed in such a way that the content of a program arises out of the group discussion. This enables the group to reach its own conclusions.

Variety of Objectives

Another characteristic of these programs is that, while each pursues different objectives in relation to very concrete problems, their aim and real effects go beyond the solution of these immediate problems.

The institutions, monitors, and groups each develop their own dynamic, which then produces effects going beyond those initially foreseen. The educational processes always involve more than just teaching; the methodological approach values the opinion of the participants, identification of a problem, and reaching an agreement on the actions necessary to alter the situation. This approach produces a notable change in cultural norms and tends to give rise to collective initiatives in other spheres; the objective is basically to generate new objectives. This is precisely where the socio-political potential of the methodology described can be found.

This demands a non-traditional evaluation of costs and benefits, since the most important effects are not those proposed by the program but are rather those achieved by the participants. In fact, the processes are more important than the results achieved. The overall success of the programs lies in their ability to adequately combine immediate objectives related to the resolution of concrete and urgent problems with broader objectives of a social nature. Without immediate goals and the activities that go with them, the meetings would hold no interest; without a broader impact, for which the methodology is the vehicle, the initial achievements would be socially insignificant.

Finally, given the possibility that this kind of methodology enables the groups to formulate their own objectives, a key question arises. In societies ridden by such deep inequalities, where the state cannot, or does not wish to, satisfy the demands and needs of the people, would that state be likely to finance programs which produce the kind of transformations that these programs do? The question of the relationship between the state and community education programs is at the heart of the considerations which follow.

Final Considerations

What might the state be seeking in designing a policy which involves support for non-governmental organizations engaged in social action and community education? At first sight, there are two obvious answers: to meet the needs of the population, or to increase the power and influence of the governing party. The third possibility, both more complex and more urgent, is that, in the light of the economic crisis and the generalized, growing impoverishment that it has produced, and taking into account the failed—or inconclusive—attempts at development made by different groups along the political spectrum (in Chile, at least), new ways of dealing with social and economic problems must continually be found.

The answer, of course, involves a combination of these three; the state seeks to meet general needs, increase its power, and look for alternatives for development. Thus the experiences described above and the suggestions made can be of use in the very form in which they are presented. In any case, we believe that it is worth exploring the meaning and tendencies that may be found in these activities, especially when the emphasis is on development alternatives.

The Sphere of Community Education

At present, projects in community education are being carried out in the non-governmental, private sphere. These projects are diverse activities, introduced individually, which makes it difficult to link them up with the state. In Latin America, local power has traditionally been developed as an administrative appendix of central power; the same occurs at the level of public services, where the state carries out national actions organized on the basis of organic laws, internal regulations, and uniform systems and procedures. The subjects of decentralization, regionalization, and the autonomy of local authorities have only very recently begun to be discussed in detail.

One of the key functions of education traditionally was to strengthen national unity.[12] To achieve this, a national education system was established. Furthermore, in order to provide equal opportunities, the state extended the educational services offered, and these became a principal factor in increasing social equality.

Later, influenced by ideas of modernization, an attempt was made to incorporate sectors of the population which had been left behind by modern society. This was done by means of employment, housing, and extending the coverage provided by the health services. Efforts were dedicated as well to changing behavior by means of social promotion.

All this did produce some results: education was popularized, services were expanded, there was a degree of industrialization, and the process of social mobility, which created the Latin American middle classes of today, was begun. None of this, however, led to far-reaching changes in society; differences and variations continued to exist. The peasants did not become a proletariat, as some theories had predicted; they either became marginalized city dwellers or remained peasants. The indigenous peoples were not integrated; they are still indigenous groups, and some defend their cultural identity more fiercely than before.[13]

Moreover, the crisis and the rapid changes in the technological conditions of production created "structural unemployment," which in Chile at one point affected 30% of the economically active population.[14] Modernization through the market deepened differences without preserving diversity, and brought further separations, divisions, and subdivisions. These differences are reflected in the existence of both formal and informal markets, peasant economies, and subsistence economies.

But is diversity necessarily synonymous with inequality? In one sense, yes. Those who are unequal—peasants, marginalized people, indigenous groups—are invariably the poor. In another sense, no—women's movements are not always an expression of deprivation. These groups, however, have common features: all are dominated, all demand emancipation, the opportunity to grow, and a sense of belonging.

Community education programs seek, at all times, to adopt the perspective of these groups. The work of community education may begin with concrete needs, opportunities for communication, and improvements in production, but its efforts do not end here. The community education that we have described is based on a concept of emancipation, the most important aspects of which are self-esteem and a re-valuing of one's own culture and community. The meeting of needs and improved production through self-organization are concerns of community education, but they are not its most distinguishing characteristic.

Community education provides a space for the initiatives of those who are different, whose potential has lain dormant, or who have been silenced. It leads to a way of understanding problems, and to the concrete experience of dealing with them by organizing. Community education encourages recognition of conflict, diversity of interests, and the need to fight for one's rights as well as to negotiate and find consensus.

This by no means implies that community education, as provided by non-governmental organizations, allows the state to evade its responsibility for providing schools, health centers, hospitals, or housing. Nor does community education replace technical assistance for peasants, materials for production, or loans; much less will it prevent people from demanding productive and well-paid jobs. On the contrary, it is possible that demands for jobs, housing, and schools will increase as a result of the increased awareness brought about by community education programs.

The Possibilities

We believe that the experience of community education opens a range of possibilities for making personal and social life richer and livelier. It also questions old methodologies and offers new methodological guides to actions and functions normally associated with the state, and gives public recognition to social activities based on private initiative.

In terms of personal and social growth, the suppression of party political activities and the drastic limits on union activities in Chile have led to a search for economically and/or ecologically more satisfactory ways of meeting basic needs. National and international resources have been sought to design and introduce approaches to these problems. The political value of these activities been recognized, in terms of both organization and cultural changes. The seeds of a more deeply-rooted, solid, humane, viable democracy can be seen here, although this may perhaps be a democracy that is built slowly.

Educational experiences of the kind described play a central role in this alternative world. They aim to produce not only a cultural but also a social change in families, schools, and rural and urban communities. Unions, for example, recover their role, but after the process of community education, they do more than hold negotiations and present demands.[15]

As far as the national services provided by the state are concerned (education, health, social security, technical assistance, loans for producers), these programs suggest new ways of taking control of, participating in, and "acculturating" them. Thus the bureaucracy, alienation, inefficiency, and inadequacy of state services is challenged. The challenge is even greater given that these services have had their budgets cut, or been commercialized or decentralized without creating opportunities for local participation. For at least the next ten to fifteen years, when there will be a shortage of foreign exchange and profound financial difficulties, the challenge will be crucial.

Some alternative approaches have already been incorporated by the public services or municipal authorities. Others remain unanswered challenges, or experiments in training (e.g. monitors), systematization, and discussion. These are alternatives waiting to see what opportunities the future may bring.

The activities of non-governmental agencies in Europe and North America have received public recognition and support in those countries. In Latin American countries, non-governmental community education institutions should also receive recognition and support for the important social contributions that they make. Here, "a specific aspect which should be appreciated is that through them a different relationship has been created between intellectuals and the community, which breaks down the stereotype both of the 'agitator' and the 'technocrat': these are not brilliant professionals who go out to poor areas to tell the people what they should do. But neither is the contribution of the educator, social worker, or technician denied. These programs seek to establish a collective process of defining problems and answers which is not technocratic but which demands science, skills and accumulated information."[16]

Some Questions and a Final Dream

There is no doubt that in this world of programs we have learnt a great deal, at all levels. But in the end, what do these programs respond to?

- The lack of other channels for political expression?
- The employment needs of professionals who have not obtained jobs in the state?
- The lack of concern by the state for sectors who are becoming increasingly impoverished?
- The offer of financial support from abroad?
- The apparent ending of the welfare state?
- The feeling among poor people who have had the doors to any kind of power, to any possibilities of expressing themselves, satisfying basic needs, identity and self-esteem, shut in their faces so many times, that these programs are a life-line, something they can cling to in order to survive?

If the answers to these questions, particularly the last one, were all affirmative, then once the "emergency" was over, the fate of this alternative world would be sealed. The opposite, however, may also occur. Once the political situation is stabilized, the economic crisis—

which remains deeply rooted—will still oblige non-governmental groups to continue their work, and make creativity in the private sphere essential. Alternatively, a new kind of state will come into being, one in which these programs will be valued as an essential element of society, related to democracy and to ecological and social health.

Whatever the future may bring, our dream is that these peasants and poor city dwellers who have been finding their feet will begin to say to each other, "We ourselves are responsible for this country. We are confident because we are learning to use the tools of victory, and we will ensure that all participate in this achievement."

If this happens, our work will be justified.

Notes

1. Iván Ortiz, "'Nos juntamos . . . Y?' Sistematización de un Programa Educativo de Convivencia Familiar." *Programas de Sistematización de Experiencias de Educación Popular.* CIDE-FLACSO, Santiago, 1985. See also: Manuel Bastías, Guillermo García, and Rosa Saavedra, "Proyecto 'Nos Juntamos . . . Y?'" CIDE, Santiago, 1981.

2. For a description and evaluation of the P.C.P., see: Howard Richards, *La Evaluación de la Acción Cultural. Estudio Evaluativo del Programa Padres e Hijos.* CIDE, Santiago, 1985.

3. Iván Ortiz, op. cit.

4. Juan Eduardo García-Huidobro, "Programa de Capacitación de Jóvenes Desocupados." *Programa de Sistematización de Experiencias de Educación Popular y Acción Social.* CIDE-FLACSO, Santiago, 1985.

5. Marianela Cerri and A. Uribe, "Una Experiencia de Capacitación: Conclusiones." CIDE, Santiago, 1984.

6. Jorge Chateau, "Programa de Educación Campesina-Cide." *Sistematización de Experiencias de Educación Popular No 5.* CIDE-FLACSO, Santiago, 1985.

7. Among the subjects of programs carried out by CIDE in 1985 were: Family and Community Health; Neighborhood Organization; Accountancy and Land Administration; Human Rights. See CIDE: *CIDE in 1985.* Santiago, 1985.

8. Quoted by Juan Eduardo García-Huidobro, "Support Programs and Community Education. A Recent Policy." In: *Methodological Aspects of Social Development Projects.* ASPAL ISUC. Estudios ILPES/UNICEF sobre políticas sociales. Santiago, 1985.

9. Howard Richards, op. cit.

10. Orlando Fals Borda, "La Investigación, Obra de los Trabajadores." In: *Investigación-acción participativa. Dimensión Educativa.* Bogota, undated.

11. On the Project to Systematize Experiences in Community Education, see: Sergio Martinic, *Educación y Cambio Social.* CIDE, Santiago, 1984.

12. Gregorio Weinberg, "Modelos Educativos en el Desarrollo Histórico de América Latina." In: *Educación y Sociedad en América Latina y el Caribe.* UNICEF-UNESCO, ECLA, UNDP, Santiago, 1980.

13. Stefano Varese, Alfredo Rojas, et al. *Indígenas y Educación en México.* Centro de Estudios Educativos, México, 1983.

14. See: "Desocupación Chilena: Diagnóstico, Impacto Social y Soluciones." *Colección Estudios de CIEPLAN No 14.* Santiago, 1984.

15. See, for example: Manuel Bastías, Miguel Oyarzán, and Jorge Zuleta, "Talleres Sindicales." CIDE, Santiago, 1984.

16. Juan Eduardo García-Huidobro and Sergio Martinic, *Las Instituciones Privadas y la Educación Popular: El Caso Chileno.* CIDE, Santiago, 1985.

3

Early Education: Children's Needs, a Shared Responsibility

Antonia Cepeda, Rosario Correa, Francisca Molina, Adriana Muñoz, and Ximena Valdés

Creation, Education, Social Mobilization (CREAS)

Introduction

In recent years, a considerable number of early education programs have been carried out in Latin America. They all deal with the same need, although there are many differences in styles of work, methodologies, and ways of integrating the participants. As a result, they have had differing impacts on the communities in which they are based.

This study gives a brief description of one such program, one which is important, particularly for Chile, for four basic reasons: (1) it puts forward an innovative concept of early education, the main concern of which is the development of the child's potential to establish a dynamic relationship with the environment, rather than with "learning" specific skills; (2) it involves the participation of women from marginal communities as educators, thus transforming them into protagonists of this program and enabling them to develop their own abilities; (3) it aims to develop a participative and democratic style of work, both in the management of the overall project and in the organization of each particular center; and (4) it is carried out within the municipal authorities' sphere of action, as a project within a local council's social services, and uses a significant amount of local resources.

In the final paragraphs of the chapter, we will identify some situations and conditions which either facilitate or hamper the program, so that this information can be considered whenever the program is introduced or extended on a mass scale.

The Problem

Consensus exists today as to the advantages of children having had some formal experience with education before starting primary school. This is particularly true for children from low-income areas, who are clearly at a disadvantage in relation to children from higher socio-economic strata. The results of the assessment test of the Program for Evaluating School Achievement (PER),[1] which was used in Chile in 1984 with a sample of 2,435 pupils who had completed their first year of primary education, confirms this.

This study shows that attending kindergarten encourages development of children's basic cognitive faculties and enables them to perform the kinds of actions appropriate for their age. Those who have not been to kindergarten, however, show limitations which will increasingly hinder them in achieving the objectives of primary education. The study also indicates that the basic faculties of children from the lowest socio-economic strata show less development, the later their education starts.

The provision of pre-school education in Chile today is extremely low. Given the country's economic situation, it will be difficult, even in the future, to allocate adequate resources to meet needs in this field. In other countries, for both economic and social reasons, there has been a rejection of the traditional high-cost, institutionalized ways of providing such services, which generally have been organized by university-trained professionals who often have no understanding of the situations in which the children live.

These facts, combined with the capacity of low-income groups, particularly in recent years, to resolve some of the basic problems which in the past were always left to the state, raise a major challenge. That is, how to find alternatives, based on the potential of low-income sectors, and taking advantage of existing local resources, to provide an efficient means of dealing with the problem of early education. The advantages of alternative programs lie not only in the possibility of reducing costs, but also, more importantly, in the potential for those involved to change from beneficiaries to protagonists, able to meet their own needs.

Early Education

The CREAS team bases its work with children under six on the concept of early education, which has been defined as "the process whereby human beings, from birth up till the time of starting general basic education, develop their potential for integrating dynamically with their environment."[2] Taking this definition, the objective of early education is *to provide children with the experiences necessary for their harmonious development*. That is, to enable them to develop the ability to talk, which is the means of communication and thinking; to develop the cognitive skills which enable them to alter their environment, react, resolve problems, make discoveries, and reach conclusions; and also to develop their emotions, so that they are able to feel, love, value, appreciate, and differentiate with respect to people and situations.

In terms of daily practice, this means providing children with experiences of play and work, contact with and opportunities to handle both manufactured and waste materials, and interaction with other children and adults. This fosters both social and emotional development, and the ability to handle and get pleasure out of the environment. An education process of this kind allows children to grow, develop their ability to think, establish relationships with other children and adults, and live each stage of development to the fullest, taking advantage of their environments.

This concept of early education differs from the traditional concept of pre-school education, where the accent is fundamentally on preparation for school, the development of concrete skills and abilities, and acquiring specific sorts of knowledge. In the model proposed here, the emphasis is on enabling children to fully live each stage of their development. This goal, if it is successfully achieved, represents the best preparation a child can have for further development.

The Project: The Community Centers for Education and Nutrition in La Florida

During 1982, the Institute for Nutrition and Food Technology (INTA)—a part of the University of Chile and of the United Nations University—on the basis of an agreement with the municipality of La Florida and with financial support from the Inter-American Foundation, made a diagnostic study of mother and child health in the southeastern sector of Santiago (the *comuna* or municipality of La Florida). The results of this study indicated an urgent need to introduce nutrition programs, especially at the pre-school level. Severe nutritional deficiencies were found in children under six years old. The study also noted the shortage of programs for pre-school children.

This situation, coupled with the increasing incorporation of women into work subsidy programs for the unemployed, led the social services team in La Florida to look for a response which could be implemented using the municipality's unemployment programs. With this end in view, a project was drawn up to create "an alternative for education and nutrition." The aim of this project—the Community Centers for Education and Nutrition or CCEN—was to "contribute to the development of children, the family, and the community through actions based on community participation and supported out of local resources."[3]

Implementation of the project began in early 1983. Four community pre-school centers were started (Los Copihues, Villa O'Higgins, San Rafael, and Trinidad). They were run with the participation of 240 women from the area, eight directors, and twelve students of social work, and received funding through the Employment Program for Heads of Household (POJH) along with some direct contributions from the municipal authorities. POJH covered the women's salaries, and those of twelve supervisors. It also provided 20% of the subsidies for CCEN expenses, which paid for food and educational materials. The objective of the centers was to provide education and nutritional care throughout the day, for undernourished children whose ages ranged from two to six years old.

Training

The educational activities of the program were the full responsibility of local women, who had had no previous experience of work with children other than their experience as mothers. During the first year of the project, priority was given to training these women. It was felt that adequate training for the mothers would result in educational activities that would encourage the children's balanced development.

The training, given by three professionals from CREAS, was held during the first three months of the project, before the children started coming. Weekly training and discussion sessions were then held in each center. This training concentrated on developing the women's own abilities as educators, starting from a reappraisal of the knowledge and experience that they had gained through their own lives. This approach was chosen because it reinforces the self-respect and self-confidence of the people receiving the training, and also develops initiative and creativity. This methodology, moreover, reflects the cultural characteristics of the communities where it is given, since the participants discuss their own experiences.

As the women begin to feel more identification with the project, their motivation and interest in participating increases. The learning process affects deeply-rooted beliefs, and is effective and lasting. Thus, to make it easier for the women to learn, and to activate their potential abilities, the educational process[4] emphasizes the following areas, which also give the program its basic format: (1) group development—the ability to work as a group, establish democratic relations, create an internal organization, take decisions, and deal with conflicts; and (2) technical training—development of potential as educators, and provision of information and skills needed to work with children.

The subjects included in these areas are examined in a specific order. The training starts by looking at the individual ("me") and ends with "the task." The decision to start with the personal level was made on the grounds that conflicts in this area hamper the group's development and ability to do the task defined properly.

The methodology used in examining these subjects can be defined as active, participative, based on personal experience, and reflective. It is active in that it requires the participants to do things (work in groups, draw, explain their own internal experiences); participative because the activities are developed by the group, with encouragement or assistance from an external agent; based on personal experience because participation is encouraged not only at an intellectual level but also through feelings and emotions—there are no "talks" or teaching, but instead the participants must experience what they learn; and reflective because the process itself is discussed, on the basis of experience, participation, and action, thus completing the learning sequence.

In this way, the three levels into which the subject matter is organized (individual-group-task) interact in an ongoing and reciprocal manner. Their relationship is one of tension, which may be exacerbated or reduced depending on the situation in the group, the individual needs of the participants, or the demands of the task in hand and the environment. As a result, whenever conflicts at the individual or group level interfere with fulfillment of the task, the group works through these conflicts before going on to look at the technical subjects.

Part of the plan was for everyone involved in the project—women from low-income communities, directors, and social work students—to take part in the training. The whole process of training was recorded and used to prepare a manual. This gives an account of the women's work, their discoveries, stories, songs, creations, and experiences. Thus the manual is an important tool to which the women can refer.

Operation

Each center was run by 60 women, divided into a morning and an afternoon shift. These women organized educational activities for the children and kept the premises clean. Meals were provided by a specialized commercial company which brought prepared food to the centers; only fresh fruit and vegetables were added there. Each shift had its own director, a professional who was also employed under the POJH scheme.

The project also benefitted from the support and participation of twelve students from the School of Social Work of the Catholic University of Chile, who were doing their social work practice. All four centers provided education and nutritional assistance throughout the day for 500 children, referred by clinics in the area, who were suffering from slight or moderate degrees of malnutrition. Their ages ranged from two to six years.

The educational activities were run entirely by the local women who participated in the project. They planned, carried out, and evaluated activities, and drew up guidelines for recording the children's progress. The educational activities in the classroom included "play in corners" and guided work. Play in corners is a methodology for working with pre-school children which invloves providing children with opportunities to use, according to individual interest and motivation, various materials that give the experiences needed for development. This occurs in a context in which the children interact with each other and with adults in the group.

After the project had been in operation for eighteen months, the social services department of the municipality asked a number of specialized teams to make evaluations of different aspects. The educational evaluation showed positive results in relation to the women's experience and the educational objectives of the work with children. Despite these encouraging results, however, the project was redesigned at the request of the Health sector, because it did not satisfy nutritional expectations.

Changes were made in the objectives of the project, its basic principles, and the role of the women within it. Nutritional concerns were prioritized, a different group of children were enrolled (only those under two years old), a trained pre-school teacher was employed at each center, and the women began to act as "assistants." The CCENs are still operating in this new form today.

The Evaluation

The project was evaluated in three areas: education, administration, and health. Here we will mainly refer to the educational evaluation, and draw on the administrative evaluation only in so far as it has a bearing on education.

Education

The objectives of the analysis in this area were to evaluate the educational process which the women went through, and the quality of the education that they gave to the children. Because of the characteristics of the educational model and the wide range of aspects to be evaluated, a strategy for evaluation was developed. It combined both qualitative and quantitative methods, techniques, and instruments, which allowed the experience as a whole to be evaluated. Care was taken to ensure that this strategy was congruent with the concept of education and the methodology used in the training.

With respect to the educational process for the women, the results showed that the objectives set had been fully achieved. The different tests used, the women's testimonies, and the information provided by other sources indicated important achievements which could be attributed to this process. Significant progress was seen in personal development (self-esteem, security, and self-confidence) and group development (working as a team, decision-making, etc). This progress is illustrated by several themes in the comments of the women involved.[5]

The women felt completely confident, sure of themselves and what they are doing:

- I think that we're quite well-prepared to look after children.
- I consider that I am trained to work in any other kindergarten, even though the other kindergardens wouldn't recognize that because I haven't got technical qualifications.
- Here we act as educators and technical workers, because we have to keep the records up to date in order to have information on each child's progress, qualifications and all that.
- The whole responsibility for educational work and organizing the activities falls on us, the helpers. We plan what we will do with the children during the week.

The women emphasized the importance of this experience for themselves at a personal level:

- It helped me to feel better about myself, because I had problems at home. It's different now, I'm working, I've got a group of friends, and I can escape from the routine of being shut up inside four walls all day.
- We used to be more oppressed. I'm speaking personally: I was more oppressed. Now I feel as though I'd like to help everyone, which is something that I'd lost. I'd lost my confidence in other people.

They also recognized that they learned to work as a team:

- What's more, working as a team has taught us to appreciate the people working alongside us, taught us to appreciate them for what they are.

- Yes, because we all have to accept the way that our *compañeras* (colleagues) are, and that's the reason why we're so united. The women who work in the mornings are very united, we always share the work.
- Here you learn that like all human beings we have our good sides and not so good sides. You get to know the women you work with, you have to be able to adapt to other people, but at the same time we are all in the same situation, which makes the task easier.

They found the training interesting and valuable:

- I was surprised by the working method we used. I was used to sitting in my place and waiting for someone to explain things to me. The dynamic exercises were new to me and I found them difficult at first. Maybe I was too stiff, I think that must have been the problem.

The women, moreover, were able to activate their own educational potential. They drew on their experience with their own children and used it to identify the characteristics of child development.[6] At the same time, they assimilated new information and concepts related to early education.

These observations were made after watching the women work in the activities room. In spite of external limitations and interference, they introduced a work routine with the children which, in many cases, demonstrated a high level of educational relevance.[7] An analysis of the registers used by the women shows their use of specialized information and capacity to employ educational techniques in daily activities.

With respect to the quality of the education which the children received, the expectations for the first year of work were "to establish a daily routine which includes educational activities, opportunities for play and recreation, and a positive interaction among children, and between children and adults." The work observed in the activities room, and the opinions of the women who worked there and of the children's parents, indicated that the quality of the children's education varied. In two of the centers, the educational activities largely matched the expectations. In the other two centers, the quality of the education given was affected by factors external to the educational work, such as inadequate space, administrative disorganization, deficiencies and confusion in the way the centers were run, and the virtual absence of appropriate materials.

Although they were conscious of the obstacles affecting their work, the women still valued their experience highly. They saw the centers as an alternative form of education to meet a real and felt need:

- In the shanty towns one often sees children who have no chance to show affection or even to show their real personalities. It (the Center) will really help these children. . . . The way these children (from the shanty towns) live is not the same as when they go to the Center. When they are with other children, they play, they have their meals at the right time. They learn to respect and to love. They learn that they have friends.
- I think that the community needs it, because there are so many children who spend their time in the street, outside, and don't have anything to eat . . . and the other thing is that they are just left to God's mercy, while here they are looked after properly, they are well cared for.
- Yes, because it's very good for my boy, for his development and later to prepare him for school, because he's already having more contact with other children—because there are children who spend the whole day alone, they're shy, while here they learn to develop.
- Because the work they do in kindergardens is the same as we are doing here, but with one difference: here we give the children much more attention than they would get in a kindergarten.

The fact that no initial evaluation of the children's development was made meant that it was impossible to measure changes. A final evaluation was made[8] in order to identify areas of development where greater emphasis was necessary, so that it could be added in programming the second year's work with the children. Comments made by parents and by the women involved indicated that they had seen significant changes in the children, particularly in their social behavior. Some accounts demonstrate this.

The women were aware that there were changes in the children:

- I was given a girl to work with a year ago. Yesterday they sent her on to another level. You should see the progress that child has made. She is a chubby girl, very pretty, smiley and playful, whereas before she was shy, silent and hardly reacted. To see that the children have made progress, and that some of the objectives have been achieved has been very satisfying for me.
- I've really enjoyed it, because here we teach the children to behave, we encourage them with love and affection. There are a lot of children who don't get any love. I've seen a lot of children who are rebellious and hostile when they arrive, but who are lovely when they leave. . . . The children start off being rebellious, then they start to play with other children, they almost stop fighting, and they learn everything.
- We've achieved a lot with the older children . . . there were children who didn't know how to eat by themselves, who couldn't talk; like Hugo, that little boy didn't know a thing, he was like a little animal, so we've done a lot.

- Because the children learn, develop. . . . We've taught them to walk, to eat with spoons. That is what we mainly do with them, because they don't know how to talk yet. At most they say, "mummy," or "mama" . . . that's all they say. We've taught them, now they play, clap. They imitate all the movements that we make. They've learned that, they've learned to walk. Some of them have even been potty-trained.

The parents also confirmed this change:

- My daughter participates, talks, tells us what she's been doing here; she likes it when you sing songs for her, and she wants to do everything by herself.
- My son has fewer tantrums. Now we talk about things, he seems cleverer.
- The children learn to develop, to play, to share things and to stand up for themselves. They don't get slapped and they don't have time for tantrums.
- My son talks more, he's cleverer; he asks me to come on Saturdays to play with the children.

Administration

According to the evaluation reports available,[9] the CCENs experienced some administrative problems which had a significant impact on the way the work was carried out. The centers' work was hampered by the lack of a set of norms and principles shared by all, which would have regulated the administration. The problem was aggravated by the fact that roles were inadequately defined; this not only obstructed the work but also created some inter-personal problems. The comments made by the directors during their interviews give some idea of this situation:

- We're never told whether we're doing things right or wrong.
- No one evaluates our work.
- In practice our work is based on intuition, we haven't had support in dealing with problems.
- We get little support in the administrative side of the work.

Furthermore, the lack of coordination between the workers on the morning shift and those working in the afternoon resulted in discontinuity in the administration and in the work with the children.

The rapid turn-over of directors, some of whom had not participated in the initial training process, led to contradictions between individual styles of management and concepts of the project. The work of the centers was also affected by the continual confusions and contradictions arising from their dual dependency on the POJH and the Social Services. This was also brought out by the directors.

- It has been difficult for us, this has been our project, not that of the people above us. There are contradictions with the model, they make demands that go against the principles of the model being used.
- We have to answer to two authorities: our relationship is with the POJH which operates independently of the municipality, but is linked with it.

The absence of proper channels for information and communication created a problem with rumors, which magnified the sense of insecurity and the permanent possibility of losing one's job. The POJH projects lasted for six months and were not automatically extended.

- You can never stop worrying, because the project might end or you could lose your job.
- The bad side is the insecurity: how long will the work last?

Along with this, the low wages, the authoritarian treatment by the POJH, and the lack of recognition, gave the women the feeling that the real significance of their work was not being appreciated.

- This project is different from the other POJH projects.
- We have much more responsibility. Nothing like the women who are in the sewing workshop, they just sew, and the ones in the knitting workshop just knit. We've got more responsibility, we have to teach the children so many things that they don't know.
- I think that if they see the work one is doing, that one is engaged in . . . we should get some recognition.
- We're different from the other POJH projects. They work the hours they have to and do what they're told. We work with children, with parents, we discuss problems with the directors.
- We've asked for some recognition of what we're doing, but we haven't been given it.

One of the major difficulties which the CCEN Project faced was the lack of basic materials needed to do the programmed activities properly. The overall project provided the children's food and funds for the women's unemployment subsidies (wages), but did not provide sufficient funds for teaching materials, cleaning, and replacement and maintenance of furniture. The women saw the problem this way:

- We said, "Well, what about the materials? How can we work if we've got no material to work with?" I don't know, but you've got to organize activities for the children. What were we supposed to do? Take the money out of our own pockets to buy some coloured paper, some glue, a little at a time, is that it? No, you can't run things like that!
- We didn't even have heaters, and sometimes we even had to bring our own heaters from home, the place was so cold.
- We are the material that the children work with; because when we're planning, for example, we say, "What material do we need? The teacher." Sometimes we're the only material they have.

It is obvious that the initial expectations of the project, in terms of the women's educational experience and the work with the children, were adequately achieved. The defects in operation, which also affected the educational activities, were primarily associated with problems in administration and overall management of the project.

Some Comments

As can be seen from the evaluation, the educational work in the CCENs produced significant results. It's worth asking, therefore, what factors contributed to these positive results? One key element was the *training*, in terms of the way it was conceived, the subjects covered, and the methodology used. Another important factor was that the women involved and the children's parents felt that there was a *real and clear need* for educational programs for pre-school children in their communities; this explains the women's commitment to the work and the value they gave to the experience.

The programs also presented problems which the women *could resolve themselves.* If we see early education as "the creation of favorable conditions for children to develop and the provision of key experiences which encourage them to relate dynamically to their environment," educational work with pre-school children is open to women from poor communities, since it is carried out through activities which they can do themselves. A final factor which contributed to success was the fact that the work was *approached from different perspectives:* mental health, education, and social work. The use of this approach was borne in mind in defining the model, in the training process itself, and in evaluating the educational work.

We feel that experiences of this kind, given their complexity and the range of factors involved, need an inter-disciplinary approach. That is, they should seek simultaneously to improve mental health, to develop organizational abilities, and to encourage action to meet basic needs.

As well as looking at the factors which assisted in carrying out the work, we need to identify those that obstructed or hampered its development. The first, and what appears to be the main, problem was the contradiction between the basic objective of the training model—to develop social actors who would be able to play a leading role in resolving their needs—and the institutional context within which the project was carried out. On this question, the team which evaluated the organizational and administrative aspects made the following comments.

- To start with, one can observe an underlying contradiction in the project which is expressed in its different activities, and which is the incorporation of an open system of organization—the project model—into an essentially closed organizational structure. This situation in itself generates difficulties which need to be resolved. And furthermore, one finds specific weaknesses in the management of technical aspects which make it still harder to reconcile the two systems.
- When one refers to the inherent difficulties involved in working with the two systems in conjunction, it should be said that this contradiction is expressed both in the ability to achieve the objectives established and in organizational aspects: decision-making, concept of the work in hand, systems of communication, exercise of authority, planning and evaluation of the work, etc.: there is a tension between the project's humanistic approach and the bureaucratic structure of the institutions involved in it.[10]

Thus the different concepts of the women's participation[11] held by the various institutions participating in the project (the municipality, POJH, the Health Service, CREAS) generated a series of difficulties which, to some extent, explains why the project was subsequently reformulated.

The *permanent lack of materials* also hampered the development of the work. This problem made the women's work difficult, both in terms of educational activities and the way the children were generally looked after. Another factor which, in our opinion, had a negative impact on the work was the *quality of the POJH project*. This was due to the low payment provided by the POJH subsidy (4,000 Chilean pesos per month in August 1984, approximately US$25), as well as to the permanent instability of the project, and to the lack of real appreciation for the work the women were doing.

The Lessons

The work in the community centers in La Florida was a difficult and complex experience. It made an important contribution, however, to the development of possible alternatives for pre-school education. Some hypotheses were confirmed and the advantages of this approach were brought out. Key elements and basic conditions, which need to be considered when introducing programs of this kind in the future, were also identified.

The CCENs demonstrated that women from low-income communities have a potential as educators which can be activated and encouraged. They further demonstrated that it is possible to develop an early education program starting from a re-examination of natural models of child-care and backing this up with the development of basic technical skills. The CCENs also confirmed that early education is a real and clearly felt need for people in poor communities. The results obtained indicated that the perspective gained from experiences such as these are encouraging, which makes the experience especially worthwhile.

Using the local women's own experience of child-care in the educational activities has emotional and cultural repercussions on the children, which heightens the educational value.[12] Making the local women responsible for the work encourages changes in social relations, since the women become social actors in search of ways to meet their own needs. This does not merely lead to satisfaction of a basic need, but also frames the experience within the broader concept of quality of life.[13] From an economic point of view, the CCENs enable better use to be made of resources, in that the community's own resources and capacities are tapped; this in turn means a reduction in the costs of pre-school care.

Another important result of the CCENs is the demonstration that early education can be organized locally. This is important for two reasons. First, it allows alternatives to be developed which are more effective and appropriate to the characteristics of each area. Second, it opens possibilities for future action within the context of the recent decentralization and municipalization in Chile.

Given that members of the community have the ability and the potential to provide educational care for their children, initiatives such as the project described could be run by social organizations. Thus local women can be trained and organized to care for children in their areas, and offer viable, efficient ways of meeting the need for early education. They can also, eventually, present projects to the municipal or other relevant authorities, and negotiate for the resources required.

As we said earlier, the CCEN project can also be used to identify some of the basic conditions required to successfully develop this type of program. The most basic condition is to overcome factors which have a negative influence.

The fundamental principles underlying this approach to early education must be compatible with the institutional context in which it is introduced. That is, if the participation of women from the community is intended to lead them to "assume the role of social actors," this role cannot be restricted solely to the classroom, but must be encouraged at all levels. This is the only way that the basic aim (to create social actors) can be kept in view without reducing the women's participation to a way of obtaining cheap labor.

Another condition is that certain basic elements are available in order to ensure that the educational work can be carried out properly. There must be a modest meeting place large enough for the number of children involved, with the potential for the space to be divided up for different activities, and with toilets (even if only a limited number) for the sole use of the children. A space outside for outdoor activities, teaching materials for specific educational activities, resources for and the conditions to prepare a light meal each day (milk and fruit or the equivalent) when the children come for half the day, must also be available.

The payments received by the local women also need to be taken into account. These women provide a service that the community needs, and should therefore receive fair payment. This will also prove to the women that the work they are doing is really recognized and appreciated.

For this work to be successful, there must be a change in the attitudes of the communities and poor neighborhoods themselves as well. That is, the community must come to appreciate this type of early education center as much as or more than the women working there. This means understanding the real importance of the centers, and not seeing them as a palliative for "as long as we are in this situation," or as a second rate alternative to proper kindergartens.

Finally, to introduce this approach on a mass scale, it is necessary to redefine the role of the professionals involved, particularly that of the pre-school teacher. This role should be to facilitate the women's work, stimulate their abilities, and jointly develop the tools necessary for educational activities with the children. It should not be the professional who works directly with the children, or acts as a model. The professional's job is to put knowledge and skills at the service of the women and show *them* that they can do the work. This change requires broader training for the professionals.

In conclusion, the community centers in La Florida have shown that it is possible to introduce an early education program carried out by the women from low-income areas themselves and using resources available in the community. A program of this kind represents an alternative form of care for children under six years old and has, moreover, proved itself both viable and efficient in providing for the educational needs of pre-school children. The repetition and eventual introduction of the program on a mass scale raises a number of problems, but given the important benefits it offers, these must be seen merely as challenges which can be overcome.

Notes

1. PER: Program for Evaluating School Achievement, whose aim, in regard to children in the first year of primary education, is to "evaluate the level of achievement in areas of knowledge and emotional aspects which are essential in order to be able to learn adequately in subsequent grades," p. 1, Doc. de Trabajo No. 51 *Análisis Prueba Experimental de 1° Básico,* Pontificia Universidad Católica de Chile, Agreement between the Catholic University and the Ministry of Education.

2. *Informe Reunión Interamericana de Consultores sobre Educación Inicial* (Versión Preliminar). Buenos Aires, 1984, CINTERPLAN.

3. "Centros Comunitarios Educativo-Nutricionales: una Experiencia de Trabajo Social Comunitario," Doc. de Trabajo No. 21, Borrador de Discusión, Escuela de Trabajo Social UC, January 1984, p. 16.

4. An educational process is seen as "the set of actions and interactions aimed at producing changes in the way that individuals or groups see their own reality. These actions or interactions have a specific purpose which may lead to different aspects or approaches being emphasized, thus creating different educational messages." Sergio Martinic, Documento No. 3, *Proyecto Sistematización de Proyectos de Acción,* CIDE-FLACSO, 1983.

5. Information obtained through "localized dynamics," a technique used to find out the participants' view of the work. See CREAS, *Evaluación Educativa CCEN,* 1984.

6. See Manual *Trabajando en el Centro Comunitario,* documento Registro de la experiencia de capacitación del Proyecto CCEN La Florida. Santiago, July 1983.

7. CREAS, *Evaluación Educativa,* op. cit.

8. We used the Denver Child Development test created by W. K. Frankerburg, J. B. Dodds and A. W. Fandal. University of Colorado. Revised edition, 1970.

9. See: CREAS, *Evaluación Educativa,* op. cit.; Jiménez and Sanhueza, "Informe de Evaluación del Proyecto CCEN," Municipalidad de La Florida, Area Social, August 1984.

10. Interview with Head of Project, Jiménez and Sanhueza, op. cit., p. 101.

11. Here we are referring to the three models of participation identified by Vicente Espinoza in *Poder, Poder Local y Participación.* Doc. de Trabajo No. 25, SUR Profesionales, 1983.

12. The most recent international meetings of experts in this field also expressed their support for the use of natural models of child-care in educational

work. On this point see: Report on the special meeting, "El Niño en América Latina y el Caribe," Mexico, 16–18 May 1979, UNICEF.; Primer Seminario sobre experiencias de Educación Inicial no escolarizada en países de América Latina, Peru, 1978, UNICEF.

13. On this subject, see: "Apuntes para Trabajo Social" No. 4/5, pp. 5–7.

4

Primary Health Care in a Local Community

Antonio Infante

If there is an ideal sphere for participative democracy, it is health.
—H. Mahler, Director WHO

This chapter describes one experience of putting the concept of primary health care into practice in a poor district (*comuna*) in Santiago, Chile. The term "primary health care" came into worldwide usage with the Alma Ata Conference in 1978 and has since been used to refer to various kinds of health work. Community participation, however, is a basic condition of primary health care. In Chile, as one meeting of primary health care workers pointed out, the term has been adopted by the Ministry of Health. In practice, the Ministry encourages a professionalization of health care at the primary level—which contradicts the real meaning of primary health care.[1]

The experience described below was possible only because nongovernmental organizations (NGOs) maintained and developed a tradition of working with the community over the 20 years in which the National Health Service (SNS) was in existence. The program also benefitted from close links with the sphere of the social sciences, which made the introduction of qualitative improvements possible.

Program Background

The Area

The work was carried out between October 1983 and January 1985 at the *Villa O'Higgins Clinic*, which is run by the Southeastern Metropolitan Health Service. The clinic is in the district of La Florida. It is supposed to provide health care for the 90,000 people now living in the area, although it was built in 1971 to serve a population of approximately 40,000 people. The population of the area is made up of a small percentage of people who work in the public services, a large number of working class families who have been allocated plots of land with only basic services through individual savings plans (*operación sitio*), and a number of very poor settlements which came into being after land seizures in 1972–1973.

The clinic was originally located in the center of the area, at a distance of no more than eight to ten blocks from the furthest point of the area served. This neighborhood is known as the Villa O'Higgins. In 1976, the clinic was moved and extended, but is still located quite centrally within the community. There has, however, been considerable growth in this sector of the city. Initially housing was built for office workers; subsequently, the Ministry of Housing built "resettlements" which "benefitted" large numbers of poor families who had been living in other districts—on land more valuable to the city.

This growth took place in an area which lacks basic public services other than schools. The Villa O'Higgins Clinic was made responsible for providing health care. The average distance that the people served by the clinic live from it is now 20 blocks; some live as far as 40 blocks away.

Of the total number of people potentially served by the clinic, only 65% (60,000) people actually use it. The rest are either enrolled in other health care systems, or cannot reach the clinic because of distance and the fact that travel by public transport is unaffordable (see Table 4.1).

In 1984, statistics of over 40% unemployment were recorded in this district. The Employment Program for Heads of Household (POJH) provided the main source of work; POJH is an unemployment benefit given through the municipal authorities. To receive this benefit, the unemployed person has to work half the day, each day, for payment of 5,000 Chilean pesos per month (US$25).

The Villa O'Higgins is also characterized by extreme shortages of other services. There is a particularly notable lack of areas for recreation, kindergartens, street lighting, basic sewage systems, and adequate housing. The conditions of unemployment and the poverty of the environment make this an especially violent area as well. There are high levels of alcoholism, serious drug problems among young people, and the streets are not safe, especially in the evening or at night, when people who go out run a high risk of being attacked and robbed.

The Situation when the Project Started

When this project was begun, the clinic did not have sufficient staff to cover all the activities required by the Ministry of Health at the

TABLE 4.1

ILLNESS-RELATED VISITS TO DOCTOR BY SECTOR OF NEIGHBORHOOD AND DISTANCE FROM VILLA O'HIGGINS CLINIC

Sector of Neighborhood	Visits per Month	Visits (Person/Year)
Close to clinic		
11	825	0.70
21	865	0.79
22	473	0.88
Distant		
9	63	0.23
10	70	0.21
12	142	0.24
13	190	0.13
14	111	0.12
26	24	0.06
27	18	0.19
28	7	0.12
29	1	0.02
30	0	0.00
31	0	0.00
TOTAL	2,789	0.38

Source: Masters Course in Public Health. "Diagnostico de Salud del Consultorio Villa O'Higgins." Escuela de Salud Publica, Universidad de Chile.

TABLE 4.2

REQUIREMENTS FOR AND AVAILABILITY OF DIRECT CARE STAFF
Villa O'Higgins Clinic, 1984

	Demand/Day		Availability	Deficit
	People	Hours	Hours	%
Doctors	13	102.9	52	49.1
Dentists	7	54.6	24	56.0
Nurses	11	84	32	61.9
Midwives	6	46.2	22	52.4
Nutritionists	2	17.5	16	8.6
Social Workers	4	32.0	16	50.0
Auxiliaries	12	92.4	26	71.9

Source: A. Infante, H. Lopez, L. Jansana and collaborators. "Personal necesario para la atencion primaria y su disponibilidad real." IV Chilean Dayschool on Public Health. 1984. Summary of papers.

primary level (see Table 4.2). Work mainly concentrated on the areas of preventive and curative care for mothers and children, and curative care for adults. Some dental treatment, basically the extraction of teeth, was done also.

This care was for the most part provided at the clinic. Since all community work had been abandoned, little educational work got done; preventive activities focused on child growth, with no time to monitor and encourage development. There was no work oriented specifically towards school children, apart from immunizations and the treatment of sick children.

The demand for curative medicine was much too great to be met from existing resources. Consequently, a large number of cases were rejected. Along with this, the number of visits per head of population was only about 20% of the recommended average.

Opportunities for participation in the clinic were nonexistent. The staff worked in isolation from one another doing routine activities. The people in the area had no channel for participation other than the possibility of writing comments in a book of complaints and suggestions.

Legal Openings

The legal rights to participate in health care are set out in various documents published by both the health and municipal authorities. The challenge presented to this progect was to put existing provisions effectively into practice. A re-examination of the definition of primary health care and the fact that Chile is a signatory to the Alma Ata agreements offered a possibility for community participation. Provisions also existed in laws relating to the municipalities that allow for community participation in District Development Councils (CODECOs), Social Action Committees (CASs), the offices for community development, the District Union of Neighborhood Councils, and associated neighborhood organizations.

All these existing provisions, however, are flawed by the vertical structure of government in which the authorities at the different levels of public administration and in the community organizations are appointed by the government and are people on whom the government can rely. This means that while channels for participation do exist, these are not used because of the lack of confidence in externally appointed representatives.

This project based its work on a functional definition of primary health care as a dynamic process involving the interaction of various components: the public health center, an organized community, and municipal authorities who represent other public institutions in the area. In this process of interaction, the community's role must be to indicate its principal needs as they are experienced. The public agencies have to be able to comprehend these needs in order to orient their activities to carry out relevant programs.

Seen in this way, primary health care involves the democratization of one specific area of life. It will only really be practiced when the majority of the population, at both the local and national levels, is guaranteed access to the decision-making process. The result of this access will be that public policies will reflect the people's basic, deeply felt needs.

This then is the conceptual framework with which the project in the Villa O'Higgins began. Three fundamental elements of the process stand out in the development of the work: the health team, the community, and the local authorities.

The Experience

The Health Team

The health team, and in it the primary level health workers, have a key role to play in primary health care. It is important for this team to collaborate in creating the structure of the health services so that it will be open to the demands of the community. The health workers must also contribute to making decisions that respond immediately to the people's needs.

When work on the progect began, there was no health team as such. There was instead a group of health workers who, as a result of an authoritarian and vertical personnel policy which left no space for staff to express their concerns, were relegated to work posts where they carried out routine, depersonalized activities. The first task in the creation of a team spirit among the health workers was to bring the mechanisms of participation—staff meetings, technical council, mother and child health committee, pharmacy committee—back to life.

The participatory activities were organized with specific objectives. The first was to take into account all the personal and professional concerns about the work. Next was a diagnosis of the state of health of the community. The objective of this was to uncover the variety of situations in the area, in terms of levels of health and access to the health center.

The result was a systematization of the information available. This made it possible to put what had been a subjective idea into objective terms. For instance, that there were deep inequalities in access to the

TABLE 4.3

CHILDREN UNDER TWO YEARS OLD ATTENDING HEALTH CENTER
Villa O'Higgins Clinic, 1984

Sector of Neighborhood	Population Under Two Years Old Total	Attending Center	Percentage %
Near			
11	563	564	100.2
21	519	549	105.8
22	256	285	111.3
SUB-TOTAL	1,338	1,398	104.5
Distant			
9	133	54	40.6
10	157	57	36.3
12	284	382	134.5
13	685	321	46.9
14	435	104	23.9
26	197	61	31.0
27	44	0	0.0
28	28	0	0.0
29	30	20	66.7
30	30	7	23.3
31	58	2	3.4
SUB-TOTAL	2,081	1,008	48.4
TOTAL	3,419	2,406	70.4

Source: A. Infante and collaborators, "Sectorizacion de la informacion: Una herramienta para programacion local." IV Chilean Dayschool on Public Health. 1984. Summary of papers.

health center was proved by the fact that it was used effectively only by people living within ten blocks of it (see Table 4.3).

In light of this evidence, the next stage of work was to design mechanisms which would give the entire population equal access to the health center and to make qualitative improvements in the care provided. The necessity to prepare people who made the greatest use of the health center as monitors became apparent. This allowed decentralization of some activities and thus the needs of patients from more distant sectors were attended. A proposal was also made to the health and municipal authorities to open another health center more accessible to people living at a distance from the existing center.

In order to introduce activities which would improve the quality of care, it was vital to transfer medical know-how to the community organization. This enabled the professionals to take on new areas of work, such as the stimulation of development in pre-school children, health education, monitoring of nutrition, family vegetable gardens, work on alcoholism, etc. As the work developed, it became evident that the health center had opened itself to the needs of the community. The staff began to act differently, taking a more welcoming attitude towards people being attended in the center. This brought a slow but sustained improvement in the working environment and encouraged collective efforts and decision-making. The results of the diagnosis by sector were used in discussions with the health authorities to support the argument for a new way of programming work, for legitimatization of the need for community participation, and increased emphasis on activities to protect and improve health.

It must be said, however, that this independent, isolated, unique experiment did face difficulties in its development. Among staff members there was concern about the direction in which the work was going, since the work was objectively very different from what was being done in other health centers in the service. This concern had a double effect. It strengthened the workers' commitment to the approach adopted, since they could see the community support for this health center compared to other centers; at the same time, it created a sense of insecurity, because the social environment was so different.

It is also important to point out that, as the work grew and matured, it aroused concern at the bureaucratic level of the health services. The local health authorities showed clear signs of discomfort; their opinions swung from praise to criticism. This authoritarian insecurity was not supported by any technical arguments, which made the lack of legitimacy of the appointed heads apparent. Evidently, the most threatening aspect was the opportunity for participation, since this gave rise to criticisms, and demands that decisions be explained and the bureaucracy be improved.

Community Health Organization

In the 1960s, together with the appearance of geographical and administrative organization in the marginal areas, there was a need for some members of the community to be "specialized" in health. This was part of a political initiative to generate community participation. Community health workers were given different names: voluntary workers, monitors, health brigades, etc. These people were, in general, unpaid, primarily women, and essentially controlled by the public health establishments that trained them and then planned their activities. Only when legislation was introduced on the formal mechanisms of community participation in health establishments did there begin to be involvement by representatives from neighborhood councils, political parties, and other organizations, the majority of whose members were men.

With the destruction of the democratic system, these forms of community organization were dismantled. Leaders who could be trusted politically were appointed to the neighborhood councils, with the result that these councils ceased to be representative or have an impact. People joined church organizations, basically in order to do solidarity work, through which a minimum level of community organization was maintained. Fortunately, as we discovered through our work with the neighborhood organizations, these traditional community activities were so much a part of legitimate community work that they had become engraved in the collective memory of the people.

Our first contacts with the community were made through its formal representatives, the leadership of the neighborhood councils, who were invited to attend monthly meetings at the health center. These meetings provided an opportunity to express opinions about the way the center was running. The opinions were very critical, focusing on the center's failure to attend to all the ill people. (In order to get an appointment, a patient, no matter how serious his or her complaint, had to get in line at 4 A.M.)

The leaders of the different sectors of the neighborhood council therefore had no way of knowing about the preventive work being done with mothers and children. In later meetings, the results of the diagnosis by sector were presented; they described the existing problems very precisely. When discussions began on how access to the health center could be improved, the leaders suggested that health monitors could be trained in each sector of the neighborhood. This confirmed that the memory of traditional forms of action was still very strong.

The Health Monitors

The sectors of the neighborhood most ready to tackle this task were those closest to the health center. These were the people who felt the greatest sense of responsibility towards the center. They were also the ones who had originally fought for the establishment of a National Health Service (SNS) center.

In selecting the monitors, the sectoral organizations adopted different methods; one used existing health groups who were working with the Church, another suggested an active youth group, which other people already involved in health activities (former SNS auxiliary staff) joined. In others, interested people were invited to enroll. The lists of names were given to the health center, so that the first meetings could be organized and a calendar of activities drawn up. Approximately twenty-five monitors were enrolled for each sector of the area, making a total of over 100. Of those proposed to receive training, almost seventy took part.

The common denominator in all the groups was the need to learn first aid, techniques such as taking temperature and blood pressure, and give injections. All of the trainings included this type of instruction. One nurse was in charge of training in each sector, which was a first step in dividing the health team between the sectors.

The training involved twelve sessions, half of which were used to provide information. The other half were for strengthening the group, using techniques for developing self-confidence, confidence in the organization, feelings of solidarity, and direct forms of communication. This training was accompanied by practical work which the monitors carried out in different areas of the health center, such as putting on dressings, giving injections, sterilizing equipment, and preparing the patients (taking blood pressure, temperature, and weight).

At the end of the course, the participants were each given a certificate from the health center and neighborhood organization, which stated that they were trained as health monitors. Each monitor was asked to make two promises: (1) to treat information as confidential; (2) not to show any kind of discrimination to a person in need of attention.

Parallel to this work and as a result of the early meetings, the groups of monitors began to make their own diagnosis of the situation in their blocks. This made it possible to get a basic idea of existing problems, to let people know about the new approach, and to legitimize this form of organization. The process was facilitated by the heavy winter rains and the subsequent support activities, mainly provided by the monitors' organization, which took responsibility for identifying problems and distributing assistance.

The Monitors' Diagnosis of Health

The diagnosis was made throughout the period when the organizations of health monitors were formed and consolidated in each sector of the neighborhood. It played an important part in helping the groups to understand what their work would be about. In order to prepare this diagnosis, a simple questionaire was designed, with input from the monitors, which allowed them to make a simple census of the population, basic health conditions, level of coverage by the health center, and variables such as employment and basic sanitation (see Table 4.4).[2]

The richness of this experience cannot be fully expressed in these few pages. Its most important effects were those within the organization and in each of the monitors. Women who were not used to expressing

TABLE 4.4

GENERAL SUMMARY OF DIAGNOSIS: SECTOR 5
Villa O'Higgins Health Monitors, 1984

COVERAGE OF SURVEY

Total No. of Lots:	951
No. of lots in survey:	925
No. of families in survey:	1,156
No. of people in survey:	5,110

VISITS TO CLINIC AND ILLNESSES

Age Group (years)	Total	Healthy child check-up		Illness Diagnosed			
				chronic treatment		curable treatment	
		yes	no	w/	w/o	w/	w/o
0- 5	578	540	38	15	-	38	6
6-17	1,554	-	-	35	16	24	42
18-64	2,666	-	-	82	60	64	51
65+	191	-	-	18	13	14	4
Total	4,989						

WOMEN OF CHILD BEARING AGE (15-44 years)

	Total	Check-ups at Health Center	
		Yes	No
All	1,424	639	159
Pregnant		37	2
No sex life	424		

FAMILY PROBLEMS

Total Families	w/ Drug and Alcohol Problems	w/ Conflicts
1,156	114	114

EMPLOYMENT AND SOCIAL SECURITY (age 18-64)

Total	Gov Employment Prog (POJH)	Unemployed	CTS	w/o social security
566	349	269	385	1,003

QUALITY OF HOUSING

Total	Drinking Water		Emergency Housing	Cesspools
	Yard	Street		
1,156	-	8	307	57

their opinions began to do so, which led to group creativity and collective work. The women talked about the impact of this work on their role as mothers and housewives; relations with their children improved, and they began to communicate on much more equal terms with their partners, who in general welcomed the change.

The group began to initiate activities such as setting up small first aid rooms and raising money for basic equipment. Fund raising involved work in each block (the basic territorial unit in the neighborhood), which led to a rebirth of local organization. New delegates were elected in the blocks and to the leadership of the progress committees, and the illegitimacy and lack of representativeness of some neighborhood leaders nominated by the mayor thus became apparent.

The process of preparing the diagnosis took about three months. The information obtained from each family was grouped first by block and then by sector of the neighborhood. The information was also transferred to maps of the sector, which gave an idea of the geographical distribution of the principal problems. The survey confirmed that the coverage of preventive activities was adequate, and showed that the major problems were unemployment, alcoholism, basic sanitation, and quality of housing.

These results gave the monitors and the neighborhood organization detailed information on the conditions in which their neighbors were living. This was frequently an emotional shock to the monitors, who never imagined that people living in their own blocks could have such serious problems of subsistence or family relations. Recognition of the situation led the monitors immediately to search for ways of solving the problems detected.

The Municipal Authorities

There has been a long history of borough-level organization in Chile, mainly concerned with cleaning and refuse collection. It has been carried out with varying levels of efficiency, depending on the wealth of, and therefore the taxes paid by, people in the area. Before the military coup, the head of the municipal authority was an elected mayor, supported by councillors who were also legitimately elected. They represented political parties, but more importantly they represented the interests of their areas.

The military coup brought a radical change. Now the mayors are nominated by the president, and are people in whom he has complete confidence; only sometimes do they live in the borough that they govern. The councillors, who to some extent acted as a collective form of leadership, have disappeared and the mayor is now responsible for putting the central government's instructions into practice. The mayor nominates the leaders of neighborhood organizations and other representative bodies related to these (Borough Union of Neighborhood Councils, e.g.). He or she is also responsible for maintaining up-to-date information on social activities in the borough.

The borough's technical staffs are generally weak, since the number of workers has been frozen due to financial problems. They are further weakened by the central government's aim of encouraging the development of municipal corporations, thus passing some sectoral programs over to the private sector. These vulnerable technical teams are appointed by the mayor, and are people whom he or she personally trusts.

Towards the end of the 1970s, it was suggested within the government that the role of the municipal authorities should be strengthened and that the administration of health, education, and recreation should be delegated to these authorities. This has been implemented in an irregular fashion by the different municipalities. The most significant change has been in the management of education. The transfer of the health centers has taken place on a smaller scale, and recreation has only begun to be handed over to the municipalities, at varying rates, since 1982. Clauses in the Municipal Authorities Law refer to the importance of community participation, and provide a basis for testing the real space that exists for such participation.

In the work in Villa O'Higgins, past events allowed the supposition that relations between the health center and the municipality would be easy. Some health professionals had participated in a joint project in 1982, involving the municipality and the university, which was intended to establish an inter-institutional coordination to improve care for mothers and children. A diagnosis of the area was drawn up, and discussed by the Social Action Committee. This work allowed the professionals to get to know the borough and the different institutions very well, and later made it possible for the health center to maintain a level of understanding with the organizations in the area it covered.

As a result of this diagnosis, community centers were created to provide integral care for preschool children. These were staffed by women from the community and financed by the municipality. The community centers belonged to the municipality, but all the institutions involved had to coordinate with each other to ensure that the best use was made of them. The health sector was responsible for the children and for assessing the state of their nutrition, which meant holding periodic meetings involving both the health sector and the municipality.

The development of this integrated work was assisted by another project in the borough. It had backing from the municipal authorities, and its aim was to find ways of meeting the basic needs of people in low-income areas through community organization. Local people had been allowed to manage municipal funds independently, and a rudimentary but promising level of local development was being achieved.

The idea developed by the health monitors and neighborhood organizations was that, once the municipality had seen the diagnosis made by the monitors and ratified by the neighborhood organizations, it could be encouraged to authorize the implementation of a project along the same lines as the one mentioned above. This would mean, basically, that people employed by the POJH and living in the Villa O'Higgins would be given work dealing with the priority needs detected in the diagnosis, and that the neighborhood organization in each sector would take responsibility for administrating the finances involved.

Discussions with the municipality were also held on the problem of alcoholism, and a brigade of former alcoholics who worked in the POJH was set up. This brigade not only met the need for a place to socialize and share problems related to alcoholism, but also created family kitchen gardens. The brigade started these gardens in one sector of the neighborhood, as a demonstration experience, to assist people to create their own vegetable gardens.

Another project on family vegetable gardens was also developed. This was supervised by staff from the health center and supported by the municipality. More than a dozen vegetable gardens were started in sectors with the most serious problems of subsistence.

These embryonic projects demonstrated the health sector's capacity to detect the major problem areas, provide an effective means of more clearly defining the problems faced by the community, and put forward relevant solutions. Thus the association with the municipal authorities indicated the prospects for some kind of link at the borough level. It also showed that the municipality could act as a powerful force in mobilizing community organizations, which quickly grasp the nature of this work and begin to develop capacities of their own, which in turn provide positive feedback.

The Outcome

It was mentioned above that this community work created a sense of insecurity in the health administration. This local problem was exacerbated by the excellent reception given to presentations of the Villa O'Higgins experience in academic meetings on primary health care.[3] This program clearly demonstrated the potential for primary health care work, in spite of existing limitations on the opportunities for participation. These factors led the heads of the Health Service to arrange for the transfer of the health center's director.

The public protest against this measure had no effect. The center's health team and the community organizations associated with the work took great pains to make clear how much damage was being done. They collected almost 7,000 signatures in protest of the measure, held meetings with different authorities, sent letters to the press. But it was to no avail—the decision had been taken by the Director of the Health Service, and there was no argument strong enough to counter it.

Six Months Later

The Villa O'Higgins health center looks clean and tidy, and members of staff have returned to work essentially concentrated inside the center. What the health authorities termed the "proselytizing work" of the health monitors has ended, and the monitors are seen as auxiliaries who carry out specific functions that are the responsibility of the health center. The municipality has left health care exclusively to the health service. Even the community centers are no longer used for anything other than the recuperation of malnourished children.

Despite this, the monitors have kept their first aid posts running and are still carrying out basically curative activities. We are still too close to the events to evaluate the implications of this experience. There are, however, some lessons to be learned.

Lessons

Health Infrastructure

The experience confirmed that health care is very unstable, in terms of both personnel and resources. This can be seen in the shortage of staff, and in the health center's radius of impact within the area it is supposed to cover. In a situation where the infrastructural services have not been expanded, the effects of the growth of peripheral boroughs, resulting from the removal of poor people from other areas, can be clearly seen. It is also clear that an urban primary health care center cannot be expected to cover a radius of more than about ten blocks, which means that the maximum number of people attended should be approximately 30,000.

Primary Level Staff

Work within the health system is of enormous importance, particularly because the health staff can play the role of "people's attorney," providing community organizations with the technical information and methodologies necessary to understand their problems and find solutions.

This "internal" work is very slow, since it involves questioning and criticizing the training given to health workers in medical schools (if they have been to university), or in the essentially hospital-based training of the auxiliary staff. There is no past experience in the history of the profession which shows how these teams should work, particularly in relation to the problems that they are dealing with and the fact that doctors are, by definition, team leaders.

Community Organization

Undoubtedly, community organizations have the greatest freedom of movement, and thus a great deal of progress can be made in this sphere. Community organizations need objectives to work for, and to strengthen their capacities. Their work can be improved through technical assistance; here both the health teams and the municipal authorities have an important role to play. A very pertinent question is how to help community organizations increase their autonomy from state institutions.

The collective memory of these organizations is of being dependent. In this case, the experience was reproduced. As a result, the people must become aware of how important the autonomy of community organizations is, since it is this autonomy which guarantees the people's ability to criticize, and thus to improve, the way in which joint work is carried out. Without autonomy, the community organizations are no more than "cheap resources" for the health sector or the municipality.

Local Government

In the municipalities, the concerns of the past continue to weigh heavily. The municipal authorities do not think in terms of local development, but rather of the decentralized administration of the state apparatus. Obviously they do not encourage community participation, nor do they facilitate the choosing of neighborhood authorities by democratic processes. Nevertheless, the great potential of these local bodies became apparent during the experience described.

Our Errors

In the first place, given that primary health care is the product of a triangular relationship, this work put too much emphasis on the role of the health center and left too little time for the community organizations and the municipality to mature. Because the work developed this way, there was a great risk that any far-reaching change in the role of the health center would have decisive repercussions on a process that was just getting under way. It is possible that a similar project could be taken further in health centers administered by the municipality, if local government is more involved in the work.

A second and ultimately decisive point was the underestimation of the importance of bureaucracy in the Ministry. In view of this, it is very unlikely that the situation in the health sector will alter substantially even when the socio-political conditions in the country change. Thus it is vital to understand the administrative mechanisms operating within the health system, and to take them into account as another condition for the development of primary health care.

Anything that suggests bureaucratic or administrative rebelliousness is much more likely to fail than to progress, even very slowly, within the margins permitted by those in authority. It was undoubtedly in this sphere that the greatest mistakes were made, given that no bureaucratic authority will tolerate having its limitations continually pointed out. We feel that if we had been more careful about these relations, our work could have continued, and we would not have risked having the health team dismantled after the great efforts made to establish it.

The Prospects Ahead

Despite the above, experiments like the one described are very relevant. There is a collective memory in the health services of a long tradition of good relations with the community. This tradition is also remembered in community organizations, which have for many years had experiences of this kind of participation.

The methodology used was appropriate. It aroused enthusiasm among the different actors involved in the process, which meant that working relationships developed, similar to the concept of primary health care.

Finally, experiments of this kind will be more easily introduced when the political will to encourage participation by the people exists, and when it is the people who decide what focus public policies should take. A detailed discussion of the bureaucratic and administrative obstacles, the roles of professionals, and the political parties' influence on this process will of course be necessary.

We hope that the experience described will be useful to all those engaged in community work in different sectors, and that they will continue to investigate new forms of participation in work which will allow the neighborhood organizations to find means of identifying solutions to their problems, encouraging local development and an extension of democracy.

Notes

1. Colegio Médico de Chile, Metropolitan Dayschool on Primary Health Care. Final Document.

2. Table 4.4 reproduces one of the forms used by the health monitors. The survey was not intended to be rigorous in statistical terms, but to reflect aspects of the conditions found in one particular area. Taken from A. Infante and collaborators,"Sectorización de la información: Una herramienta para programación local," IV Chilean Dayschool on Public Health, 1984.

3. Presented at the Workshop on Public Health at the Universidad de Chile (Escuela de Salud Pública), Workshop on Primary Health Care held by the Servicio de Salud de Valparaíso and the Metropolitan Dayschool on Primary Health Care organized by the Colegio Médico.

5

Experiences in Community Education and Health in Latin America

María Teresa Marshall and Luz María Perez

Latin American Council for Adult Education (CEAAL)

The underlying issue in this chapter is the relationship between educational practices and primary health care programs. Educational practices as part of the community education process, and primary health care as seen from the perspective of the "Health for All by the Year 2000" strategy, are two indications of the desire for a project to transform society in Latin America. They also both contribute resources to effecting this change.

Educational practices and primary health care programs each have a specific contribution to make towards the lofty goal of transforming the structure of health care. It is our great aim to assume the right to be the protagonists of our own lives, our own health, and our own countries. This enormous task must be furthered by many different initiatives. One of the most important is to learn the language of democracy and put it into practice in our lives, seeing this as a process which grows out of individuals and rises to the heights of social and political power.

The strategy of primary health care embodies a wide-ranging desire for social participation. It demands that we weave broad webs in our societies with threads that extend into all social relations; it calls on us to redefine health in decidedly social terms, and to break the authoritarian, hierarchical monopoly on decision-making held by the state and health institutions. The experts must cease to be the only people who can take decisions or intervene in our lives; instead it should be each and every one of us—those who are directly affected—who decides what we need.

This call for social participation goes hand in hand with the need to demand and create opportunities for social organization based on collective interests and needs. The extention of networks that express our desires cannot be achieved by decree; it requires a long period of collective work. The essential component of this work is a process of education and training, in order to produce a mass resocialization and enable us to accept the challenge of assuming responsibility for our own health. This task involves great numbers of people, and can only be accomplished if the broadest range of disciplines, know-how, practice, and experiments are included.

At present, in the sphere of primary health care and community education are many programs of different kinds, with varying degrees of coverage, institutionalization, stability, etc., which have achieved varying degrees of success. Some—in Cuba and Costa Rica, for example—have had a great impact on the population as a whole. Others are small-scale and almost invisible, but have a "symbolic importance, a prophetic force which enables one to imagine and think about the process of social transformation in a new way."[1]

This chapter starts by giving a summary of some thoughts on the concepts of primary health care and community education, in order to delineate the area with which we are concerned. We argue that both the underlying principles and the breadth of the two concepts allow what is possible to merge with the utopian, and the narrow bounds within which we commonly act to be broken.

In the second section, we describe programs concerned with health and community education in Latin America. This does not attempt to be an exact account but is, on the contrary, our reading of these experiences. We collected, from libraries and documentation centers, all the publications on such programs. Since this is the first exploratory study of developments in this field in Latin America, we opted for a survey that excluded information obtained directly from participants. Assessment of that information will have to wait for a second stage, dedicated to comparing hypotheses with the challenges faced today.

The material collected contained a considerable amount of information and details about health and community education practices. By making a comparative analysis of the different programs, then measuring the analysis against the concepts of primary health care and community education, we created a basis for transforming this information into a proposal for discussion.

Finally, the last section marks out the field of debate. This is an increasingly urgent task, involving the exchange of experiences and information in order to meet the challenges head on. At the level of debate, by making use of past lessons, we project our aspirations towards the future.

Convergent Strategies: Primary Health Care and Community Education

The concept of primary health care is used regularly by health care workers employed by state institutions. In this context, the phrase refers merely to a "level of care," and education has no other role than to transmit norms and information. At the other extreme, in the margins of the state sector and public policies, the concept of primary health care is rarely used. A great deal of trouble is taken, however, on paper and in discussions, to give the concept of health care a universal character that goes beyond the bounds of illnesses and their cures.

Thus it is worthwhile to clarify concepts in order to make a reading of our practices. This reading will broaden the range of analysis and enrich daily activities with new approaches. The term primary health care, coined in 1978 at the Alma Ata Conference, reflects both a consensus on and a strategy for achieving the goal of health for all in the year 2000.

There are those who think that international declarations, agreements, and documents are worth no more than the paper on which they are written. This is a great mistake, because ideas which reflect needs and which are supported throughout the world can provide a way to project local experiences on a wider scale. An educational approach developed over a long period of time with small groups, whose principal merit is a practical application with a creative and innovative potential, will necessarily have a great deal to offer in deciding how to implement the educational work that accompanies a primary health program.

At the Alma Ata Conference, it was stated that primary health care is the key to achieving health for all, meaning "obtaining for all people the highest possible levels of health."[2] This declaration expressed a coming together of ideas, and reflected a consensus on development by recognizing that health transcends the bounds of illness and cure.

This integral approach refers to causes of an economic, political, cultural, and social nature, and is aimed at achieving a global concept in which health is not merely the absence of illness but also quality of life, including the physical, intellectual, and emotional well-being of individuals, families, and communities. Holistic solutions are put forward by emphasizing the capacity to meet the challenge of creating health for all through participation and organization. The concern is not simply to achieve intangible levels of participation, but rather to underline the need to create opportunities for participation in the planning, organization, operation, and control of health activities in the community.

The concept of primary health care rests on three basic criteria which must be part of a broader development policy: equality, sectoral coordination, and the development of independent capacities.

Equality, because primary health care is a basic human right. The fight for health for all is part of the fight for social justice. A redistribution of resources and priorities is called for, as well as access to basic services for the entire population. This redistribution must be made because of the vast inequalities between countries, with the high cost of health care and technological development increasingly widening the gulf.

Intersectoral coordination is a response to the problem of planning and manipulation of public policies by regimes, the problem of parallelism, and the duplication of activities which results in a waste of already scarce resources. It is also a call for collaboration and cooperation between different social and economic sectors: agriculture, recreation, education, etc.

The development of independent capacities has many implications, which taken together basically confirm that individuals and communities must take control of the care and protection of their own health. In Latin American countries, development of independent capacities allows the underlying criteria of primary health care to be identified more clearly. As a strategy, the development of independent capacities is not located in purely individual terms, but instead within a social context, which implies local and national initiatives. The aim is not self-sufficiency; it is recognized that intersectoral and international support and solidarity will be needed to overcome obstacles.

The three principles of equality, sectoral coordination, and developing independent capacities give a distinctive stamp to this health strategy, which calls for the pivot of health activities to be moved from within the structure of institutions out into the organized local community. This is a new way of looking at health. The sole responsibility for introducing this view cannot be left to those working in the sphere of public policy. The move from institutions to community is a necessary task for development, and a challenge to all social sectors to coordinate their efforts in agriculture, housing, employment, industry, education, recreation, and communications, to name but a few.

The strategy of primary health care defines the role that must be played by local groups and organizations in achieving health for all. This goal cannot be reached without the active, organized involvement of the community. From the perspective of primary health care, community participation, as Rajesh Tandon points out, is both a principle and an essential component. Participation may be at different levels, from acting as a mechanism for increasing health provisions to establishing rules which enable local organizations to influence the planning, management, and control of health services.[3]

The term 'participation' has been given different meanings. In Latin America, the experiences of participation have been so different that a form of classifying them has been developed. Here we refer to the four categories of participation put forward by Patricio Hevia, on the basis of experiences in Latin American countries: (1) community volunteers; (2) local health committees; (3) local councils; and (4) health brigades.[4]

Just as the concept of primary health care has introduced a number of new approaches in the field of health, the concept of popular education also opens up new horizons and extends the range of educational activities. Any comparison between the two concepts must take into account that they have different starting points. The underlying postulates and concepts of popular education have been clarified in the course of its development, while the development of primary health care has been reached by international agreement.

The practices of popular education have provided a basis for development of a broad movement in Latin America, identified by a particular style of education which involves community organizations. This education is associated with the experience of mobilization of various sectors and oppressed classes, and is intended to further this mobilization.

The underlying principles are basically the same as those of primary health care, although in education the emphasis is on community organization, consciousness-raising, and implementation of integrated programs and activities. These principles are expressed at the local level, in specific actions intended to contribute to developing the hegemony of the people and as an alternative project for social change.

If we were to establish a bridge between the two concepts, what would be their common contributions and challenges? The work in popular education has successfully responded to many of the demands being raised by community groups, organizations, and social movements. In particular, it has opened up a space for participation, communication, and the exchange of ideas. These are clearly spaces that such groups consider their own, where respect for the individual and his or her culture and aspirations for social change are expressed in a common political will.

Popular education has been able to introduce innovations in methodology and techniques which make it easier for individuals to participate in community actions, and provide a foretaste of democratic social relations. At another level, it stimulated research into the reality of low-income sectors, with a view to revaluing the culture of the people; this research also involved the participation of individuals and groups directly involved. Finally, the educational work was assisted by social agents (mediators, given different names in different contexts) and constantly attempted to systematize its experience, as a basis for the exchange and enrichment of practices.

By bringing these educational practices together with the strategy of primary health care, new challenges are created. On the one hand, primary health care is a global challenge, a call for intersectoral coordination and the development of independent capacities. Popular education, on the other hand, is a demand for social change, and the development of methods and practices which contribute to this process and prepare the way for democratic relations.

These two concepts are complementary, in the sense that each fills gaps in the other. Primary health care can easily be transformed into a practice for community development, and thus lose its revolutionary potential; popular education has a bias towards community or local actions directed away from the critical challenges of the present. If the two strategies are combined in a common effort, they offer a way of achieving the goal of health for all by the year 2000.

Different Approaches

In Latin America, the number of examples and the extent of the development of community health programs that incorporate education as a component is much higher than anyone could have predicted. The experiences have been multiple and diverse, with a variety of styles and processes of development. Each provides examples of a wide range of strategies and techniques to deal with poor and deteriorating conditions of health.

Our aim in the following paragraphs is to show the different ways in which health work and popular education are organized. The comments and analyses provide a summary of experiences in these areas. The material available is highly disparate, but it allows us to set the scene, describe the actors, explain their approaches to health and education, and most importantly, put forward propositions as a basis for future discussions.

We suggest one way of analyzing and organizing the different projects, but it should be borne in mind that each project was developed in unique conditions. While we talk about how and from what perspectives this work is carried out, we must not forget that these groupings include a multiplicity of individual factors: political systems, health indicators, cultural characteristics, etc.

These programs have been developed by governmental and non-governmental groups. The latter include development agencies, church associations, and autonomous groupings. In each case, the parent organization is reflected both in goals and in styles of work. It leaves its mark on the levels of coverage, the potential for innovation and creativity, styles of management, and how results are evaluated. Perspectives differ and are at times antagonistic, but the work is firmly grounded and neither governmental nor non-governmental agencies try to work completely on their own, ignoring the other.

For purposes of discussion, we have classified this set of experiences in terms of objectives in the sphere of health. The reason for using health rather than education is empirical; in the material analyzed, the conceptual approaches to health and primary health care are set out more coherently. To organize these experiences in terms of educational practice would mean starting from that practice itself, and such an approach is only possible through discussion and exchange of opinions with those directly involved. The classification used here provides reference points for further discussion. With this in view, the experiences have been grouped in three categories.

Care for the Population

This category includes all primary health care projects or programs whose main concern is to ensure that adequate numbers of the population are provided with health services or to extend existing services. This particular characteristic is most often found in officially-run projects either directly or indirectly associated with government policies. This explicit concern for problems of coverage is seen in precisely those countries or regions where levels of care are low, and where people either do not make use of existing services or where these services are inadequate or ineffective.[5]

In this type of project, the strategy of primary health care is set out explicitly. Special emphasis is put on aspects of care associated with community participation and incorporation of resources available in the community itself. Community participation is the identifying feature of this category. Given that it is an underlying principle, and in light of the history of "experiences of participation" in Latin America, it is worth asking what the aim of this approach is, and what the possibilities are for this approach to be put into practice in an institutional setting which excludes participation.[6]

The results obtained by programs for community participation run by authoritarian, exclusive institutions (such as most medical institutions in Latin America) indicate that there are obstacles that can only be avoided with difficulty. The basic problem lies in the type of relationship that has been established between staff working in the health services and people seeking attention. There is a polarization between western forms of medicine and traditional practices, and an authoritarian relationship is established. This is expressed in distrust, fear, and, evidently, in a submissive attitude by the community towards the health staff.

From an educational perspective, a different assessment of these experiences can be made. This type of education is based on a positivist approach, and aims to transform the consciousness and health practices of the population by teaching new information and skills. The educators argue that inadequate practices for health care, hygiene, diet, and dealing with common illnesses are used in the community.

Educational work generally concentrates on two areas in which it is vital to improve health indicators: hygiene and nutrition. This form of education has absorbed modernizing influences, and rejects approaches which involve the direct imposition of information and relegate the community to the passive role of listeners. Instead, approaches which encourage participation, group discussion, and techniques for self-expression are being adopted. This participation, dialogue, and self-expression, however, continue to take place in an authoritarian context, in which the health staff has the last word. This is not simply because the staff wants it that way, but also because it is what the community expects.

As long as these educational activities are part of primary health care programs whose basic concern is to expand the coverage of the health services, they will be subject to needs and priorities established at the central level. These are generally either temporary projects or occasional campaigns around specific problems such as environmental sanitation, breast-feeding, early stimulation, etc.[7]

In spite of the rigidity typical of most programs run by official agencies in extending and maintaining levels of coverage, these programs do have advantages. There has clearly been a progressive improvement in indicators of child health, number of mothers giving birth in hospital, child malnutrition, and number of visits to the doctor per year, in countries which have achieved satisfactory levels of coverage.[8] Nor can it be forgotten that in these areas the changes can be attributed to a long process of education on a massive scale. This is the situation in Chile, where mass-level involvement of the people in health activities is a habit already being passed on from one generation to the next. These changes affect the daily lives of families in both urban and rural areas, and their area health center or health post has become a place that people visit regularly. This massive presence at the health centers explains the government's pride in the level of community participation in health programs, but attendance is not the same as participation.

The strategy of primary health care in the experiences referred to, because it is carried out within the framework of the official institutions, might well be in a position to suggest or implement changes. No intersectoral coordination, however, which would provide a basis for development, can yet be seen. Even if a strategy for integral development is put forward by the health sector, it is not easy to get other services also concerned with basic needs, such as housing, agriculture, or recreation, to adopt it.

Along with this integral concept of health is the idea of "caring for oneself." The use of this term in areas of poverty and marginalization can be extremely dangerous. In the first place, how can one care for oneself when the basic social and economic conditions for this do not exist, and in a situation characterized by unequal distribution of resources and abilities? Inevitably, the result will be unequal care, with care for the poorest groups in the population being very unreliable, while high technology is available to the sectors that can afford it.

The concept of self care, which does have potential validity, must be translated in different terms in Latin America. In Chile, it should involve the social appropriation of health. While the fight to increase coverage is clearly a priority, it is nevertheless only one element in a development strategy aimed at improving the health of the population.

Although self care is a valid concern, the path taken by those countries which have achieved acceptable levels of care must be borne in mind. Their experiences suggest that efforts to extend coverage must go hand in hand with measures to improve the quality of health care and to extend community involvement. And the great danger of health institutions establishing authoritarian structures which exclude and dominate those they serve must not be forgotten.

Linking Health and Organization

Under this heading we have grouped all programs intended to improve health conditions in the population by means of educational activities and community organization. "Education for organization" is a key factor in bringing about social transformation.

The great majority of these programs developed as reactions. Some are a response to inadequacies and defects in existing health systems, others to military regimes that have denied all possibilities of carrying out programs with poor communities. These regimes have unintentionally encouraged a search for and creation of alternative spaces in which to develop work on health care, education, and organization around health issues.

But it is not merely the inadequacy of existing systems that gave rise to this new approach; issues which have not been dealt with publicly have also contributed to its emergence. Women, indigenous peoples, and marginalized social sectors all have very particular conditions of living which are inevitably ignored in the uniform approach taken by official health systems. As a result, projects have been introduced to raise consciousness in these sectors, so that they can begin to look for ways to control their own bodies and the health of their families, and recognize the specific oppression they suffer.[9]

Our concern is not so much with the origin of these initiatives as in seeing how they relate to the primary health care strategy and examining the experience in terms of community education. At first sight, it is surprising that the concept of primary health care is not mentioned in the documentation of these programs. Nevertheless, this approach is firmly rooted in the dominant principles of the strategy.

These projects are based on the integral concept of health as one component in a process of development and improved quality of life. Health conditions in the communities where these projects work are defined not only in terms of health as an absence of illness, but also as directly related to the material conditions and specific oppressions suffered by indigenous people, women, peasants, etc.

The predominant concern is with organization. In many cases, this organization goes beyond the work on health and relates to a set of demands arising from the daily lives of people in poor sectors. When the program is developed under repressive political conditions, the possibilities of strengthening the organizations and encouraging social participation represent a still greater challenge. This political scenario also imposes limits on the area in which the grassroots health organization can work.

These projects maintain a predominantly local character if political conditions do not allow them to be extended. This work has particular characteristics; it is intensive, and based on small groups which have little communication with other groups. The strategy they adopt is ultimately one of self-reproduction, with national issues not taken into account. To a great extent, efforts tend to be spent on reproducing associated organizations rather than coordinating with other initiatives in the community. Thus there will be a health committee, a women's workshop, and a people's medicine chest—organizations given their validity by local conditions.[10]

Running through all of these community organizations is a sense of precariousness and instability. In many cases they have emerged and exist because of the project, and their survival will therefore be affected if the project ends or declines. This situation, which is a recurring problem, has meant that the work has been most successful in the experience of individuals, rather than as part of the history of the community.

As stated above, political concerns are latent in these experiences, but the emphasis is on issues of the moment, and action does not always extend to putting forward proposals. This is confirmed by the fact that these projects rarely make alternative proposals for health. The vision of a utopia and the dreams of change, with their great capacity for analysis, criticism, and inventing new forms of organization and mobilization, have faded away. Immediate demands, political repression, and the challenge of just keeping going have worn down the people's capacity to take hold of the future as their own.

Some of the most important achievements and advances made by health promotion can be found in the sphere of education. The local and intensive nature of health promotion has opened a space for innovation and creativity in education. The experience of popular education has been enriched by the process of developing an alternative political and social project, and forming the actors to participate in it.

The broad challenge to make changes in daily health activities has resulted in discoveries and achievements as well as mistakes. The issue of health has made introduction of specific methods of education necessary. Community groups concerned with health matters do not meet just to discuss their "reality" and the "present situation"; they also have an urgent practical need to discover, learn, make changes, take action, and exercise an influence. They must dominate an area of knowledge, in order to develop effective tools for transforming daily practices such as diet, hygiene, first aid, recognition of common illnesses, and use of herbs.

Reading about the experiences of these projects, one can see the relationship that was established between popular wisdom and medical knowledge. The general tendency was to overvalue popular wisdom, referring to it as autochthonous, native, and pure, terms which suggest a populist approach in which the only thing that counts is what the participants say and do. This creates a situation where new information must be introduced in tune with the pace and rhythm of thought and action of the groups involved.

In educational work, the goal was most often to train health monitors or promoters to act as mediators between the institutions and local groups. The groups involved were not untouched by processes of modernization and the spread of information, and thereby the demand for medicalized health. Particularly in urban areas, there are demands for very specific information. This can be used to enter the medical marketplace, as with courses on first aid which enable the person to give injections, or for personal benefit, as in learning about child development in order to be a better parent.

The ability to go beyond individual demands, to root activities in the field of social needs, has involved slow, systematic work, backed up by the organizational experience of these projects. Clearly, the presence of and membership in a grassroots organization enables participants to understand the limitations of individual aspirations and the need for collective demands and efforts.

This kind of project represents, in both education and community organization, a call for communication, exchange of opinions, and proposals. These experiences, under the adverse conditions of silence, exclusion, and repression, have developed a form of operation characterized by innovations in methodologies and contents. The challenge they represent, however, has still to be taken on by society as a whole.

Extending Horizons

Under this heading we have included a number of projects combining different strategies that enabled them simultaneously to develop social organization and participation, and introduce alternative educational approaches, in both cases with a view to improving conditions of health in the population. The concern with coverage and with community organization to raise demands and take action on health issues are among the aspects taken into account in creating an alternative for development. These projects have emerged from the convergence of several conditions in the socio-political situation, and in particular from the political will to make changes in traditional methods of health care. They are also the result of the development of community organizations, and technical teams with a long history of involvement in social demands for community health and education.

These various factors have merged and produced a style of work that can serve as a preparation for substantial change. The concern for care and organization can thus be combined to form the basis for an alternative form of primary health care. An explicit future projection or the elaboration of a utopia is a characteristic result of experiences in these projects. In some cases, the vision is being transformed into reality (as in Cuba), while in others it remains a thing of the future, with realization depending on outside forces (as in Chile and Peru).[11]

All the work on primary health care based on a global approach is not being developed by governments. The Chorrillos (Lima) health project,[12] for example, was put forward as an alternative approach to health run by the people. It did not relieve government agencies of their responsibilities but made the formulation of an alternative approach to primary health care its goal, with the active involvement of the local community, and sought to consolidate grassroots organizations and participation in the work of improving local health.

In the discussion of "extending horizons," we focus on aspects of projects that emphasize health as a tool for achieving social development. This type of health care is developed through a process of community participation and organization, and depends on a number of factors ranging from the state's resources to levels of organization, control, and capacity for management in the community. Thus it cannot be visualized separately from the rich fabric of organization, consciousness, and social mobilization of which it is a part.

From an educational point of view, these projects have a wide range of focusses. Among them are recognition of the urgent need for education for the health groups themselves; the idea that education must respond to a variety of demands, such as learning about the human body, life, and illness; the need to learn about social mobilization and organizing collectively; and learning to establish and manage democratic relationships after breaking with authoritarian and bureaucratic traditions. There is a great educational challenge to create appropriate techniques and methods in the course of such experiences.

Flexibility and the capacity to build upon past experience and recognize existing limitations and new demands are among the outstanding features of the examples discussed. Today the Cubans are talking about the need to deal with authoritarianism and bureaucracy in health care. This problem has finally been recognized after years during which the emphasis was on quantitative progress. Those involved in the work in Chorrillos recognize its limitations as a pilot project, but also see its importance in terms of putting forward alternative models of care. This ability to project into the future breaks the narrow bounds of a local experience and is the most important challenge to programs which have limited themselves to local action.

To sum up, a number of different factors contribute to the experiences of these programs and projects: existing situations, political will, experience in community health, strengthening of local organizations, and the willingness of the health teams themselves. Common to all is the search for a primary health care strategy which combines education, organization, social mobilization, and a global concept of health as tools for personal and social development.

From the Present Towards the Future

This review of experiences in programs that combine primary health care with community education gives an idea of the strong force growing out of their presence in the daily life of the communities. They are part of a movement that becomes more consolidated day by day, and a foundation for plans for the future. A discussion of this future must be started in order to make the best use of the potential represented by our activities, to take control of our own health and lives, and as a first step towards what sometimes seems far off and unattainable.

We begin with a series of stages which we consider priorities, bearing in mind that for this discussion to be productive, many other actors must also become involved.

Health, a Priority for Public Policies

In order to imagine the situation of health for all in the year 2000, priorities for public policy-making that are very different from present priorities must be established. We first examine the role of the state in providing and distributing resources to develop the strategy of primary health care.

From an economic point of view, given that there have been a number of failures, opting for primary health care involves far-reaching changes. This choice implies both global and radical changes. Global, because they will affect the distribution of resources in other areas of national life. And radical, because there will have to be a redistribution of priorities and efforts within the health systems. The tendency towards high levels of medical specialization will have to give way to systems that respond to the most common, frequent problems.

When the strategy of primary health care becomes a priority for national policy, a tendency to impose uniform norms, programs, and methods of attention develops. The risk of creating a single program or national plan which everyone has to follow is very common in health and education programs. These rules and norms may seem to be universal and efficient, but in fact are based on an authoritarian approach.

It is easy and tempting to take this path, because of both the lack of resources and the inertia in the way activities are carried out. One of the great challenges involved in primary health care is to find ways of avoiding uniformity. The question is how a national policy can be combined with respect for the heterogenous nature of society?

The best answer is flexibility. From the start, each community should be encouraged to find concrete forms of controlling its own health, according to its own characteristics, conditions, and priorities. This train of thought leads to a second issue.

Collective Tasks

When any community or any social movement initiates a process of taking increased responsibility and becoming increasingly organized in order to introduce primary health care, it is laying the foundations for a system which will respond to the needs, beliefs, and characteristics of each social sector. Health is not a statistic; as Valentina Borremans says, ". . . it is that special vitality, which is always surprising and which is the expression of a culture."[13] It seems contradictory, therefore, that health should continue to be seen as the particular and exclusive responsibility of the staff of hospitals, health centers, or primary health care posts. There must be a far-reaching process of change, so that health becomes instead the concern of each individual and of the totality of our social organizations.

At first sight, however, this change does not appear easy, since it implies a change not only in social and power structures but also in ways of thinking and behaving in relation to health. Any attempt to take control on an individual or collective level encounters obstacles rooted in the social order. The greatest obstacle is the authoritarian, elitist relations which have for centuries characterized the medical and health system.

It is therefore not surprising that any proposal for change must involve changes in social and cultural relations as a whole. This implies something as simple—but at the same time as difficult and problematic—as a social process to democratize power relations. This in turn raises the question of the democratic exercise of power, taking it as not only a mechanism of representation but also as involving direct management. We are talking about the socialization of power, so that responsibility for our health can be taken collectively. There have been significant developments in both the literature on power and its socialization and in social experiments which contribute to debate and practical action.

Included here are discussions on local development and self-management, which have resulted in a call for the reconstruction of the fabric of social relations in order to overcome the inertia and authoritarianism of the state bureaucracy. This new social structure would give expression to daily life in poor neighborhoods, factories, schools, and rural areas as a vibrant, active whole, able to break the barriers of silence and exclusion. It would lead to a definitive process of development and the decentralization of local communities which, by developing new social relations and organizations, thus would reject the institutional formalism of the existing medical system.

By placing the strategy of primary health care within the concept of the development of local communities, it can be extended and enriched. At the same time, new possibilities and perspectives for social participation are opened up. This gives primary health care a position and a concrete role in improving the quality of life in the community, by involving its members but also respecting their history, culture, and pace of life. The similarity between the views and processes of primary health care, in conjunction with the practice of community education, will ensure that this utopia does not die an early death, or remain closed within the narrow confines of a local community.

The criticism of medical institutions as part of an authoritarian and elitist system obliges us to go on to a third stage, in order to refer to the social group composed of mediators or agents who provide medicine and health care within this system.

The Health Services Staff Today

Between the institutional structure of public policies and the local community is a group of people who physically provide care and health services. Health staff do not represent a homogeneous whole, so any generalizations will fail to express the wealth of differences among them. They range from doctors to medical auxiliaries, and include nurses, midwives, and social workers. Each category has its own academic training, with different languages, codes, and status. In providing basic health care, these workers are obliged to carry out a routine series of predetermined activities which leave little opportunity to make use of skills or creativity.

These groups are all engaged in a single task but each has specific activities to carry out. Here subordination and hierarchy are accentuated; doctors are at the top of the pyramid, with a monopoly on power, authority, and prestige. It is this hegemony of medicine that, day in and day out, undermines the integral concept of the strategy of primary health care.

While doctors have a monopoly on prestige within the health team, in the local community prestige extends to all staff working in health institutions. The daily relations established by the community with this world of health officials display extremes of admiration and rejection. The community admires the power that health services staff have over their lives, especially in times of illness, pain, or insecurity. It also rejects the bureaucratic, rigid attitudes of the staff, especially when they are unable to respond to expectations of a cure. These clearly are complex relations, and contribute to deforming the practical application of the strategy of primary health care.

Once again there is a barrier; the health services staff has recognizably failed to satisfy the conditions necessary to make primary health care a reality. We cannot forget that all primary health care strategies rely not only on developing local communities and community education, but also require the encouragement and participation of health services staff. The daily work of the staff must necessarily feed into and carry forward any initiative in this sphere.

Special educational activities therefore need to be organized in this area. They should be wide-ranging, covering not only technical retraining but also, more particularly, the resocialization of health workers to prepare them to work side by side with the local community. It is an ambitious task, which should be supported by public policies and involve multiple initiatives. The fruits of this work are realized only in the long range, but the educational process involved does forge an integral concept of health.

Invisible Themes and Excluded Actors

The breadth of the primary health care strategy can only be achieved by opening up new horizons. When we look back at actual practices, however, it is surprising that certain themes and actors are either absent or not mentioned. The priority given to certain problems such as nutrition, hygiene, or common illnesses, have relegated to a secondary position issues which, while crucial, do not give rise to visible dramas.

New problems have arisen in society in Latin America: violence, repression, neurosis, depression, lack of opportunities for self-expression and recreation, destruction of the environment. These are issues about which a primary health care strategy must take a position. Some progress can be seen in the work of non-governmental organizations. These issues present another major challenge; socializing responsibility for health means not ignoring or filing away certain problems, but dealing with each and every one of them.

It must also be recognized that there are social actors who are given no part to play in traditional health practices. These are people who have been excluded and marginalized because they are different, they criticize existing norms, and they cannot be made to conform. An important aspect of the wealth of our cultures lies precisely in these minority groups, who do not conform to social norms. Because it is difficult to accept things that are different, these people are avoided. Health work is characteristically dogmatic in dealing with them, due to the overriding tendency to make everyone the same, to fit them into pre-established molds. In fact, this process results in a loss of potential for personal and collective growth.

If health is seen as a coming together of life-styles, an expression of vitality, and a symbol of culture, it demands that minority groups, marginalized sectors, and those who are different receive just treatment. To break with systems of domination also involves accepting as equals people with mental illnesses, homosexuals, and people of other races. The common—and now institutionalized—attitude of marginalization ensures that a structure of exclusion is preserved. This exclusion is based on the belief that some men are better than others, and that men are better than women. Any strategy which aims to achieve the goal of health for all in the year 2000 must question all these different and invisible mechanisms of domination.

Popular Education as Part of This Future Task

We have referred to different issues which suggest the need for educational activities as a key to meeting the challenges identified. We see this activity being included in each of the different aspects of primary health care, and thus as an appeal for a different approach in the field of health education. What is needed is an approach to education which supports processes of social organization and mobilization, gives rise to new ways of understanding, behaving, and providing health, prepares for the restoration of personal and collective control, and tests alternative methods of transforming relations of authority and exclusion. Ultimately, this educational practice must unite efforts with and increase the potential of the primary health care strategy.

This set of requirements seems huge; it is difficult to imagine that there could be adequate proposals in all areas of action. Community education, however, enters the sphere of primary health care with a number of advantages. In the first place, it is a discipline founded on practice, and does not rest on a structured, rigid body of theory. Its usefulness lies in this incomplete process, the ongoing search, criticism, and transformation. Community education bases its proposals on the conditions and demands of the groups with whom it works. These characteristics are an advantage, because they give the flexibility to adapt to the challenges presented by the primary health care strategy.

A second advantage is the concern to preserve and revitalize expressions of culture and daily life. It is in this everyday culture, in the specific ways that every human group develops to defend life and create health, that basic health practices are found. These are simple methods, invisible rites, actions of women and children, which combine to make life better and provide ways of dealing with pain. Seemingly insignificant practices are engraved on the history of the poor, and have been transmitted orally and by imitation from one generation to the next, from the countryside to the cities. History reveals practices and beliefs which have converged as a unity of distinct elements, where the boundaries of the natural, mythical, and emotional worlds merge into one another.

A third advantage is that community education acknowledges its involvement with actual events, with the present and the future. This concern is expressed in efforts to deal with the challenges of each period, and to seek appropriate ways to make the process of transformation more effective. It is a discipline that does not simply support social movements, but takes up challenges related to politics and culture as well. In this sense, community education is able to respond to the need for a primary health care strategy and introduce initiatives appropriate to the stage of development of specific social movements and to the most pressing health problems.

The fourth advantage we should mention is that part of this discipline is the ongoing task of systematizing the work and knowledge that have been accumulated. Thus community education is, simultaneously, trying to influence actual events, respond to existing needs, and preserve traditional educational processes. This concern, however, has ensured that the complex and at times chaotic process of community education maintains an underlying thread which in the long term can be seen and evaluated by those involved as well as by outsiders. When educational work is combined with health activities, it becomes even more important to study and evaluate its impact.

Given these advantages, community education should be able to offer specific alternatives for putting primary health care into practice. This process must involve a consensus covering all the different activities taking place in this sphere—those carried out by the government, as well as those in the non-governmental sector. The specific solutions offered should take three dimensions into account: information, organization, and participation. These fields are relevant for both educational activities and primary health care.

Community education has developed a body of ideas and practices relating to popular knowledge, a diffuse and sometimes intuitive form of knowledge which has a wealth of expressions, and is born and grows out of everyday life. It is important to investigate this form of knowledge not only to understand it but also to transform the information to make a person's control over his or her own life effective and powerful. This involves getting to know his or her own body, understand its reactions, learn to look after it, and eat properly. Health, the body, sex—these cannot be kept a mystery any longer.

Discovery of and control over one's own body helps in understanding that the body is not just a machine made for working, having children, and eating. An understanding of anatomy as the harmonious relationship between parts and the discovery of sexuality, pleasure, and recreation, enable a person to dominate and manage the different aspects of life. This process starts with getting to know one's own body, goes on to controlling the various spheres of one's social life, and makes a transformation of both health and life possible.

Taking control of information also means enriching popular knowledge through new approaches. There is a daily bombardment of news and information about science, technological advances, and new experiments in health. If the gulf between the two types of knowledge is maintained, the result will be a chronic state of marginalization.

Organization is the structure which feeds into and coordinates the different initiatives of social life. Popular education has been preparing the field of organization by means of very varied activities. It is through organization that individual demands, needs, and suffering can be seen from a collective perspective.

The practice of primary health care requires an educational approach which not only allows the internal structure of organizations to be strengthened but also moves outwards to strengthen the local community as a whole. This educational practice must also feed into and broaden existing horizons, at the same time as it initiates work, recognizes achievements, and sets new goals. The need to emphasize the educational aspect of development is especially significant in organizations that have stagnated and become merely reproductive agencies as a result of too much importance being placed on petty achievements.

Health problems are a permanent challenge. Local organizations continually need to find innovative solutions in order to meet needs and mobilize the different social actors. One achievement of such educational practices has been the creation of opportunities for participation and involvement. This is a crucial factor in societies where participatory relationships are being progressively worn away. Today many people come to local organizations looking for refuge and support, for a space where they can talk, discuss problems, establish relations of solidarity and friendship.

Popular education has been able to respond to this demand for involvement by employing techniques to improve communication and self-expression. In health work, the dynamics of participation are crucially important; in times of pain, illness, or insecurity, a network of solidarity can have a restorative effect. It is at this level that these experiences of popular education have made their greatest contribution. They provide a simple, accessible way to find solutions to the most basic and routine human needs, while at the same time bearing in mind the importance of social transformation.

APPENDIX 5.1

REGISTER OF PROJECTS REVIEWED

1. Chile: Santiago, La Granja.
Women's Project - Friends. Ref.: Educacion Popular en Chile: 100 Experiencias, CIDE-FLACSO, 1984.

2. Chile: Santiago, South-eastern Area.
Educational program in Perinatal and Mother and Child Health. Ref.: Educacion Popular en Chile: 100 Experiencias, CIDE-FLACSO, 1984.

3. Chile: Santiago, Southern Area.
Development of the Villa 14 de Enero Community. Ref.: Educacion Popular en Chile: 100 Experiencias, CIDE-FLACSO, 1984.

4. Chile: Southern Area.
Health Education: guides on primary health care for community agents. Ref.: Primeras Jornadas Metropolitanas de Atencion Primaria, Colegio Medico. Santiago, January 1985.

5. Chile: Santiago, Lo Hermida.
Study on Scabies in the Lo Hermida Area, Health Groups, Lo Hermida, San Roque Local Clinic. Ref.: FLACSO, January 1985.

6. Chile: Santiago, Northern Area.
An experience of Health Work in the Northern Area: Fundacion MISSIO. Ref.: Primeras Jornadas Metropolitanas de Atencion Primaria, Colegio Medico. Santiago, January 1985.

7. Chile: Santiago, Pirque.
School for Parents Project. Ref.: Primeras Jornadas Metropolitanas de Atencion Primaria, Colegio Medico. Santiago, January 1985.

8. Chile: Santiago, Rural.
Training for Rural Teachers and Parents. Ref.: Educacion Popular en Chile: 100 Experiencias, CIDE-FLACSO, 1984.

9. Chile: Copiapo.
Health Agents Program: IEP. Ref.: Educacion Popular en Chile: 100 Experiencias, CIDE-FLACSO, 1984.

10. Chile: Rancagua and Talca.
Health Agents Program: Emaus. Ref.: Educacion Popular en Chile: 100 Experiencias, CIDE-FLACSO, 1984.

11. Chile: Linares.
Work with Groups in Poor Neighborhoods: Department of Fraternal Support. Ref.: Educacion Popular en Chile: 100 Experiencias, CIDE-FLACSO, 1984.

12. Chile: Chillan.
Parents and Children Program. Ref.: Educacion Popular en Chile: 100 Experiencias, CIDE-FLACSO, 1984.

13. Chile: Chillan.
Development of Sanitation in Rural Communities. Ref.: Educacion Popular en Chile: 100 Experiencias, CIDE-FLACSO, 1984.

14. Chile: Santiago-Copiapo-Chillan.
PAESMI: Alternative Program for the Extension of Mother and Child Health. Ref.: Que es PAESMI? Santiago, 1985.

15. Chile: Cachapoal Valley.
Peasants and Health. Ref: Primeras Jornadas Metropolitanas de Atencion Primaria, Colegio Medico. Santiago, January 1985.

16. Chile: Temuco.
Community Development: ACE. Ref.: Educacion Popular en Chile: 100 Experiencias, CIDE-FLACSO, 1984.

17. Chile: Concepcion.
Experiences and Results of School, Family and Community Education Program. Ref.: Primeras Jornadas Metropolitanas de Atencion Primaria, Colegio Medico. Santiago, January 1985.

18. Bolivia: Ocuri, Potosi.
IPTK: Tomas Katari Polytechnical Institute. Ref.: IPTK, 1983. Dr. Franz Barrios Villegas.

19. Bolivia.
Warmi Wawantin: Community Participation Program. Ref.: Encuentro Andino sobre Educacion y Participacion en Salud Comunitaria. La Paz, January 1984.

20. Brazil: Rio de Janeiro.
Women of Paraty: Education for Health Project, Institute for Cultural Action. Ref.: Contact, October 1984.

21. Costa Rica: San Ramon de Alajuela.
Hospital without Walls Program.

22. Cuba.
The Cuban Revolution in Health Care. Ref.: World Health, WHO, December 1980.

23. Ecuador.
Program for Extending the Coverage of the Health Services, Primary Health Care and Community Participation. Ref.: Programa de Gobierno, Ecuador.

24. Guatemala.
ASECSA: Association for Community Health Services. Ref.: ASECSA, Ap. Postal No. 27, Chimaltenango, Guatemala.

25. Honduras:.
Description of a poor neighborhood in Central America. Ref.: World Health, WHO, October 1982.

26. Mexico: Tlalpan.
Project for Research and Community Education with Women. Ref.: "Desnutricion, su diagnostico, prevencion y Primeros Auxilios," Mexico, 1985.

27. Mexico.
Universidad Autonoma Metropolitana, Unidad Xochimilco. Ref.: Juntas Aprendemos.

28. Nicaragua.
A revolution in health. Ref.: Organizing for Health, ICAE, Toronto, 1984.

29. Peru: El Cuzco.
Cuzco Regional Experience. Ref.: Encuentro Andino sobre Educacion y Participacion en Salud Comunitaria, La Paz, January 1984.

30. Peru: Lima, Chorrillos.
Alternative Community Health Program. Ref.: La investigacion-accion, vieja dicotomia. Leila Lima Santos. CELATS, Lima, 1983.

31. Puerto Rico: Estacion Hato Rey.
Women's Health Program. Ref.: Taller Salud.

32. Dominican Republic: Santo Domingo.
CIPAF, thematic guides: Women and Health. Ref.: CIPAF, Edic. Populares Feministas. Santo Domingo, 1984.

33. Venezuela: Paria, Estado de Sucre.
Centro de Capacitacion Los Pinos, CESAP. Venezuela.

APPENDIX 5.2

TABLE 1

AVAILABILITY OF BASIC HEALTH SERVICES IN AREAS WITH LESS THAN 2,000 INHABITANTS, 1971
(Population in thousands)

Country	No. of areas with less than 2,000 inhabitants	Areas with access to services	Population without services (thousands)	Population without services %
Bolivia	3,144	1,595	1,857	59.1
Costa Rica	946	904	682	72.1
Chile*	2,636	1,975	659	25.0
Ecuador	2,365	1,134	1,192	50.4
Guatemala	3,523	2,385	1,577	44.8
Honduras	1,866	939	1,414	75.8
Mexico	20,992	6,124	18,263	87.0
Nicaragua	1,070	321	736	68.8
Peru	6,555	3,933	4,862	74.2
Venezuela	2,888	2,454	295	10.2

* Less than 3,000 inhabitants.

Source: PAHO, Evaluation of the Ten-Year Health Plan for the Americas 1970-1980. Initial Evaluation, Mexico, 1976.

TABLE 2

LIFE EXPECTANCY AT BIRTH AND INFANT MORTALITY
(Latin America, 1975-1980)

	Life expectancy at birth (Men/women)	Infant mortality (children under one year per 1,000 live births)
CENTRAL AMERICA		
Costa Rica	68/72	30/25
El Salvador	60/64	56/45
Guatemala	57/59	81/71
Honduras	55/59	109/97
Mexico	64/67	74/66
Nicaragua	54/57	128/115
Panama	68/72	49/44
CARIBBEAN		
Bahamas	67/71	27/23
Barbados	68/72	30/24
Cuba	70/74	21/22
Dominica	65/70	-
Dominican Republic	58/62	102/90
Grenada	65/70	28/19
Haiti	49/52	137/123
Jamaica	68/72	16/14
Puerto Rico	70/76	23/17
St. Lucia	65/70	-
Trinidad and Tobago	66/72	34/24
TROPICAL SOUTH AMERICA		
Bolivia	48/53	176/159
Brazil	61/67	115/113
Colombia	61/64	84/71
Ecuador	58/62	74/66
Guyana	67/72	52/46
Paraguay	62/65	67/60
Peru	55/58	97/87
Surinam	65/70	33/21
Venezuela	65/68	50/40
TEMPERATE SOUTH AMERICA		
Argentina	66/73	48/42
Chile	62/69	42/38
Uruguay	66/73	52/49

Source: World's Women Data Sheet of the Population Reference Bureau, Inc., 1337 Connecticut Avenue, N.W., Washington, D.C. 20036, U.S.A.

Notes

1. Sergio Spoerer. *América Latina: los desafíos del tiempo fecundo.* Siglo XXI–ILET, Santiago, 1984.

2. *Global Strategy for Health for All by the Year 2000.* WHO, Geneva, 1981.

3. Rajesh Tandon, "The interlinks between primary health care and adult education." *Convergence.* Vol. XV, No. 2, 1982.

4. Patricio Hevia, *Participación de la comunidad en la atención primaria de la salud.* Mexico, 1984.

5. See Appendix 5.1, experiences in Bolivia and Peru (El Cuzco), Nos. 18, 29, and 30. In Bolivia, 70% of the population has less than 0.2 medical appointments per person each year; WHO recommends an average of one appointment per person per year for adults, and 1.5 in the case of children. Furthermore, Bolivia's vaccination program does not cover even 20% of the population at risk. Source: "Bases para la política de Salud del Gobierno Democrático y Popular." La Paz, 1983.

6. Jane Cottingham, "Women and Health." In *Women and Development.* ISIS, Geneva, 1983.

7. See Appendix 5.1, Nos. 19 and 29.

8. See Appendix 5.2, Table 2: Latin America (30 countries): Life expectancy at birth and infant mortality, 1975–1980.

9. See Appendix 5.1, Nos. 18, 20, 31, and 32.

10. See Appendix 5.1, Nos. 1, 3, 4, and 6.

11. See Appendix 5.1, Nos. 14 and 30.

12. See Appendix 5.1, No. 30.

13. Valentina Borremans. *Lo inverso de la salud medicalizada.* Mexico, 1978.

6

Appropriate Technologies: A Way of Meeting Human Needs

Blanca Velasco and Arodys Leppe

Center for Experimentation in Appropriate Technology (TEKHNE)

Our civilization has reduced the definition of human needs to needs of a purely physiological nature. Cultural, social, and emotional needs have been given only secondary importance. We therefore use the term "basic needs" to refer to the whole set of demands whose satisfaction is essential for human survival and is the fundamental basis for individuals to act in society.

Basic needs include food, housing, and health, as well as education and work. But these are only the most basic requirements. Both practical social action and new theories indicate that basic needs should be extended to include other aspects which make the human experience more complex and rich in variety.

Humans beings have sophisticated needs and requirements, such as the ability to love, to understand the world around them, participate in social activities, enjoy their leisure time, be free, create, and transcend individual existence by making contributions to science, art, technology, etc. Most people, however, have developed mechanisms which fundamentally tend to meet needs associated with survival and ownership. These mechanisms function to the detriment of the person as a human being.

To the extent that human needs have been reduced to physiological needs, only the physical aspects of life are taken into account in finding ways to meet them. Thus the goal of western models of development, in both "free market" and "centrally planned" economies, is satisfaction of easily measured and quantifiable material needs. Western development concerns are basically production, exchange, and consumption of objects.

> It should therefore come as no surprise that there is nothing more important than income which, in the language we use, is the supreme yardstick, the ultimate need and the crucial possession. If the language we speak gives it a higher place than anything else, it is inferred that our instincts must be to value it above all else. Development is measured by income, welfare is a function of income, inflation is income that has been generated in the wrong way, and unemployment is the failure to generate income.[1]

Is it because of the difficulty of quantifying non-material human needs that they tend to be forgotten in development? Or is it that only the individual's physical aspects are considered because apparently only the physical being is useful for production? There is no simple answer, but human beings have clearly structured their world in terms of possessions; it is the number of goods produced, exchanged, and consumed that demonstrates human development.

At TEKHNE, we have chosen a different starting point. Orienting ourselves essentially in accordance with Max-Neef's approach, we focus our view of the world, society, and development on people, not on objects. As stated above, we therefore see basic needs as all the requirements of a human being, both those related to subsistence and those necessary to fully achieve the "human" character that makes men and women diametrically and qualitatively different from other forms of life on this planet.

Among these needs we include those required for individual and collective development, those whose satisfaction strengthens and improves relations between traditional human groupings (families) or new types of groups (social groups organized by sex, age, or common interests). We use the term "satisfactor" to describe mechanisms or relationships which the use of or participation in allows a human need to be satisfied. We also assume that fundamental human needs are by no means as abstract, ethereal, difficult to classify, and infinite as they might appear.

In order to develop a language with which to better understand and assess the level of satisfaction of needs than can be done with the precise terminology of statistics, it is necessary to accept and to use our essentially human sensitivity. We therefore take a position somewhat different from the concept of basic needs. "Basic" implies the establishment of priorities, which reduces the breadth of human nature and tends to exclude efforts to deal with those less quantifiable demands that are also an inherent part of the human condition.

Our basic argument is thus that development should have to do mainly with people and not with objects. We start by rejecting the definitions of technology as nothing more than "the science of mechanical and industrial arts." In fact, technology in its many different forms is a significant element in the human world. Its structures and processes have altered, influenced, and are now part of the structures of human consciousness, society, and politics.

We define technology as a set of tools, materials, information, and skills used to satisfy the needs of an individual or a community. We also include the mutual relations established through the use of technology in its definition. Thus technology may be regarded as an expression of social action, in which machinery and tools provide the means for organizing and carrying out that action.

When we use the term "appropriate technologies," therefore, we imply that these technologies are appropriate because they respond to the needs of a particular human group. This group might, for example, live in a certain geographical area, have a specific culture, its own scale of values, and/or its own specific requirements. These requirements, as we have seen, are to be found in all spheres of human existence.

If technology is an instrument for satisfying needs, it should therefore try to provide for the simultaneous satisfaction of the maximum number of existing needs. If that is not possible, technology should at least not make the satisfaction of some fundamental needs impossible in return for the satisfaction of others. For example, an individual who feels impotent because he or she is being controlled or manipulated by other people or by a computer, has been forced to abdicate the rights to understand, create, participate, establish personal relationships, and take decisions about the world in which he or she lives, in the crucial area of work. All this is surrendered in exchange for a salary which offers only the *possibility* of satisfying the need for food and shelter.

The means are part of the end and ought, therefore, to reflect that end.

Thus the first essential aspect of our definition of appropriate technology is that it should be developed for the purpose of satisfying the fundamental needs of a particular community, rather than in response to the economic demands of a market, particularly a market unfamiliar to the producers themselves. This definition implies that appropriate technology will produce the goods and services needed by the group it serves. Also implied is that appropriate technology should be simple in conception, thus allowing the people who use it to understand, develop, and employ it autonomously. It should also preserve rather than pollute the balance of the ecosystem.

The second essential aspect of this definition deals with the problem of resources. In order to allow the autonomy necessary for the population to participate actively, the technology must essentially use resources available in the physical, economic, social, and ecological environment in which the proposed development is to take place. Particularly in an urban context, the technology to be used should recognize the economic limitations and other restrictions imposed by poverty. This means that appropriate technology is characterized by the small amount of capital required, and by intensive use of labor. In general, it is also likely to be small-scale, being operated, maintained, and managed at the local level. There is also a need to use natural resources rationally, as a contribution to the welfare of future generations.

The third factor which should be borne in mind in this definition is social environment. The education, culture, customs, and values of the population cannot continue to be seen as obstacles to development, which is how they are seen from the viewpoint of the dominant interests in society. These characteristics must instead be accepted as the foundation on which each group will build its own development.

The dominant concept of development as based on "modern" technology emerged primarily out of post-war Europe. Transferred to underdeveloped countries, the problem seemed relatively simple: these countries would have to follow the same path of development that the now-advanced countries had taken. In practice, however, a rich, complex process of evolution was reduced to a process of industrialization.

In this approach, cultural differences were completely ignored. The specific characteristics of poor societies were evaluated almost exclusively in terms of their usefulness in furthering industrial development. Wherever cultural characteristics became obstacles to development, they were treated as signs of backwardness which would inevitably disappear. In other words, cultural differences were implicitly treated as only a stage of economic development, as though the desire for industrial development was the overriding aspect of any particular human society.

In our approach, the fundamental conditions for the assimilation of a technology into the social and cultural environment of the people who are to use it include their participation and the development of their creativity. These conditions are therefore indispensable if a technology is to be appropriate. The traditional approach sees technology as an inevitable factor of development, as though it were an unchangeable force to which all other needs must give way. We take technology as an important variable, one whose role should be defined in relation to other needs, resources, and the environment.

This approach neither accepts nor rejects machinery as such; nor does it see machines as either bad or good. Instead, it assesses them as instruments by means of which the community is either enabled or fails to satisfy its fundamental needs. Any machine, tool, or process which enables a community to satisfy its overall human needs, in our opinion, merits the title of "appropriate."

A labor process carried out by using a technology that allows individuals to establish harmonious relations with the work tools, the environment, and the other people involved in the work, is a process which satisfies fundamental human needs.

Diagnosis of Social Conditions

In Chile, the introduction of neo-liberal policies that concentrate economic power and are socially exclusive and politically repressive has had a much greater impact than can be conveyed by the disastrous effects shown in economic indicators, and has significantly altered traditional social and cultural patterns. In an analysis of urban sectors of "critical poverty," it is important to emphasize that changes in cultural and socio-economic patterns and in traditional mechanisms for the economic insertion of individuals in society, have made the situation of the worst-off sectors much more complex.

This complexity is also indelibly marked by the myth of industrialization. There is now little employment in industry, and the organization of industrial workers has been broken; they have been excluded from the "productive" sector. In industrial societies, the sense of belonging to a reference group with real social importance comes from factory employment and is based on an awareness of common interests. With the dismantling of Chilean industry, this pattern has been broken. The people thus excluded from the system have suffered damages not only of an economic nature but also psychological and human damage.

This paradigm of industrial development and its universal and individual consequences is as true of "free market" as it is of "centrally planned" economies. The requirements of industrialized production and the corresponding organization of the population have been imposed. The interests, and economic and cultural activities, of the rest of the population have been subordinated to those requirements.

The resulting crisis in the social system has made necessary some alterations in the model of development. More complex assessments of the various forms of social organization and the changes in cultural patterns must be made. For example, the rise in male unemployment and the increase in the active female labor force brought[2] a change in the traditional view of the "head of household." The characteristics of a male head of household are, generally, that he is a factory worker with a relatively stable job who provides money to cover the costs of his family's subsistence. He also has no specific responsibility for domestic work, which is done by his wife and the older children.

The female head of household, who has emerged over the past decade, does not usually work in industry but in the service sector, and in general on an informal basis. This implies an ongoing search for work, since she has no security of employment. This insecurity results in the development of survival strategies based on collectively-organized activities, which require the new head of household to take an active social role in community organizations. The woman must also continue to be responsible for the domestic work. In short, the female head of household—found in one in every five homes—has a more complex role than the male head of household. In drawing up and putting forward social policies designed to improve the living conditions of children in areas of exclusion, the needs of these women and of community organizations the majority of whose members are women, must be addressed.

Over the past 40 years, there have been significant alterations in eating habits, and the importance of childhood has been recognized.[3] As a result, it is now possible to have a direct impact on the living standards of the child population in marginal sectors by influencing the nutrition, psycho-social stimulation, and education that they receive.

In almost all Latin American countries, urban areas of exclusion have many characteristics in common. The people who live in these areas do not have access to the socio-economic benefits provided by the system. The areas themselves are usually geographically peripheral to urban centers, and characterized by their overall deterioration—nearby rubbish dumps, polluted atmosphere, proximity to industries without planned systems for waste elimination, shortages of housing, overcrowding, promiscuity, lack of basic services for domestic hygiene, distance from educational and health facilities, inadequate transportation, insufficient sewage systems and street lighting, lack of parks and play areas, along with other problems.

Campamentos (squatter settlements), *poblaciones* (poor communities), and *conventillos* (slums) are three specific types of areas of urban poverty. There are differences in the kinds of people, levels of subsistence, and temporal stability of each type of community.[4]

The population of the *campamentos,* where the problems described above are acute, is composed of people who have been removed from their previous homes in more residential areas (in general, people from several neighborhoods are brought together in one *campamento*) and who usually own nothing more than a meager amount of domestic equipment and some dilapidated building materials. Not only have they been geographically and socially marginalized, they also have no title to the land they occupy, which means that they are repeatedly moved from one site to another.[5] There is no sense of belonging, and therefore no long-term commitment to a group or community.

The *poblaciones* have often also been formed as the result of the removal of a group of people from their previous homes, but here the land is allocated to them, which is a qualitative difference from the *campamentos.* The income of people living in *poblaciones* is relatively higher than that of people in *campamentos;* they have, or have had, more stable jobs, although today unemployment in this sector is high. Each home has a sanitary unit (bathroom and kitchen), to which the family's fragile wooden dwelling (*mediagua*) is attached. An important difference is that the people here are not vagrants but residents, which affects the nature of social organization and provides a perspective of community life.

The other type of impoverished urban dwelling is found in the city centers, generally in large, old buildings with an extremely high level of overcrowding and promiscuity. These are known as *conventillos* or *cités.* The physical structure of this housing is different, but the conditions are as unbearable as those in the *campamentos* and *poblaciones.* The large number of families living in a single house (there may be as many as 30 people living together), with men, women, children, and old people crowded together, produces a deterioration in human and social relations not seen in peripheral areas. People in this kind of housing generally do not consider themselves marginalized, and tend to set themselves apart from the people in *campamentos* and *poblaciones.*

The economic characteristics of the sectors described here include a constant struggle to survive, periods of unemployment and underemployment, employment in various unskilled jobs, low wages, child labor, a chronic shortage of money and no savings, lack of stocks of food, no access to social security and medical systems, etc.

This situation of people living in uncomfortable, overcrowded conditions, without private lives, and the existence of *allegados* (families who share another family's home), has become a national institution. There are also high levels of malnutrition, alcoholism, drug abuse, and child prostitution. Violence is a frequent part of day-to-day relations, along with an exaggerated encouragement of machismo.

Living conditions such as these normally give rise to strong feelings of marginalization, dependence, and not belonging anywhere. However poor and marginal a particular group may be, it will nevertheless always establish some form of economic life. Faced with conditions of this kind, community groups, support institutions, churches, and other organizations have developed many types of assistance.

The phenomenon of outside assistance has been expressed in a very particular way in Chile. Associations have been established to deal with immediate economic, social, and cultural problems. This is done by means of concrete economic activities, and/or production and sale of goods and services, and/or obtaining goods and services for their members.[6]

The people who participate in the programs provided by these associations make equal contributions and collectively manage their own resources, as well as any resources they may be able to obtain through donations or social activities. They thus manage to establish themselves, to some extent, in the market or in the informal sectors of the economy. An important characteristic of these organizations is that their values are not individualistic, but based on solidarity and mutual support. Sometimes they are economic units which are alternatives to the capitalist institutions that predominate today, and in this capacity indicate paths towards the transformation of society and the liberation of the people.

As well as these organizations, there are other forms of economic, political, social, and cultural life, which share the concern of finding ways to deal with the problems and basic human needs which cannot be satisfied by means of the group's own collective efforts.

A sense of solidarity, democratic internal relations, a concern for autonomy, the sense of belonging to a community, participation, integration of private and public issues, are some characteristics common to grassroots organizations and which may be the seeds of a new culture in the poor sectors of the cities.

Forms of Social Intervention

Today the city of Santiago alone has a population of 4.5 million people, 22% of whom are living in conditions of extreme poverty. Our work, as a form of social intervention, focuses on the use of appropriate technologies to deal with urban problems. As the discussion above has indicated, the central objective of our work is to assist the people who are at present living outside conventional economic and social structures in finding ways to satisfy their fundamental human needs.

We have chosen the development of appropriate technological solutions as the instrument for this work. Appropriate technologies make possible or facilitate the production of goods which help to meet the requirements for survival. At the same time, appropriate technologies can generate or develop a new relationship between people, one which is more egalitarian and balanced, and allows for participation, creativity, affection, self-esteem, and, ultimately, a respect for human dignity.

The specific objective is thus to support grassroots organizations through technological solutions which offer the possibility of autonomously meeting basic needs, reinforce the values of solidarity, provide opportunities to develop social relations, and to use and develop latent capacities. The severity and urgency of the problems, the level of consciousness among those affected by them, and the activity and organization to which the situation has given rise, are all factors which help in the development of this work. The virtually complete lack of economic resources, the total absence of government support, and the limitations imposed by the present economic situation on all work involving social action or autonomous organization, are obstacles which can make the proposed goals impossible to achieve.

The method used generally involves six main phases. The first is *direct contact* with the organization or group requesting support. Getting to know the members of the group, their characteristics, skills, and limitations; the group's history and degree of organization; and the types of relations between members, etc., is crucial to further development. The only requirement in making the decision to support a particular group is that its members be fully and absolutely clear that the problem is theirs, and that finding a solution is their own responsibility. The group itself, therefore, makes the decisions, determines the pace at which the work proceeds, obtains the materials, and organizes activities. In some cases, however, donations and/or loans may be requested.

The second is *identification of needs.* In fact, it is not difficult to "identify" a need. The problem, for a person who lives outside the community, is identifying which need is the most urgent, will most effectively galvanize the group into action, and can be dealt with by using the resources to which the group has access. Usually the members of a group already know what their major problem is, and ask for support in finding a way to resolve it.

The third phase is the work involved in *research and development* of a technology that will offer an appropriate way of resolving the problem. It is important for some member of the group to participate in this phase. The problem is first taken on as a challenge to the imagination, knowledge, and experience of the professionals. In the second stage, the methods used to deal with similar problems in other places are looked at. Experience has shown, however, that technologies developed in other countries can rarely be adapted to the social, economic, political, and cultural context of people in urban areas of Chile.

Once a technological solution has been found, tests are made, discussions held, and those involved *decide* whether or not to adopt it. If the decision is positive, then the necessary measures to implement the technology can be taken.

Next is *implementation* of the technologies. This usually involves training sessions, during which the whole process is carried out collectively. When the solution is a machine, a piece of equipment, or a set of machinery, these instruments are built, tested, and put into action through the joint efforts of all the people taking the training.

The final phase is *monitoring* the work, which actually means an ongoing involvement with the group. This is necessary because of the risk of a lapse in the work, generally due to the social dynamics of the community organization. To fail to understand, to deny, or to ignore this problem can result in an evaluation of the technology being made only in theoretical terms, not as the technology operates in real circumstances, full of potential and frustration, subject to change, and where progress is always accompanied by some reverses.

This is only a general outline of the work method. These stages are not always carried out exactly as described, nor are they necessarily consecutive.

Virtually all the problems of subsistence are related to nutrition, energy, housing, and health. The problems found in many different poor communities are similar. Thus the ongoing research into these issues has resulted in the development of a variety of alternative solutions which can be used in different urban environments.

The general policy in putting these solutions into practice has been that the people who will benefit should themselves provide the materials and tools necessary. The acute lack of resources, however, has on many occasions meant that a link was established between the grassroots organization and other institutions. These other organizations can provide resources, either financial or human, that allow the planned work to be carried out.

To sum up, our activities focus on research, training, and technical support, and have two main objectives. First, to provide grassroots organizations with simple technologies which assist them in dealing with problems of subsistence. Second, to develop technologies which are the basis for setting up units of production or workshops whose members produce goods for either collective consumption or exchange in the marketplace.

Some Conclusions and Perspectives for the Future

The work we have been doing makes it possible today, on the basis of concrete evidence and an analysis of past experiences, to put forward a number of preliminary conclusions.

The scale and complexity of the problems faced at present mean that they can no longer be dealt with using conventional methods. The structural deterioration of the economy rules out any possibility, in the short- or medium-term, of fulfilling external obligations as well as responding to the growing number of internal needs. Thus the sectors excluded from the system as a consequence of the economic and political situation are likely to remain excluded for some years to come.

The various grassroots organizations that have emerged in poor neighborhoods in order to demand rights or meet needs can no longer be considered a transitory phenomenon. They have become a structural element in society, and contribute new values and cultural tendencies as a result of their participative, supportive, democratic forms of social action.

In these circumstances, appropriate technologies have proven to be a valuable galvanizing factor, a tool which enables these sectors to deal with problems of subsistence, and a reinforcement of the human values developed in daily social actions. These technologies have encouraged certain changes in cultural patterns of development. They support a change in relations between individuals in order to help them to achieve their demands, and thereby develop the concept of a different type of community and social interaction.

The development of appropriate technologies in urban areas has had a particular character. The recognized sphere of appropriate technology has thus far been limited almost exclusively to rural settings and therefore related to agricultural production or animal rearing. In developing appropriate technologies for peripheral urban areas, the question of resources immediately arises. In cities, everything must be paid for, whether it is water, earth, sand, or stones. There are few trees, little space, and the air is poisoned by high levels of atmospheric pollution. Thus the natural resources of cities have virtually zero potential. There is, however, abundant waste material in cities, and although everything has its price, the rubbish dumps, rag-and-bone men, flea markets, etc., provide low cost materials, and can be useful resources.

The abundance of available labor power, the tradition of involvement in groups, level of organization, influence of the mass media, intensity of urban life, and participation, skills, and technical background of the participants make the results of a technological catalyst much more rapid than is possible in rural areas. This very speed of action, the urgency of the problems, and the social dynamics of the urban environment impose demands on the technical support team which lead to a further conclusion: technological solutions should be generated, basically, from Chilean imaginations, using Chilean knowledge and skills. There is not enough time to seek advice or ideas from appropriate technology centers in Europe or North America. New relations of dependence should not be established, nor should technologies be taken from catalogues. Also, the way technological training and/or the introduction of a technology is experienced by people who have been involved in the creation or development process is very different from the attitude of people using a method brought in from outside, in which they have invested neither their knowledge nor their commitment.

This brings up another point, demonstrated by the work: the multiplier effect of a technology is much greater when it has been wholeheartedly adopted by a group which other groups identify as their equal. From this point of view, the time and work spent on, and the people concerned with, investigating and testing technologies aimed at the common problems of many similar groups, is fully justified. The energy generated by this approach is encouragement to continue working along these lines.

The characteristics of the work described, as well as the conclusions drawn from experiences so far, suggest new scenarios where different kinds of actors will emerge.

Taking preparation, training, and organization to be basic needs, our work, similar to that of other institutions, has developed in the way described above. We see horizontal communication between groups as crucially important, and therefore support and encourage coordination between similar types of groupings. On the same principal, our institution seeks out others of the same kind in order to implement support policies.

The first steps in coordinating support efforts involved other similar institutions, and were by sector. Thus the focus on development policies is from a local perspective. Indeed, the physical environment, the social actors, and the nature of both the problems and the instruments to be used, provide an especially appropriate basis for encouraging local development.

The objectives of central government today are hardly compatible with the interests and styles of action of local social groupings. A development project based on the use of appropriate technology implies a set of values and a working method which are essentially opposed to the present government's form of local planning. It is, however, possible, on certain occasions and for specific purposes, to make use of available government resources to further local development. We believe that it is necessary to support co-ordinated, operational initiatives which bring different interests together in order to create the foundations for a participative system of development, one in which appropriate technology encourages and supports changes in cultural patterns of development.

Finally, there are the productive workshops. They are small- or medium-sized workshops which produce a greater quantity of goods than can be consumed by their members. Thus the surplus can be distributed to or exchanged with other individuals or groups.

Progress in this field has been hampered by two different kinds of problems. The first difficulty lies in the absolute lack of resources for an initial investment. However minimal this investment may appear, it is still beyond the economic possibilities of these groups. The general problems faced in everyday life, along with the total unavailability of loans or backing from higher institutions, mean that in most cases the group is unable to overcome this initial obstacle, regardless of the members' determination and/or their access to a technology appropriate to their needs.

The second problem is lack of management skills within the groups. The degree of organization that has developed in response to past needs may be compromised, weakened, and sometimes even destroyed when the collective has to take responsibility for managing a business. However small the business may be, it requires that they perform roles for which they have no preparation.

In these cases, we may be able to provide support in terms of some technical training in administration and accountancy, but it is impossible to communicate, in brief training sessions, the security and confidence needed to take decisions and act in a previously unknown sphere. This knowledge can only be gained through experience, but the group cannot afford to make any mistakes in this process. Because of the minimal room for maneuver, any error may mean the failure of the experiment.

Technology clearly influences and is influenced by social, political, economic, and cultural aspects of society. The prospects for this work are thus linked to the degree of change that a particular society can absorb. It is evident that work of the kind described strengthens the process of change in cultural patterns of development.

The growth in the number of grassroots organizations and the increase in local action are giving rise to types of community participation which are different from those found previously. Community soup kitchens, consumer collectives, production workshops, all arise from collective efforts involving creativity, discussion of ideas, and the search for and implementation of solutions to needs. At the same time, individuals cannot fully satisfy their need for creativity, participation, and autonomy in a society where freedom is in chains. To the extent that appropriate technologies are able to satisfy needs, they encourage and increase the desire for freedom, and indirectly influence or give rise to political behavior by the people who use them.

In order to illustrate this, we give below an account of work with a community soup kitchen in Santiago, in a neighborhood called Población La Alborada, Peñalolén. This account is taken from social activities and interviews with women who participated in the soup kitchen.

Stories from a Soup Kitchen[7]

The story of the community soup kitchen in Población La Alborada is the story of a series of coincidences, shared efforts, learning processes, and experiences of working as a group. The soup kitchen was developed in order to satisfy the fundamental human need for food.

Población La Alborada is in the eastern area of Santiago, in the *comuna* (borough) of Peñalolén. Like many other poor communities in this sector, it was established as a result of the "removal," in 1982, of people living in squatter settlements in other *comunas* in the eastern area of the city. These people were moved in order to "clean up" the elegant parts of the capital, basically the *comunas* of Las Condes and La Reina.

The people living in La Alborada came from *tomas de terreno* (illegal land seizures) and from long-standing squatter settlements along the avenues of Las Condes, Colón, and Bilbao. From there they were moved to empty sites in the foothills of the Andes, in Peñalolén.

Karina recalled: "We were moved out in truckloads. We were allowed to take with us whatever we could get into a medium-sized truck. My family had to leave behind the wooden panels that had been the walls of one room, and part of the floorboards."

Gloria added: "Each family's piece of land had been marked out, and had a connection to the water mains and the electricity supply. But even so it meant starting over from scratch."

La Alborada lies between two canals, Canal San Carlos and Canal Las Perdices, on a fairly pronounced slope where the mountains begin to rise. Beside the *población* there is a piece of waste ground, which is to be converted into a sports center by the General Directorate of Sports (DIGEDER). Meanwhile it is a cross between a rubbish dump, a football field, and a recreation ground, and provides material resources for the fertile imaginations of local children and adolescents.

Due to the slope, rainwater and water for irrigation often overflow into the streets, flooding the land and creating a permanent problem of dampness. This is not the only difficulty. Overcrowding and physical discomfort do not improve human relations, nor does the fact that the authorities arbitrarily grouped together people from different sectors, with different traditions, habits, and forms of individual and collective behavior.

There are problems, but there are also people who knew each other from former neighborhoods, and who had been involved in collective action. Thus a new learning process slowly began. The road from understanding and accepting other people's different characteristics to altering cultural patterns and establishing relations of solidarity is long and difficult.

First Steps

The first effect of the move was a noticeable decline in incomes. In their previous neighborhoods, domestic work in private homes was easily accessible to the women. In Peñalolén, the proximity to and thus the possibilities for such work declined considerably, and very few of the women now have jobs.

The type of work available for men also changed. The majority were gardeners, plumbers, or handymen. Today, a minority are employed by the local authorities on the PEM or POJH employment programs,[8] and the rest are unemployed.

These conditions gave rise to the idea of a "Fraternal Soup Kitchen." A nun and the most active people in the community nurtured the initiative. Little by little, the people came together and began to get support.

"The first soup kitchen was called San Pedro, and it was started in another part of the *población*. I was involved when it started. This is the second soup kitchen—the first and second soup kitchens are working together," said Peta.

"We have been working for more than a year, and have had support from the Church and also from other institutions. . . . This support has been in the form of food, firewood, and help in building the hearth where we cook, and the oven," explained Esperanza. She added, "To begin with there were about 30 families, now there are 69 of us. That means 335 meals a day. The work has doubled. And of course we now need twice as much food."

Gradually, at least one member of each family has become involved in the soup kitchen's activities. It has been a slow process. To admit that one is hungry and doesn't have the means to feed the family is difficult. The shame of not having anything to eat is only overcome after many conversations with neighbors, friends, in meetings, and while doing one's rotation in the soup kitchen. Still, there are families who, although they do need to eat better, do not participate in the soup kitchen because they consider themselves "above it," or because they see it as a political activity.

Sometimes "we women realized that it was a good idea to get involved in the soup kitchen, but what a job it was to convince the men! . . . Our husbands would say that we only went to gossip. But when they saw we brought food home with us, that silenced them."

The level of participation is uneven—"it's always the ten of us," the most active women. The difference in participation is one of attitude. There are some people with a history of active participation, who put the group first and are concerned with creating a sense of solidarity among the inhabitants of La Alborada. Others are content with solving their own family's problems. The physical proximity of the houses and the families living in them, however, makes it almost inevitable that problems are socialized, and so the second category is small.

How a Community Soup Kitchen Works

The work involved is distributed according to each participant's available time and personal characteristics. "There are six shifts, from Monday to Saturday, as we don't cook on Sundays."

No one is in charge of the shift. Some feel that things would work better if someone was in charge, but "of course someone always ends up organizing the lunch." Although it is not explicitly stated, the person who organizes takes most of the responsibility.

The president and some of the other women get the food, which is stored at the nun's house. They bring it to the people working that day's shift, and also give them money to buy vegetables. If there is not enough food, a pool or a house-to-house collection is organized for donations.

"The people on the shift are only responsible for the cooking." This means preparing the food, washing vegetables, peeling, chopping. The quantity of ingredients and seasonings to be used must be calculated; there is the fire to light, firewood to chop, and ashes to be cleaned out. Cooking also involves making sure that the food is neither over- nor undercooked, serving the rations, and monitoring distribution of the food.

Then comes the work of clearing up, and cleaning the room and the equipment used. The pots are washed out with ashes, which is very effective and makes up for the lack of detergents. Also involved are washing up the rest of the equipment, collecting rubbish, and generally tidying up the room.

The teams in charge each organize their different shifts in their own way. Some work particularly well; others don't. The problems are discussed in the General Assembly, or with the president. "If there are problems with one of the shifts, you try to sort them out and not exaggerate them. You give your point of view and they explain theirs," said Patty.

The Major Problems

The main difficulties in making the soup kitchen work properly are obtaining food, finding a suitable place to work, and making the fire for cooking.

The problem of the fire is not insignificant. At first gas was used, but it was very expensive. Finding four or five thousand pesos a month (US$20-25, at 1985 prices) became an insuperable obstacle for a group with an economic life virtually untouched by monetary transactions.

They started cooking on open fires. Firewood was collected and the fire made on the ground; the cooking pot was balanced on stones. "We had to light the fire at about six in the morning. It took ages to bring the food to a boil. Sometimes the food was still not ready at one o'clock."

"We didn't know whether we would be able to go on like that. It was too much work, and there was nowhere to get more firewood," added Karina.

That was when they made contact with us. "Some women from the Human Rights Commission called us," explained Carmen. "They knew the kind of work we were doing and they asked whether we could give any help in La Alborada. We just agreed to go and see the situation, in order to get an idea of the problem."

That was how Manuel and later Santiago arrived in the *población*. "They were cooking in a tiny courtyard," said Manuel. "They made a fire in a sort of hole in the ground and the pots would sometimes fall over, people would get burned, and they also wasted food."

Then they moved to a new place, which gave rise to the idea of building a proper hearth. It was designed and built, and some things began to change. "Now we start cooking at nine in the morning and by one we're having lunch. And we use very little wood," said Peta, the president of the soup kitchen. In fact, the amount of wood used has been halved; it is now only five or six kilos a day. They contacted an institution which financed the purchase of a good supply of firewood, and began to talk about the need for better organization.

More people joined the soup kitchen, and weekly meetings were held. The idea that the group should build and equip its own kitchen was put forward. A number of designs were made and some resources obtained, but all efforts to find a site for the building were fruitless.

Then the soup kitchen moved again, from the garden of one house to the garden of another, whose owner was an active member of the group. "Now that we're working at this house, we're more independent. Yes, we've had problems in other places. We really need our own place. Here the owner of the house doesn't complain about the smoke or the number of people coming in. She knows what's involved," said Gloria.

A number of the group's plans have been carried out in this new location. A hearth and a clay stove were built, with a roof and wooden walls for protection. "Actually, this oven was originally designed for a bakery, but the number of people receiving food from La Alborada's soup kitchen justified building one here. We suggested that they build it and . . . well, that design has now served a new purpose," said Santiago.

The warmth of the hearth began to be felt in other places. The first one was built in La Alborada, using "guesstimates." Later its design, dimensions, and materials were perfected, and an instruction manual on how to build it was prepared. Another hearth was built in the *comuna* of Conchalí. Since then, ovens and hearths have been built, with the Central Coordination of Community Soup Kitchens, in Conchali and Lo Hermida, as well as in Maipú, Puente Alto, and other places.

Other new technologies to improve subsistence activities have also been developed or introduced. They include organic vegetable gardens, food conservation, and "magic" cooking pots to save fuel. In the La Alborada soup kitchen, a pit was dug beside the water tap. The bottom was filled with large stones, so that the cooking equipment could be washed without flooding the house.

The members of the La Alborada group found better ways of using their time and resources. For example, to stop the pots from getting covered in soot from the fire, "we now coat the outside of the pots with mud, and it's no trouble washing them," explained Graciela, a grandmother.

They also divided up the work involved in cooking, and improved the organization. "The shifts (cooking) are functioning better, people are less ashamed to come to the soup kitchen," said Esmeralda.

A short time ago, leaders were elected. The purpose of a leadership was to improve the work, and send official representatives to other organizations in the area. The members feel more in control of their activities, and there is increased stability and greater continuity.

The knowledge that the benefits of their work are distributed daily among the inhabitants of La Alborada motivates the participants. They see their work as a collective effort, which has resulted in a marked improvement in the organization.

What Is Changing?

There has been a change in the women's self-image, and in the interpersonal relations established in the process of working together. The shared experience of building an appropriate technology to improve working conditions and better utilize available resources has encouraged unity, a socialization of activities, and greater solidarity. To go from "I'm hungry" to "we make bread and food for the community" required a process of learning about both technical issues and human relations.

"Whenever I have a bit of time, I come to help, because there's always someone with a problem—their children may be ill, for example. . . . And if we don't help, the soup kitchen will end, and then what will we eat?" said Patty.

The soup kitchen is a meeting place, a place to share with others. "During the shift the women talk, we get to know each other, we discuss our problems, we give each other advice and support," said Bernarda. "My daughter says, you spend all day at that kitchen: do you think you'll get any thanks from the other women? I tell her, I'm not doing it for the other women. I just want to help, that's all."

"You're kept occupied here, you forget about your own problems. I'm always making jokes," said Patty.

"A group has started meeting to find out more about nutrition, and there we also talk about health, children, sexuality, domestic violence and violence elsewhere," said Karina.

"When we built the oven, that was really hard work. We had to prepare the clay, find bricks and iron rods. . . . And some of the women went to learn how to solder, so that they could make the top parts—it's good to learn new things," said Peta.

Learning involves observation, and the ability to perceive the world that lies beyond one's own house or community. Some of the most active women in the soup kitchen have taken part in meetings with other women, such as peasant women, women from Indian communities, and from other *poblaciones.* They've also participated in meetings organized by the Coordination of Community Soup Kitchens in the area. They have seen how people organize in other places, and others have come to tell about their work, give advice, and share ideas.

These exchanges (among women) have been positive and valuable for the organization. "We've realized that you have to have a leadership, because one person cannot take responsibility for all the work on their own," explained Gloria. "We all learn this way."

"And perhaps we'll organize ourselves better, because there is so much work to do, and we could be doing it better," added Esmeralda. "But it doesn't mean just ordering people about."

Contact with peasant women during a meeting in Santiago[9] made the women realize that they could do other productive work to help the soup kitchen and their own families. They could do knitting, sewing, other crafts, or make jams and preserves. The idea of getting organized to produce and sell was novel and exciting; now they are looking at ways to do it.

This is a story without an ending. Every day, every week, a few more pages are written, based on nothing more than the events of daily life.

A course on nutrition has been planned, so that the women can learn how to make a balanced diet using the resources available. Women from another soup kitchen are going to teach them how to make blood sausages. Soon they are going to make *empanadas* (meat pies) on the weekends to raise funds to put the soup kitchen on a firmer footing. One woman is already using the embers in the hearth to cook a traditional type of Chilean bread.

And so, day after day, the story carries on. This is La Alborada—clear proof that a sense of solidarity can develop, even among people who hardly know each other, people who live on a steep slope beside a piece of waste land.

Notes

1. M. Max-Neef, C. Mallman, and R. Aguirre. *La sinergia humana como fundamento ético y estético del desarrollo.* 1978.

2. The total female labor force rose from 768,000 women in 1971 to 1,104,100 in 1982, with the majority of these women working in marginal occupations. Working document. PROSOC, Santiago, 1985.

3. Benavides, Morales, and Rojas. *Campamentos y Poblaciones de las Comunas del Gran Santiago. Una Síntesis Informativa.* FLACSO, Santiago, 1983.

4. D. Marcotti. *La mortalidad infantil en Chile.* PET, Santiago, 1983.

5. This is the case in the Carampangue *campamento* in the VIII Region of the country.

6. See Luis Razeto, *Las Organizaciones Económicas Populares en la nueva Coyuntura.* PET, May, 1984.

7. This community soup kitchen has been in existence since September 1984, and provides for 44 families out of a total of 160 who live in the community. Every day 212 rations of food are prepared in shifts which change every month. The teams which work the shifts are made up of one delegate from each family who, here as in many other cases, are all women.

8. Programa de Empleo Mínimo (Minimum Employment Program) and Programa Ocupacional para Jefes de Hogar (Employment Program for Heads of Household).

9. Meeting of peasant and native women organized by PEMCI, a program organized by the Center for Women's Studies (Centro de Estudios de la Mujer) in June 1985 in Santiago.

7

Socially Appropriate Technologies and Their Contribution to the Design and Implementation of Social Policies in Chile

Manuel Baquedano

Center for Studies in Appropriate Technologies for Latin America (CETAL)

Background

The contribution that non-governmental organizations (NGOs) working in the field of socially appropriate technology (SAT) could make to the design of social policies and programs for the worst-off sectors of society is difficult to analyze. The political situation in Chile today does not favor interaction between NGOs and official agencies. This has prevented these organizations from participating more actively in development actions which involve the formulation of broad social policies and programs. The work of technical support institutions is relatively recent and not widely known, which makes our perspective on the central theme of this book unique.

The contribution of NGOs to society as a whole is basically made by characteristics and activities of the institutions themselves. We will therefore discuss the question of their contribution by giving an account of three experiences, presently being carried out, which represent a contribution to local and national development.

A Short History

The movement for socially appropriate technology has evolved through three successive stages of development, which we will describe briefly.

India was the birthplace of both the concept and the main prophet of socially appropriate technology: Mahatma Gandhi. Gandhi was one of the first people to draw attention to and question the effects of applying a specific model of technology which is part of a broader system of domination; he was also the first to point out that technology is not neutral. Gandhi taught that, if a technology has been used as an instrument of domination, it can also be used by the oppressed for their own liberation.

His campaign for the use of the spinning wheel is enlightening:

> I would be prepared to encourage the use of the most sophisticated machines if this would bring an end to India's poverty and to the unemployment resulting from it. I suggest that people use spinning wheels because I see this as the only means of warding off penury and providing a minimum of work and resources. As for the spinning wheel itself, it is also a type of machine, with a warmth of its own; using the limited means available to me, I have managed to make certain improvements in its design, to adapt it better to the particular conditions found in India.[1]

Although Gandhi's work gave rise to a movement which spread throughout India, it never achieved more than a relatively marginal position there. Certainly there were no significant attempts to apply his methods in Third World countries. Thus the development of appropriate technologies entered a stage of comparative stagnation.

There was little progress until an English economist, E.F. Schumacher, spent a great deal of time in India and made, by no means accidentally, the same criticism of western industrial technology, the authority and importance of which had been unchallenged. Schumacher called his proposal "Small is Beautiful," and started the famous Intermediate Technology Development Group (ITDG) as an instrument to develop appropriate technology (which at that time was called "intermediate technology"). This technology was inexpensive and labor-intensive, thus offering a middle way between traditional and modern technologies. Other agencies, such as Volunteers in Technical Assistance (VITA) in the United States and the BRACE Research Institute followed in the footsteps of the ITDG. All focussed on the adaptation and transfer of technologies for the Third World.

A parallel movement was developing in industrialized countries. It involved students such as those who took part in the actions of May, 1968. They questioned the highly technological, industrialized nature of society, and criticized nuclear energy, pollution, the arms race, etc. They also saw appropriate technology as the basis of a strategy for change aimed at creating an alternative type of society.

The movement for SATs achieved its present importance due to the convergence between what was essentially an intellectual movement that criticized industrial society from the inside, and a small elite who were working on development problems in Third World countries. The failure of classic development strategies based on industrialization could be clearly seen in these countries. Thus the leaders began to look for new and different approaches and arrived at the idea of appropriate technology.

The majority of well-known appropriate technology centers now in existence were established: Meso-American Center for Studies in Appropriate Technology (CEMAT) in Guatemala, Andean Center for Rural Development (CATER) in Ecuador, Environment and Development in the Third World (ENDA) in Senegal, Dian Desa in Indonesia, Center for Studies on Appropriate Technology for Latin America (CETAL) in Chile, and Center for Agricultural Mechanization and Rural Technology (CAMERTEC) in Tanzania. These are only the NGOs in the field of SAT.

It was no accident, therefore, that it was a representative from the Third World who proposed to the World Assembly of Socially Appropriate Technology International Information Services (SATIS), the umbrella organization for SAT Centers, that SATIS be an instrument to achieve a new international order in technology. This would mean encouraging close co-operation rather than conflict between the industrialized countries of North America and Europe, and the Third World nations of Central and South America.

Thus a strong movement developed, which forced governments to take an interest in its proposals and programs. This interest was then expressed in economic support—in some countries, such as Germany, Holland, and the United States, on a significant scale. Only later did agencies associated with the United Nations, such as the ILO, FAO, UNEP, and UNICEF begin to take a similar interest.

Paradoxically, as the movement has grown, its initial cohesion has weakened. There are two principal reasons for this phenomenon; the first can be found in the industrialized countries themselves. As governments and intergovernmental institutions became committed to work involving the use of appropriate technologies in the Third World, they also needed specialized technical staffs. The only people both willing and able to accept these jobs were the very people who criticized modern society.

The same individuals and groups who encouraged the development of SATs have moved from working in independent organizations to positions in the state, or in intergovernmental institutions. The movement has lost some of its dynamism, as no new generation was waiting to take the places of those who left. Yesterday's appropriate technology fundamentalists are the realists of today, who must take into account the interests of the governments or intergovernmental institutions that employ them. Thus relations which originally were mainly between NGOs in industrialized nations and NGOs in underdeveloped countries have changed to include government institutions.

Another weakening factor is the explosive growth of organizations in the Third World working in the sphere of SAT. SATIS, which currently has a membership of 27 organizations (25% are agencies in industrialized countries), has received requests from over 130 new organizations seeking to be accepted as members at the next World Assembly. Ninety percent of these are from the Third World.

This increase has not been accompanied by a similar growth in SAT organizations in the industrialized countries. The level of international resources available has also remained the same, but these resources must now finance an ever larger number of activities and groups in the Third World. This is the end of the second stage of the SAT movement, and the start of a new period of crisis and, therefore, evolution.

The continued need for the development of SATs makes it vital that the movement be brought back to its place of origin: the Third World. The North-South relationship which predominated during the second stage must be replaced by a South-South relationship, or the movement is likely to die. This situation is a great challenge to organizations working on SATs in Third World countries. The previous stage, based on North-South co-operation, allowed a significant degree of experimentation but only a limited dissemination of developments. This new stage, however, demands that the use of SATs must be extended on a mass scale; otherwise the movement will not achieve the internal consensus required to survive and expand using local resources.

Concepts

In order to facilitate understanding of the following discussion, we will first give a precise explanation of some concepts implicit in our argument. This brief review will make no attempt to justify the use of these concepts, as this is not the place to go into each in depth.

We use the concept of technology as defined by J. Galtung,[2] that is, as a set of technical methods placed in a specific structure (Technology = Technical Methods + Structures). Thus "technology" refers to technical methods and what surrounds them, which may be social, political, economic, environmental, cultural, or other factors. Seen in this light, technologies are part of social processes, and cannot be understood without knowledge of the process of which they are a part. Technology is one of the components which establishes a society's framework of action. It is not a tool for decision-making, but is rather a product of earlier decisions of varying kinds—political, social, cultural, economic.

A key concept in appropriate technology is its rejection of the idea that technology is neutral. Technology is not autonomous or uniform, nor does it have universal validity. Technical developments are not based on "natural laws" which society must discover or accept as inevitable. In the words of A.K. Reddy, technologies "bear the genetic code of the society that produces them," and therefore seek to reproduce the conditions in which they were created.

Science and technology are part of the same reality: "the conditions for the production of knowledge are not independent of the knowledge which is produced, just as the social conditions for the production of technical developments not only determine the techniques developed, but also provide the context in which they operate."[3] If technology is not neutral, then a difference cannot be established between the spheres of technology and science. It cannot be that technology is historically determined, while science is universal.

Technology is almost always associated with machines and tools, with things that are visible and tangible. But along with the tangible there is also an invisible aspect, such as information, practical knowledge ("know-how"), or organization, without which the physical side would have no meaning. The development of SAT is based on the hypothesis that it is possible to replace capital—a scarce resource—with a more intensive use of knowledge and organization. Third World countries can therefore find the most important resources for development among their own people, as long as a genuine policy of investing in human resources is adopted.

When the processes of transformation are not in tune with social needs, society intervenes. From the moment that technology ceases to be taken as the parameter of social change and becomes only one variable in such change, it is possible to develop a concept of technological intervention (actions which produce a deliberate change in ongoing technological processes). Technological interventions can be made in different spheres and at different levels, as shown below. The areas of intervention are of various types, such as communities, productive or service organizations, institutions, technological policies, research policies, etc. In every case the objective is the same: to alter ongoing processes for a particular purpose.

Technological interventions must be made with great care when the systems affected are fragile and vulnerable. This requires a detailed knowledge of the system, the ability to identify real or potential factors of change, and to act according to a strategy of intervention. Technological interventions always arouse resistance, and success often depends on the ability to identify areas of resistance, understand their causes, and find ways of overcoming them. This can most easily be accomplished by dealing first with the more minor points of resistance.

The concepts of technology, non-neutrality, material and intangible aspects outlined above, all bring us closer to the real meaning of SAT.[4] Put simply, a technology is appropriate when it helps to meet the objectives of development, and can be adapted to the local conditions in which it will operate. No technology can be considered a priori appropriate. "As a current of thought, appropriate technology does not work like a new religion; it proposes nothing more nor less than the possibility of identifying themes, systematizing and rationalizing technological decision-making, that is to say, of intervening in a very ancient process, but one which has been characterized by its unconscious, implicit, prejudiced, and uncontrolled form of development."[5]

The Features of Technologies

If technology is analyzed as a dimension of the production of goods and services for a particular situation, then its productive function involves five variables: (1) nature (N)—all production uses inputs from nature, such as air, water, fire, etc.; (2) work (W)—the human activity used to transform nature; (3) capital (K); (4) research (R); and (5) organization (ORG)—administration. The last two factors represent the non-material, invisible side, the technological dimension of productive processes. Together these five factors create the alchemy of production.

The features of three principal types of technology in existence today can be established according to their relatively greater (intensive) or lesser (light) use of each factors in the process of production (see Figure 7.1). These features should be kept very much in mind in the analysis of concrete examples of appropriate technology in later sections.

Present Role of SATs in Development: Three Basic Hypotheses

One: Appropriate Technology as Technology for Survival

The first approach is to see the use and development of SAT as a short-term response to a specific, exceptional situation in Chile. Some see this exceptional condition as a consequence of an authoritarian regime coming to power. This regime, through implementation of liberal economic policies, is responsible for economic and social conditions under which major sectors of the poor have neither employment nor income, and find themselves in a situation where they can barely

FIGURE 7.1

PROFILES OF TYPES OF TECHNOLOGY

a) Profile of Industrial Technology

Use of factors of production	INTENSIVE
	LIGHT

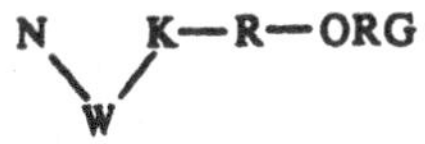

b) Profile of Simple Technology

Use of factors of production	INTENSIVE
	LIGHT

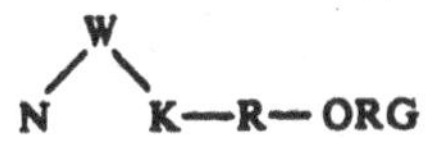

c) Profile of Socially Appropriate Technology (SAT)

Use of factors of production	INTENSIVE
	LIGHT

survive. For others, the exceptional nature of this situation is not so much the product of the existing socio-economic model as it is the result of an external variable. The world economic crisis has had repercussions which have prevented Chile from achieving development targets and a more equitable income distribution.

Proponents of the first hypothesis see SAT as a useful, direct aid to survival. It employs resources that are not scarce, are easily accessible to the people using them, and/or involve little investment. They justify the use of such technology for as long as this state of exception, defined as transitory, continues.

These technologies reflect a deterioration in the standards of living and level of development achieved by the country; thus the fact that it is necessary to use them is an embarrassment. They are also labelled "technologies of shame" and it is therefore felt that they must be eliminated as quickly as possible. If the state adopted policies more oriented towards redistribution, such technology would not be necessary.

According to the above interpretation, SAT is a response to an essentially transitory phenomenon and has no long-term role in the development of the country. If it does, this role is so marginal that it is not worth taking into account in drawing up public policies.

The experience with "family kitchen gardens in the cities" can be used as as illustration.[6] All measures dealing directly with problems of basic consumption are given high priority, especially those related to diet. Family kitchen gardens in the cities are being widely publicized at present, and have given rise to great expectations, although there is still not adequate data available as to their real contribution to family diets.

Organic kitchen gardens, where the principles of organic farming are applied, have generally been adopted. This system has certain characteristics, such as using less water than the traditional system of periodic flooding to water the plants, use of organic manure provided by domestic waste, and more intensive use of the arable land, which make it attractive. Observation and analysis of different experiences, however, particularly in the Fifth Region of the country and Santiago,[7] reveal certain features which show that these organic technologies have only been considered from the point of view of survival, and their development has thus been limited.

The main motivation of the participants who cultivate their own kitchen gardens is that these gardens will enable them to deal with the immediate problem of subsistence by providing the vegetables needed for daily meals. From this point of view, the success or failure of these kitchen gardens is determined by whether or not they are effectively able to meet the level of expectation of those cultivating them. A recent estimate, on the basis of the situation in two *poblaciones* (poor communities) in Santiago where kitchen garden programs are working, indicated that in most cases the gardens had not fully lived up to expectations; an average kitchen garden provided only 25% of the food required each day.

Organic kitchen gardens involve the use of technologies which are basically foreign to life in poor communities. Although the gardens cost very little to cultivate, they are the product of a mature, sophisticated technology which, while the capital used is low, demands an intensive employment of information. Thus a significant element of ongoing support is required for the introduction of kitchen gardens in poor sectors. This makes it very difficult to generate autonomous development and short-term expansion of the technology.

The work of cultivating an organic kitchen garden, moreover, is done entirely by women. Among other reasons, men see gardening as domestic work and therefore below them. This often prevents involvement of the whole family in these activities.

Finally, we should say that an adequate implementation of organic kitchen gardens implies the investment of greater resources than would be justified by a temporary activity. As a result, it has not been possible to demonstrate the effectiveness of SAT in gardening, since all the necessary resources, properly trained people, and enough time have not been available. These weaknesses further reinforce the idea that SATs are an uncertain and temporary solution.

Traditional kitchen gardens have no cost problem, need little capital, and the people already have the necessary knowledge and experience. Traditional gardens, however, require intensive use of resources. In urban areas, this results in low productivity, with little to offer people who have a limited amount of space available.

An analysis of the technological characteristics of the organic kitchen garden shows that it differs from the traditional kitchen garden in its dependence on research. Organic cultivation requires ongoing advice and support from specialists. Programs working with organic kitchen gardens must take into account the need for ongoing technical assistance. Such programs often fail because they are merely being monitored.

Two: Appropriate Technology as Organizational Technology

The second approach to SAT in Chile is as a new means of creating participatory organizations. This view coincides with the first in that it sees the use and development of SAT as a response to an essentially transitory phenomenon. It gives SAT a much broader and more long-term significance, however, since the process of encouraging organization and participation is concerned with more than the problem of survival.

The potentially instrumental character of these technologies is the basic factor in this second approach. SATs are useful, not only because they optimize production processes or increase the viability of productive activities, but also because their existence in poor communities facilitates the creation, continuation, and development of organizations. From this point of view, it does not really matter if a technology is abandoned and another activity is adopted; the important thing is that the organization remains.

The evolution of solutions to the problems of fuel in the community soup kitchens in Santiago illustrates this. In many poor communities various methods are being tried to provide food for basic consumption. One of the most important is the community soup kitchen, in which a group of families from a particular community or sector prepare their daily meals collectively.

In Santiago alone, there are at the moment over 250 community soup kitchens, in which about 20,000 people participate. In the beginning stages, virtually all of these used gas cookers to prepare the food. Due to the high costs involved, they began to cook with firewood as fuel. This change was made spontaneously, and the people tended to use open fires, a method commonly used in poor communities to boil clothes for washing.

Although the change made it possible to lower fuel costs, the cost of firewood is also high, and it requires more effort to collect or purchase. Fuel is currently one of the major problems facing these organizations. Why then have none of the activities of the community soup kitchen been aimed at direct improvements in working conditions and optimizing the scarce resources available?

If the open fire was replaced with a properly-built clay oven—as occurred in the community soup kitchen in Nueva Amanecer—there would be an immediate savings of 40% on firewood consumption.[8] Thus, with only minor innovations and investments, substantial improvements could be made in hygiene and environmental conditions in which food is prepared and cooked. According to this interpretation of technology, technical innovations are only necessary when the shortage or complete lack of one or more factors of production threatens the survival of the organization itself.

Three: Appropriate Technology as Technology for a New Style of Development

The proponents of this third interpretation do not deny that a large sector of society lives at subsistence levels and that something must therefore be done very quickly for these people. Nor are the proponents unaware that the organization of these sectors is a crucial element in any process of participative development. They argue, however, that the principal purpose of SAT is to contribute to the viability of a new form of organization and action which will transform society. SAT should also help ensure the satisfaction of fundamental needs, which implies an alternative form of development.

According to this view, in Chile and the rest of Latin America the mechanical association between the development process and industrialization has been definitively broken. Development does not necessarily mean industrialization, but rather the achievement of a certain standard of living. This standard should be achieved through the satisfaction of needs by the most direct, immediate means possible, without waiting for the indirect benefits of a hypothetical stage of industrial development which Third World nations will never reach. From this point of view, modern industrial technology and socially appropriate technology are antagonistic.[9]

One example of the practical implementation of this approach is CETAL's introduction and development of sanitary manure-producing latrines for urban areas, a system based on the domestic recycling of human excrement. At present, the only way to dispose of excrement in communities where sewage is not provided is in cesspits. While cesspits solve the problem in the short range, in the medium and long range they themselves become the source of difficulties which eventually become insuperable.

Infections, flooding, the limited space available on individual plots of land, the bad smells produced, etc., have transformed this traditional solution into a problem. Until very recently there was no alternative method as cheap as the cesspit in areas without sewage. Thus it was important to introduce and test systems to recycle the waste and convert it into manure, using modern concepts of bio-technology.

These manure-producing latrines could become a very important alternative to cesspits. Today ten latrines of this kind are operating successfully in Valparaiso, and a further 200 are programmed to be built in the San Antonio area. If this solution is successful, there could be whole groups of houses and communities without sewage, where waste is recycled locally.

To sum up, technologies appropriate to a new style of development take as their starting point a real situation (of subsistence) to which they propose solutions that encourage organization. These solutions should be oriented towards a kind of development in which the satisfaction of fundamental needs results in the achievement of a reasonable standard of living for the entire population.

Organizations Working with SAT: Activists in Local Development

The non-governmental organizations working in Chile can be divided into three categories, according to which interpretation of SAT shapes their overall framework of action.

First-Generation NGOs

These are, firstly, agencies and institutions that do not question the fundamental principles of the present model of development but rather seek to limit and mitigate the damage caused by the application of this model. These organizations range from purely charitable institutions like CARITAS-Chile (a Catholic Church organization) to agencies created by private companies and run by businessmen who are open to change and interested in small-scale production and intermediate technology. Agencies such as the CIDEREs,[10] particularly in the Biobio region and Valparaiso, support programs to improve the economy in deprived areas and non-productive sectors of society.

The term first generation organizations is used because these organizations play an extremely important role in areas with problems of subsistence. To a certain extent, they provide a means of responding to these conditions. These agencies, in the conditions existing in Chile today, have the greatest scope for action and possibility of official recognition.

Second-Generation NGOs

There is a second group of agencies and institutions which do not accept the present model of development, but seek to introduce another model. Their common characteristic is the conviction that, if technology is not introduced as part of a process of structural change, it could instead be a demobilizing factor. From this perspective, technology must be above all an element which strengthens grassroots social organizations.

SAT is not, however, a long-term priority of these organizations and institutions. They believe that if SAT enables grassroots groups to survive and maintain their organizations, this alone is enough to justify its existence. According to this view, needs will ultimately be satisfied as the result of efforts to democratize society. A strong economy will thus be developed, involving the state and the private sector, and its main mission will be to encourage the re-industrialization of the country.

SAT's role will be to strengthen the economy by contributing to a reduction of pressure by the poorest sectors on the state to find ways of satisfying their basic needs. If these needs were met immediately, it would then be impossible to accumulate the capital needed to invest in the process of re-industrialization. NGOs have taken a key role in developing public and social policies in the recent processes of democratization in Latin America. They have also provided the public officials to implement these new policies.

These agencies are second generation because their most important role will be in a future period, in Chile's democratization phase. Institutions such as CIEPLAN, CED, organizations linked with the Academia de Humanismo Cristiano such as PET (Programa de Economía del Trabajo—Labor Economics Program), GIA (Grupo de Investigaciones Agrarias—Agrarian Research Group), ILET (Instituto de Estudios Transnacionales—Institute for Transnational Studies), etc., are representative of this second generation.

Third-Generation NGOs

Finally there are the organizations and institutions which oppose the present model of development and are working for an alternative, where not only is the model different but also the kind of development. These institutions start from the assumption that it is impossible to transform the economic order without at the same time questioning the technological order on which it is based.

In contrast with second generation organizations, which support an autonomous national development model based on a real redistribution of incomes, the third generation believes that it is impossible to generalize the distribution of technological products at present found only in the dominant social classes.

The technology found in the dominant classes has been designed for use by a minority. In Latin America, and even less in Chile, entire populations cannot solve transportation problems by the use of cars, nor problems of excrement disposal by sewage systems, nor nutrition problems by prioritizing the consumption of animal proteins. The generalization of the fruits of the dominant technology is impossible in terms of the model itself, and undesirable in terms of development.

In this sense, the technologies developed by first- and second-generation NGOs will in the long run adapt themselves to the logic of traditional development, in which the motor force is industrialization. The socially appropriate technologies promoted by third-generation NGOs will create the conditions for a new kind of development.

Although they are actively involved in finding solutions to problems of subsistence and support the processes of democratization, these organizations will play their most important role at an even later stage. This will occur when the limitations of development based on re-industrialization are revealed, and the focus is shifted to satisfying the basic needs of the population by bringing about a real redistribution of products. Organizations and institutions working towards this end are called third-generation agencies.

The Sphere and Significance of CETAL's Work

The Work Environment: Reality of the Worst-off Groups

One of CETAL's basic objectives is to find socially appropriate technological alternatives for use by the poorest people in the country. Our methodology takes the form of technological intervention, which means that the organization is not involved in any one area on a permanent or long-term basis. Work is rather carried out in response to requests from grassroots organizations or other support organizations working in a particular community. Certain criteria are necessary in deciding when and where to intervene. The groups or sectors we define as poor include "those people who are unable to satisfy certain requirements considered to be fundamental in areas such as diet, health, education and housing."[11]

Several studies show that Chile's urban poor consist of a wide range of heterogenous social groups. The poor are not concentrated in any one branch of the economy, in cities, or in specific neighborhoods. Due to this heterogeneity, we have chosen to use the *comuna* (borough or district of a city) as the unit in which to measure indicators of levels of poverty.

The *comunas* in Santiago with the greatest relative poverty are La Florida, Pudahuel, and La Granja. It is there that CETAL concentrated its work, developing wood-burning stoves for community soup kitchens in La Florida, urban manure-generating latrines for the *campamentos* (emergency settlements) in La Granja, and the use of medicinal herbs by health groups in Pudahuel.

Another criteria in the profile of poverty is the degree to which people are unable to satisfy their basic needs. Nor is poverty in Chile a temporary situation, affecting specific categories of people such as young people or pensioners. The welfare policies adopted to deal with poverty are clearly limited, and the potential capacity of groups defined as poor to create sources of productive employment for themselves must be evaluated. Taken together, these features provide a profile of poor groups to which we refer in deciding what kind of intervention to make.

The main tools of CETAL'S work are technological measures, actions which serve as a catalyst to produce a deliberate change in existing technological processes. Thus, once we have decided that it is worthwhile to support a group, other important elements are taken into account. We need to know what support institutions and organizations are already working with these groups on a more permanent basis. And, it is important to bear in mind, from a technological point of view, the needs and requests put forward by the community.

The need to introduce a technology is experienced in terms of what already exists and what the community assesses as a positive development. Nothing unreal, nothing that people do not already know about, can generate a need, and still less a technological change. Experimentation and the dissemination of results on a limited scale can demonstrate alternative approaches, which could be developed on a much wider scale if adopted by the relevant authorities.

Three examples of prior work illustrate the philosophy underlying this form of action.

The Work of the Medicinal Herbs Group (GPM)

First, work with medicinal herbs was an attempt to integrate traditional medicine into primary health care. This work on medicinal plants started as a response to the findings of a study on health conditions in Chile published by the magazine *HOY* in February, 1980. The study showed that over 50% of the Chilean population did not have sufficient resources to obtain medical attention. A further 40% could only partially cover their needs for medical attention, and only 7% could fully cover the costs of health care. This situation has in no way improved since the report was published, and all recent information suggests that it has in fact become worse.

One of the principal factors in this situation is that the medicines are so expensive that the worst-off sectors cannot obtain them. The scale of the problem led many health workers, doctors, and others concerned with the welfare of the population to take the position that traditional medicine should be reevaluated. In particular, it was felt that existing knowledge about medicinal herbs in local communities, universities, and research centers, should be used in order to incorporate use of these herbs into primary health care services.

Although there is still a certain degree of knowledge among members of the community about the use of medicinal herbs, this knowledge is disappearing, principally as a result of the scorn poured on traditional practices and remedies by the officials of western medicine. In 1980, the medicinal herbs group (GPM) was set up, with the aim of reappraising traditional, alternative forms of medicine in Chile, and encouraging integration with elements of western medicine. GPM is composed of health professionals working in different fields.

To achieve its aims, the GPM established two general objectives. First, to restore the communities' confidence in the use of medicinal herbs, by increasing and generalizing scientific knowledge of their properties. Second, to progressively incorporate the use of medicinal plants into the work of organized health groups and primary health care activities in the official sphere of public health.

A three-part strategy was drawn up to meet these objectives. The first involved making contact with poor communities and traditional health workers working with herbs, and systematizing their empirical knowledge. The following results have been obtained after several years' work in this sphere.

A diagnosis of the use of medicinal herbs in poor sectors was made. The most important points of this diagnosis were: (1) medicinal herbs continue to be used widely, both in urban and rural areas; (2) these herbs are often used for the wrong purposes, not used properly, and may even be used counterproductively, since there is a lack of knowledge about, and no means of testing, the medicinal properties of the various plants; (3) people prefer (if they can afford it) to treat illnesses with industrially-manufactured medicines, since their effects are swifter and better known; (4) the use of medicinal herbs is considered a throwback to ancient superstitions, although they are often used to treat ailments which do not respond to treatments prescribed by western medicine; (5) the Common Pharmacopoeia of Chile does not include the medicinal uses of many plants which are, however, very common in the country; and (6) the opportunities to learn about these plants are limited because of the pressures of daily survival. People in poor sectors have a low capacity for assimilation, concentration, and interest. Any program of social action needs to take these factors into account, especially in setting realistic targets.

The systematization of common knowledge of the medical uses of different plants was begun. Among the results of this work are the catalogue of medicinal herbs published by CETAL, and a data bank on medicinal herbs, in preparation at the time of this writing.

Written material on the medicinal properties of the most widely used plants has been checked by tests and scientific experiments. This scientifically verified information has been disseminated in poor areas, in easily accessible educational manuals.[12]

These activities gradually provided the elements for an evaluation, which convinced the GPM that it should move on to work with people organized around health activities. This second stage involved training health groups in the use of medicinal herbs. Health groups are community organizations, essentially made up of women, who look for ways deal directly with the health problems most common in their sectors.

With support from a range of NGOs promoting community work, these health groups have achieved varying degrees of development and stability. They have a very wide range of concerns, covering a large proportion of the health problems found in poor areas. The GPM has made a survey of about 300 groups, the majority of which are based in cities such as Copiapó, Valparaíso, Santiago, Concepción, and Temuco.

In January, 1985 the GPM started training courses for health groups, to teach the precise medical use of medicinal plants. The courses were intended not merely to give practical information but also to increase the groups' autonomy in producing their own supplies of medicinal plants by introducing techniques for collecting, preserving, and producing medicines locally. The basic training in this kind of treatment was intended to be given over a period of two years.

The GPM has a small training and experimentation center called Hierba-Vida (Herb-Life). This center is now producing a variety of medicines prepared from herbs. After the 1985 earthquake, a special program to produce essential medicines was set in motion. Under this program, 18,000 doses were distributed.

To encourage the autonomy of local health groups, there is a plan to set up local herb gardens within each community, to be administered by members of the health groups. Hierba-Vida will provide support for the creation of local herb gardens, and act as a centralized distribution point.

There has been a slow but positive change in the attitudes of health professionals, particularly doctors. This may be because they see herbs as a means of survival, and thus valid only in the present circumstances. An increasingly significant number of doctors are nevertheless taking a growing interest in the use of medicinal plants, often as the result of pressure from health groups seeking to incorporate them in day-to-day work. In 1985, the GPM made a presentation of its work to the Chilean Medical College, which gives some indication of the changes taking place.

Once the health groups have been trained, community herb gardens created, information on the scientific uses of the principal medicinal plants in Chile disseminated, awareness created in the scientific community, and some degree of willingness to use this approach shown by health professionals, it will be possible to move on to the third stage. This stage involves gaining official recognition and introduction of medicinal plants into the primary health services—that is, incorporation of herbal remedies into the National Health System.

It is unlikely although not impossible that this process could begin under the present regime, although the predominant concept of health is non-participatory. During a general process of democratization, however, medicinal plants would of course be accepted and incorporated. It is inconceivable that the process of democratization could fail to consider the work of the health groups, or the techniques they use.

Thus it is possible for NGOs to have an important role in bringing about changes in the way public policies are designed and formulated in the long-term.

Expanding the Use of "Magic Cooking Pots"

The economic crisis, unemployment, and excessive optimism as to potential uses of alternative technology (encouraged by this technology itself), have created a great demand in poor areas and among community development workers for assistance from institutions such as CETAL, and others working in the field of alternative technology. In order to respond to this demand, a new stage of action must be entered. This involves the introduction, on a mass scale, of techniques which have had successful results. SATs must be capable of resolving certain problems for the entire population, and offer solutions that can be copied and reproduced.

One of CETAL's major tasks will be the introduction of energy-saving insulated cooking pots. CETAL has chosen to expand the use of this particular technology for many reasons. Fifty percent of the energy used in cooking food can be saved by using these pots, which implies savings representing 8% of the total income of a poor Chilean family.

The technology can be combined with any of the different kinds of energy used in cooking (firewood, gas, coal, electricity). This flexibility means that the same process of publicity and distribution can be used universally. The production costs are low (US$8), so even the poorest families can afford one of these pots; the cost is equivalent to two months' savings on fuel.

Jobs are created manufacturing and selling the pots; with two workers in each workshop, the optimum production rate is 160 pots per workshop per month. Decentralized production in independently-run workshops is one of the first attempts to produce a simple technology in small technology workshops. This could be the foundation of a totally new industrialization strategy in Third World countries.

The precise calculations relating to this technology are as follows. In Chile, a poor family of five uses a minimum of one 15k canister of liquified gas a month in the preparation of food. In 1985, the cost of a canister was 1,300 Chilean pesos, or about US$8. Taking the minimum family income in 1984 as the wage paid by the PEM (US$90 per month), the cost of cooking food represents at least 10% of family incomes.

The calculations made during the first few months of promoting and selling the ECONOMITA magic cooking pots indicate that, if these pots are used daily, an average of 50% of fuel costs can be saved (minimum, 40%; maximum, 60%). This means a savings of half a canister of gas per month, or 650 pesos, just over US$4. Since the ECONOMITA cooking pot sells for US$8, the full cost is recouped in fuel savings during the first two months of use.

The ECONOMITA is to be produced, and publicity prepared, in special workshops. At the time of this writing the first pilot ECONOMITA workshop is in operation in Viña del Mar. The ECONOMITA workshops are autonomous economic organizations, basically run by the workers and dedicated to production. Each workshop is responsible not only for production of the cooking pots but also for publicizing, promoting, and selling them.

Promotion takes place in training sessions of approximately five hours. The participants are taught to make a basic model which can be used by families who cannot immediately afford to buy the ECONOMITA model. At present, CETAL has 120 agents throughout the country who publicize and give advice on the use of appropriate technology. These people have all attended training sessions on the cooking pots, and assist at workshops promoting their use.

The School for Socially Appropriate Technology

The school's purpose is to train primary-level promoters of appropriate technology for the community. From a technological point of view, communities almost always express their needs in terms of *existing* technologies, and in a form strongly influenced by the dominant ideology in the community. Any organization attempting to assist a community to take responsibility for and participate in its own development must act in relation to the way that needs are expressed.

To inspire technological changes and innovations originating in the community itself, there must be local people capable of recognizing needs, putting them into words, and making them part of the collective consciousness. The SAT school attempts to prepare this kind of leader. The objectives are to train community agents in technologies being developed by CETAL which are appropriate for subsistence activities, and then establish grassroots economic organizations, by providing basic training for people involved in introducing technologies and a more advanced training for those who have taken the basic course.

The school is organized around two courses, basic and advanced. The emphasis of the advanced course is on the development of small units of production. Three areas are covered in each course: (1) Technology and Society; (2) Health and Diet; and (3) Energy Technology.

People taking the basic course can chose between Areas 2 and 3; Area 1 is taken by all participants. Those in the advanced course continue in the area chosen in the basic course. Two sessions have been held, and 104 people have been trained either as promoters (on completion of the basic course) or advisors (on completion of the advanced course). Their practical achievements have been encouraging.

The identification of the need to train primary-level appropriate technology workers from the community, implementation of pilot training program, and creation of a system of technical support for participants undoubtedly represent one of CETAL's major contributions to the development of an appropriate technology movement in Chile.

Conclusions

Every form of production of goods and services requires a combination of physical technology and social organization. Technology cannot be seen independently from the socio-economic structures within which it operates. We believe that industrial technology has exaggerated the usefulness and the role of physical technologies in the production process, and that many goods and services could be produced with less materials and machinery, and with more organization and research—that is, by using knowledge more intensively. Socially appropriate technology puts this idea into practice, and is vitally important in new models of development, particularly in the formulation of new social policies.

The current belief has been that the only social wealth is material wealth, amassed by the rich, whether rich nations or social classes. We believe that the strategies for survival developed by the poor sectors of Chile in recent years have shown that there are other forms of wealth quite different from existing ones, which have not yet been recognized. NGOs, in this specific case those working in the field of socially appropriate technology, play a very important role in reappraising the value of resources and information which can be used to create new wealth. The examples given in this chapter support this assertion.

Development agencies should therefore create new indicators and methods of economic and social evaluation which reflect the new situation, and replace traditional systems of evaluation which cannot be adapted to this new approach. To give one example, how can the impact of a reappraisal of the value of medicinal herbs on a specific sector of the population be evaluated? Is the change merely a matter of substituting one kind of medicine for another, or is it part of a new way of looking at health?

The way in which NGOs working in the field of SAT participate in drawing up and carrying out social programs is today one of the most important factors in defining the role of NGOs in local or national development. In fact, NGOs are increasingly coming to be seen as effective agents for implementing programs to popularize and/or provide technical education in poor areas, and less as institutions for research, development, and technological innovation. People responsible for promoting development programs frequently request that NGOs take on a role which could equally well be filled by other community agencies (for example, managing programs to assist families to build their own homes, programs for rural development, health programs, etc).

Community organizations are small and have limited resources. The role of NGOs should be to act as catalysts for change, innovation, and the introduction of new technologies in the community, rather than taking responsibility for carrying out programs. That role should be shared by the other various organizations in the community.

Notes

1. M. Gandhi. *Todos los hombres son hermanos.* Editorial Atenas, 1973.

2. J. Galtung. "Por una tecnología que favorece la autonomía." CNUSED, June 1978. (Text in English).

3. Economic Commission for Latin America and the Caribbean. "Tecnologías para los asentamientos humanos: Un marco conceptual." E/CEPAL/HEX/1982/L.4/R.1.

4. See also: M. Baquedano, "Qué son las Tecnologías Apropriadas?" CETAL. *Serie Alternativas Tecnológicas* No. 3.

5. ECLA. Op. cit. p.17.

6. We will limit our discussion to vegetable gardens in urban areas, since this is the sphere in which CETAL's work mainly takes place.

7. Verónica Vargas. "Evaluación del Proyecto MMP/CHI/019." FAO, June 1983.

8. Figures provided to the Fund for Small Projects with Appropriate Technology in a meeting of experts working with family vegetable gardens in urban areas held in Santiago in July 1985.

9. W. Riedijk, (ed.). *Appropriate Technology for Developing Countries.* Delft University of Technology.

10. CIDERE: Corporación para el desarrollo regional (Regional Development Corporation).

11. Pilar Vergara, "Necesidades básicas y políticas contra la pobreza; la experiencia de Chile." CIEPLAN, No. 27, September 1978.

12. See: *Cuadernos Populares de Plantas Medicinales,* Nos. 1, 2, 3 and 4, and the *Fichero de Plantas Medicinales,* CETAL Publicaciones.

8

Organic Agriculture: Questions and Challenges

Center for Education and Technology

After 1973, private groups and institutions in Chile assumed, for the first time, a significant role in social work. As a result, several concepts and ways of responding to the situation of poor people can be identified in these institutions. Some concentrate on investigating and developing an understanding of the new conditions in the country and the different sectors of society; for others, the basic concern is the defense of human rights. Finally, there are those whose work focuses fundamentally on social advancement. Here we are interested in conceptualizing the activities that have taken place in recent years. This will be a retrospective analysis, looking at results achieved and contributions made by these organizations to social work.

The first initiatives taken at the end of 1973 were essentially a response to the fact that major sectors of the rural and urban poor, having lost their sources of income or the various kinds of state support, were plunged into extreme poverty. Changes in economic policy and state action to a great extent explain why these sectors found themselves so utterly without protection. The challenge facing the newly created non-governmental organizations was how to meet the basic needs of poor people, in particular the problems of hunger and lack of employment, without the work being reduced to social welfare, and ensuring that the work was founded on a rough estimate of the scale and likely duration of the economic, social, and political changes that had taken place.

The majority of social actions in this period were organized by the churches in urban areas, and by other religious institutions in the countryside. Children's dining rooms, groups offering support and encouragment for self-help action by the unemployed, production workshops, and programs providing advice of different kinds in rural areas are clear examples of the sort of work carried out. These actions were intended to be symbols of solidarity, and effective means to arrest the increasing fragmentation of social relations among the poor.

By two or three years after the change of regime, both the non-governmental organizations and the poor themselves had realized that the situation was likely to be permanent, due to the neo-liberal economic policies and the fact that the political regime excluded all opposition. This made the kind of social work provided inadequate. Existing organizations stagnated, no new leaders came forward, and actions originally developed in response to an emergency began to take on a paternalistic character. At this point, more autonomous social groupings emerged, along with non-governmental organizations which had no direct links with the churches.

Thus movements based on concrete demands developed among the unions and community organizations. This made improved organization necessary, in order to achieve objectives and to involve people with higher degrees of social awareness and commitment. This need, although not clearly articulated by the social movements, gave rise to the formation of new non-governmental organizations concerned fundamentally with grassroots education.

The actions which took place in urban areas during this period were strongly influenced by the union movement's demands for better wages, and land seizures by community organizations pressing for a solution to housing problems. These actions were based on the assumption that both employers and the state would agree to the people's demands if sufficiently high levels of consciousness and organization could be developed. In retrospect, despite awareness that the regime and its economic policies had achieved a level of stability, people had not yet fully understood the nature of the regime. Thus the organizations were unable to develop into mass movements and, when they attempted to mechanically copy forms of social mobilization that had been effective in the 1960s and early 1970s, the leaders found themselves in small groups divided along ideological lines, and cut off from the grassroots.

In the countryside, division of land into small plots, opening the market to imported goods, and development of export-oriented agriculture had at least two significant effects. First was the expulsion of the rural labor force. Then came the increasing indebtedness of farmers who had been allocated small plots of land during the agrarian reform, which often resulted in farmers losing their land to the banking system.

In rural areas, non-governmental organizations focused their efforts on providing advice for peasants in the reformed sector, and raising the issue of the landless poor. Since the reforms, there had been an explosive growth of people without land who still lived in the countryside. There was also a new realization of the importance of a productive sector which had never—even during the agrarian reform—received any attention: small landowners.

Towards the end of the 1970s, the peasants and urban poor began to see that their poverty and exclusion from the system were part of the same pattern of development that had denied them a role of any kind, and that these conditions were becoming increasingly acute. Non-governmental organizations were also very conscious of this phenomenon. Thus the concept of "independent capacities" arose, along with the closely-associated idea of alternative technology.

The first steps in actualizing these concepts were mechanical; information on alternative technologies which might be useful for people living in poverty was collected. This work was well known at the institutional level. It hardly touched the lives of the peasants and urban poor, however, since it did not taken into account the logic of survival which necessarily underlies development in poor sectors.

CET's Work

The team of workers at the Center for Education and Technology (CET) was formed in 1981. It was composed of people who had been working, most of them since immediately after the military coup, in other non-governmental development organizations. Initially, the team saw its task as that of responding to the following challenges: (1) dealing with the basic needs of people in poor sectors, rather than concentrating solely on organization and social awareness; (2) meeting these needs in a way that would encourage autonomy and not dependence; (3) identifying the most deeply-felt, widespread, pressing needs of poor people—based on analyses by other groups and the opinions of urban and rural poor people themselves, the priority issue is clearly diet; and (4) finding ways in which both urban and rural poor can produce food using their own resources, which makes a fresh look at agricultural production necessary.

The above points demonstrate the importance of organic agriculture as a cheap, efficient method of producing food for consumption by the people who produce it. This raises some further questions, however. What technical validity does this technology, developed in other countries for other purposes, have in Chile, and what is its social value for the poor? Is it easy for them to use? Does it provide a real way to resolve their problems, given the conditions in which they live? Can it be linked to other elements of development? Can it be rooted in the culture and idiosyncrasies of people in poor areas?

The technical challenges involved led us to set up a small experimentation center where the appropriateness of these methods to the conditions could be tested. The decision on where to carry out experiments in organic agriculture was based on two fundamental criteria. First, the center had to be near Santiago, since most programs, both urban and rural, are there. Second, the land had to have similar characteristics to the land of poor people, that is, soil of only average quality.

The first concern was to discover what a peasant, or an urban resident with no money and only a small plot of land immediately around the house, could do to produce food. A kitchen garden that would produce a large quantity and variety of vegetables throughout the year, enough to cover all the needs of a family, was designed. The results achieved during this stage of experimentation were extremely positive,[1] providing initial proof that the system was technically viable. This gave a firm basis for going on to consider social validity.

The first work with the urban and rural poor started in northern Santiago. In Concepción, 500 km to the south, a second experimentation center was created in a peasant community. During this stage the centers played a dual role. The results of the experiments were a motivating factor, and the gardens served as places where local people could receive training.

People elected by local groups went to the centers to learn how to set up kitchen gardens, then returned to their own communities to teach other members of the group. The nature of the work required a type of training which would respond to needs expressed by the groups. The training was therefore divided into units of technical and educational activities.

The training workshop based on the first unit of activities normally lasted five days and covered three basic areas. The first area dealt with the technical steps required to set up, tend, and keep a kitchen garden producing throughout the year. A literal interpretation of the educational principle of "learning by doing" was applied, and explanations and theoretical arguments underlying the techniques were provided in the course of the practical work. The second area included an unravelling of the reasons for choosing a non-conventional technology, and discussion of the history, present situation, and relations with other social sectors of each particular group of peasants or city dwellers. The technical activities themselves generated the basis for these discussions. Third came plans to share techniques with others in the communities, as well as to support existing organizations and to create conditions for organizations to develop where they did not already exist.

The technical worker participated on equal terms with the rest of the group in manual work. This encouraged the participants to recognize the importance of manual activity, and established a foundation of common experience on which to introduce the discussion of social questions. The technical worker also participated as a member of the group in discussions, ensuring that everyone contributed to the conversation.

The technical elements included in the first training workshops were systematized and provided the material for a leaflet, "Intensively Farmed Family Vegetable Gardens," the first in the series "Somos Capaces" (We Can Do It). The parts referring to social issues are presented in the form of points for discussion.

The immediate result was that the participants began to regain their self-confidence. This came out clearly in the evaluation with which each training workshop concluded. It was expressed in comments such as, "we have seen that there are things we can do," "a peasant's work requires intelligence," or "we've discovered that there is some hope."

The follow-up after the workshops showed that the participants not only learned to create their own vegetable gardens but also how to teach others.[2] Those who had never been community leaders saw that they could fill this role. Leaders recognized by the community were provided with a working instrument that enabled them to make contact with, in particular, people who ordinarily did not participate in organizations. A clear example is what happened in one area affected by the earthquake of March, 1985. The local community chose the same people who had been trained in setting up vegetable gardens to organize the work of reconstruction.

Another result of the workshops is the participants' desire to extend their knowledge of the subjects covered. This was demonstrated by the fact that they took the initiative in looking for and trying out ways of adapting the technology. They also requested more advanced workshops.

Planning and carrying out practical work also brought out the need for organization and discussion. It is often better to do this kind of work as a group, rather than individually. This happened, for example, in preparing the land (raised beds), the monthly seed nurseries, and collecting manure.

The work of creating and maintaining the vegetable gardens broadened the participants' awareness of issues beyond vegetable production. For example, they began to think of ways to deal with other problems linked to diet. They have also used the same alternative style of approach to meet other urgent and basic needs. The participants' interest obliged the centers to provide a series of other units of technical information on domestic greenhouses, beehives, solar fruit-driers, hand pumps, food preparation, raising domestic animals, tree nurseries and the care of trees, and making furniture for the home.

People in rural areas have begun to discuss what could be done with larger plots of land. Their ideas include organic vegetable plots, rearing and maintaining bigger animals, seed production, adaptation of machinery, building stables and chicken coops, etc. Responses to these concerns were transformed into new technical and educational units, taught using the same format as the Intensively Farmed Family Vegetable Gardens: practical work, technical discussion, discussion of social questions arising out of the technical contents, and how to program work in the community.

Along with the achievements of this process there have been difficulties, accentuated by the situation of poor people in the present period. The level of unemployment has remained constant at between 50 and 60%. During the workshops, young people said that they had never had a stable enough job to allow a minimum of organization in their family lives. In contrast with workers from the industrial sector, now unemployed but accustomed to the discipline of work, these people find continuity hard to maintain. The growing discouragement produced by the lack of possibilities for the future has had a similar effect on family stability.

On top of this, there is high level of social fragmentation and mistrust generated by the deprived conditions in which poor sectors find themselves. These conditions are a result of the economic policies implemented by the government. This is particularly true in a country such as Chile, where the poor have traditionally been able to get their basic needs met by making demands on the state apparatus.

To sum up, two central elements have emerged from the work so far. The first is the importance given by the urban and rural poor to activities which guarantee subsistence, especially in food production, as a foundation on which other objectives can then be proposed. The second, resulting from the oppression, despair, and frustration of the poor, is the restoration of self-confidence and a decrease in feelings of fatalism and dependence generated by the situation in which they live.

Along with the wide range of participants' demands, other national and international non-governmental development organizations also have needs. These organizations have requested training for technical staff and grassroots leaders in the technologies developed at the centers. This double demand meant that research had to be defined as a permanent area of work in order to make effective responses to the problems being put forward and to supply fresh material for the technical training given by the institution.

The requests for training made by other institutions, many of which have direct links with the churches, made organization of specific training workshops for these groups necessary. A third center was also set up in Temuco, to the south of Concepción. For similar reasons, a Latin American seminar on "Organic Agriculture and Social Development" was held. It was attended by NGOs from seven countries and gave rise to a constant flow of technical workers on study trips to the centers.

At this point two new challenges were identified. The development programs had mainly been organized among landless peasants and people in squatter settlements in the cities, since these groups received the least amount of support from other programs. The demand for training by other institutions made it necessary to initiate new programs in grassroots communities, involving the participation of other representative sectors of the poor peasantry and poor city dwellers. It was vital that the technical and social validity of the approaches developed be tested in these sectors also. The other challenge was to transform these more or less short-term actions into increasingly complex, ongoing programs which the communities themselves could control more autonomously.

The work of community members trained in the kinds of activities described above has produced changes in the attitudes of their communities. These communities are reassessing traditional methods and ways of working. Some peasant communities have begun to reconsider the way they raise poultry, how pastures are organized for grazing, and their methods of sowing corn, beans, and sugar beets. In urban areas, people are looking at ways to maximize savings on consumption, how time is employed on productive activities, housing problems, and making local authorities use government resources to support community initiatives.

The analysis of each activity involves discovering and then explaining clearly how the activity is carried out, how much time it takes, how it has traditionally been performed, which members of the family are responsible, what difficulties they face, what the objective is, and what the problems are. It also means making plans for action, and deciding at what point the plan should be implemented. In short, the group unravels the logic underlying the ways they have traditionally acted and discusses how innovations that they see as appropriate could fit in with this logic.

The technical worker's role is to participate in this process, to help the group organize and systematize the discussion of alternatives. On no account should the technical worker diagnose the problems for the people concerned. This methodology has enabled the groups to identify the different levels at which their activities are carried out: individual plot of land, community, local area, other social sectors, the general situation in the country.

They can then identify the major obstacles to development and their causes, and find the most realistic, appropriate measures to deal with these problems. They began, for example, to analyze the relationship between production for family subsistence and production for the market, and discussed how to establish an effective balance between the two, defending their own interests. This same methodology was also used in the seminars held for technical staff from other institutions.

As part of this process, community members have allocated certain places (the home of a member of the urban community, or a peasant's plot of land) for holding trainings or carrying out local experiments. These places are also where meetings and discussions are held and community activities planned. By this stage, the centers had become a technological reference point for the communities. In the centers they could find answers to their questions, which allowed them to deal with new problems such as the question of housing, and make the best use of local resources and the capacities of the people concerned. The centers also acted as a point of comparison with the achievements of the community, providing a basis for discussion of ways to improve the work.

The development of this work by the peasants and urban poor aroused interest among other social groups, such as researchers, teachers, university students, professionals from a variety of fields, artists, and members of other non-governmental development organizations. All these people have found the space to make a systematic, creative contribution, and in the process have also discovered the seeds of an answer to many of their own concerns about development in Chile. In the initial results of this work they saw what could be the basis of a new society.

One concrete example is the degree of maturity reached in research carried out in the centers. This research was formalized by the creation of the Commission for Research into Alternative Agriculture (Comisión de Investigación de la Agricultura Alternativa—CIAL). This commission is made up of university professors and students who do their practical work, write their graduation theses, and carry out research directly related to the problems of the poor.[3]

The interest aroused by this work among non-governmental development organizations inside Chile can be seen in the fact that 42 such organizations have participated in seminars for technical staff organized by CET. Twenty NGOs have also signed the Colina Agreement, committing themselves to support one another in training staff and carrying out joint actions to analyze and share information on the different kinds of work undertaken.[4] NGOs from other Latin American countries have also shown interest in this work. Eighteen have either participated in a seminar organized in Colina, or sent technical staff to CET on study visits.[5]

In 1984, two members of CET's staff led a seminar in Paraguay which was attended by 17 Paraguayan NGOs.[6] Two similar seminars were requested for 1985, one of which was to be held in Brazil with the participation of 20 technical workers, and the other in Chile, to be attended by about 20 people from seven different countries. CET was also invited to hold a meeting in Peru in 1986, with a group of local institutions.

Questions Raised by CET's Work

This discussion of the work raises a series of questions. These cannot be dealt with fully here, but we would like to bring out some aspects which we see as central. We will look at the work in relation to the following questions.

What Is the Central Element in This Concept of Development?

As stated earlier, we see development as a human process, the material results of which (production of goods to meet needs), while important, do not express the whole nature and dynamic of the process. We do not believe, therefore, that development can be measured and evaluated solely in terms of the quantity of material goods generated.

The central element in this process of development is the mobilization of a social actor who takes responsibility for his/her own needs and adapts tools in order to satisfy these needs. Through this kind of action, the individual increasingly develops as an active subject. This enables him/her to suggest more far-reaching, integral, and lasting solutions to new needs.

It follows, therefore, that the key result of this concept of development is that the nation becomes the agent of its own destiny. The poor are the majority of the population, the sector in which the most severe social problems and contradictions are concentrated; thus transforming the attitudes of the poor will produce a transformation of the nation as a whole.

On What Foundations Does This Process Rest?

If a group of people are to make themselves masters of their own destiny, then they must develop in at least three areas.

The first is to develop an adequate and efficient organization. A group of individuals with no connections between one another are not a social actor. Social actors emerge when groups of people come together on the basis of common needs and interests, which allows them to discover, through the concrete activities they carry out, the importance of organization as an effective tool for action.

As a group begins to tackle the more radical issues affecting its situation at different levels, it generates community, local, or social organizations of a size and character proportionate to these challenges. At the same time, leaders capable of doing the work required by the organization will emerge.

Secondly, a level of consciousness that implies a recovery of social identity must develop. This involves a clear understanding of what the group represents as a sector of society, where its real problems and interests lie, and how it has come to be in its actual position. Discussion and study of the group's history is one of the most important elements in understanding the present situation.

The development of awareness also implies discovery of the relationship between individual problems and social reality, and thus of the root causes of these problems. The removal of these obstacles to understanding is what ensures that the process of development can continue.

The third essential development is related to the idea of an alternative model of society. This model is a response to the group's interests, allows the identification of appropriate, effective actions, and makes it possible for the group to take these necessary actions. Increasing clarity of awareness is achieved, to the extent that the group continually reviews the actions in which it is engaged, and analyzes their successes, failures, and limitations.

Along with organization and increased consciousness, a social actor is constructed by the development of this actor's ability to resolve the group's needs.

In countries such as Chile, the tendency in society has generally been to exclude and marginalize poor people. One of the clearest changes imposed by the present military regime has been in the role of the state. From being a state that sought to integrate different sectors, it has become one that excludes the majority, to such an extent that the vital problems of survival facing the vast majority of the population are, in official discourse, referred to as merely the social cost of the new economic model.

In the past, the poor presented their needs to the state, which responded by providing more or less adequate solutions. This practice gave rise to a type of organization and social consciousness focused almost exclusively on the problem of power. Today the poor are beginning to discover, almost instinctively, that in order to reverse this exclusion they themselves must initially take the first steps to resolve their most basic needs, by using the resources available and developing their own individual and collective capacities.

For this to be possible, technological tools geared to using available resources, easy for the group concerned to obtain and use, and whose emphasis is different from that of conventional technology (for example, labor valued more than capital) are essential. When people in the cities and the countryside begin to dominate technologies such as organic agriculture, they gain greater autonomy and self-confidence. They can then respond to their own needs, and in the process generate new forms of organization and social consciousness.

This point is of great importance today, and will be even more relevant in taking up the challenge of development and dealing with the problems that Third World nations will face in the coming decades, whatever the nature of the government in power.

The Principles of an Appropriate Methodology

The work carried out thus far had concentrated primarily on two points in the process of development. First is the starting point, where the process of development is set in motion with the recognition that the individuals and groups involved are divided, worn down, discouraged, and have low self-esteem. Thus a changed attitude towards one's self and one's capacities is required. This unblocking of the mind is achieved by and in the process of carrying out simple actions which result in successful experiences and increased self-esteem.

The second key point comes when people discover the links between short-term actions and other activities which affect the group or community at deeper levels.

In order to maintain and expand the process of development, a group must be able to analyze its own traditional practices. The group can then establish priorities for actions to be carried out over a period of time, having identified their real objectives, the obstacles which block or prevent improvements, and links with other spheres in which the group's daily life develops. This analysis enables the group to systematize the steps being taken, and therefore ensures that progress is always built on a firm base.

Between 1976 and 1980, a clear idea emerged of who brings about development, and what exactly this actor does. Only from 1981–82 onwards was there any clarity about how to bring about this development.

Contributions to the Process of Global Development

By centering attention on the actors in the development process rather than on the results, the role of individuals and groups is emphasized. The people who participate are, in general, not taken sufficiently into account in either national projects or projects at a global level.

In accepting responsibility for resolving their own problems then taking measures to deal with them and in discussing their work and decisions, the individuals and groups involved operate according to democratic principles. In practice, this makes the process an education in democracy and participation. From the start, the activities develop critical awareness, self-esteem, and self-confidence. Participants begin early on and continue to recognize the need for social change, for a more just and fraternal society.

This kind of work emphasizes the use of local resources, the importance of labor rather than capital, the need for autonomy in relation to outside input, and for a technology suited to local idiosyncrasies and culture. Thus light is shed on important questions, questions often not taken into consideration by programs on a broader scale.

Challenges Presented to NGOs

The chief role of an NGO should be to accompany poor groups in urban and rural areas through a process of development which the people themselves gradually construct. The NGOs are not meant to substitute action by these sectors with their own work. They should rather help to discover obstacles and identify appropriate ways of dealing with them.

As this process involves a variety of spheres (technology to meet needs, education to teach new approaches, methodology for ongoing support, etc.) which together make up a single whole, input from all these spheres is needed. Specialization in a limited field is thus an inadequate preparation for the support requested from NGOs. These requests often oblige NGOs to go into areas that in other cases would be considered outside their spheres of action.

A direct consequence of this need for an open approach is that technical staff must receive a broad-based training; they are the ones directly involved with the groups and communities. Given that the scope of the NGOs' action is limited, however, their role can only be to give an indication of what a more global, far-reaching process of development might involve.

Finally, the size of the NGOs gives them much greater flexibility than larger institutions, making it possible to carry out experiments whose cost, if they are unsuccessful, is not too heavy.

Challenges

The experience we have described and analyzed raises an infinite number of challenges for NGOs seeking to respond to the demands generated by social processes and the increasingly specific needs being put forward by the poor. We have chosen to discuss three of these challenges.

First, training a team of workers. To think in terms of an alternative form of development when one has been trained to implement conventional approaches, demands a review of technical knowledge, the ways we communicate and educate, and the way professionals in different fields coordinate their work in a development process. This is a particularly complex task, given that today there is no opportunity for this new kind of training other than practical work in the field and interaction with other groups carrying out similar work.

Second, making the most of local contributions to the process of alternative development. Bringing together and mobilizing the nation's resources and specialists in science and technology is a priority. A concrete expression of this is using the research facilities of universities and centers of learning to find simple, low cost ways to resolve the basic needs of peasants and poor city dwellers, and to involve students studying subjects relevant to furthering an alternative form of development.

Third, raising the support needed for this work. The novelty and complexity of this alternative approach accentuates the need for open discussion and exchange of opinions on experiences elsewhere in Latin America and with other co-operation agencies. Thus other contributions can be obtained, making it possible for this work to continue.

Notes

1. Measurements of the productivity of the Intensive Family Vegetable Gardens taken over a two-year period gave the following results: 32 different kinds of vegetables were grown, and yielded a daily average of 1-1/2 kilos of edible material throughout the year.

2. Up to December 1984, 3,160 families were involved in cultivating vegetable gardens or similar activities in programs directly linked with CET, and 790 monitors had been trained. (*CET Report,* December 1984).

3. At present 12 graduate theses are being prepared, as well as 40 research studies (*CIAL Report,* December 1984). Staff from CET have held four seminars in universities, and a request has been made that the organization give a course

on "Technology and Development." In January 1985, 30 students of agriculture did their practice in the experimentation centers and development programs.

4. *Colina Agreement,* (October 1984).

5. Report of the Latin American Seminar on Organic Agriculture and Social Development (January 1983).

6. Report on the Seminar in Paraguay (September 1984).

9

Support for Income Generation in an Economy of Poverty

Arno Klenner and Humberto Vega

Labor Economics Program (PET)

Poor people, having been forced out of the labor market over the past decade and having had their incomes drastically reduced, have nevertheless found creative ways to meet the challenge of subsistence. In the process, a new phenomenon has arisen: the Popular Economic Organizations (OEPs). Productive workshops, consumer organizations, housing committees, health groups, etc., have come into existence in poor communities in Santiago and other urban areas of Chile.

The Academy of Christian Humanism's Labor Economics Program (PET) has focused one area of its work on the OEP sector. PET has provided research and analysis as well as technical assistance, training, communications, and support for extending such experiences. Through its work and along with other support institutions, PET has formed an institutional network designed to promote and support self-help activities within the economy of poverty.

Characteristics of Popular Economic Organizations

These are subsistence organizations. Their members face difficulties in satisfying basic needs. OEPs are principally concerned with the economic sphere, and receive institutional support and services in this area.

The economic sphere refers here mainly to income generation. It can mean the addition of new income to the family, for example when a family member previously unemployed finds paid work. The economic sphere can also refer to economies or savings in the family's expenditures in order to satisfy other basic needs, which produce an effect similar to an increased income.

In general, as will be shown in greater detail below, these organizations are small groups of people experiencing a similar situation in the same way. Together, these people look for a means of resolving an immediate economic problem. The original link which brings them together may be that they live in the same neighborhood, they were employed by the same company, belong to the same religious community, or hold similar political views.

A study made in 1983[1] identified five different types of popular economic organizations.

Productive Workshops

These are small economic units, employing a limited number of workers. The division of labor is rudimentary and the organization is run by the workers themselves. In some cases, the members do the productive work in their respective homes.

An important differentiation between these workshops is whether their productive activities are permanent or occasional. Further distinctions can be made between permanent workshops operating full-time, permanent workshops functioning part-time, and occasional workshops that function only at specific times of year (Christmas or the start of the school year, for example), or in response to specific campaigns or events (Sunday markets, sales to raise money for particular objectives, etc.).

Organizations of the Unemployed

These differ from the productive workshops in that their subsistence activities do not necessarily involve either the production of goods or the provision of services.

The first organizations of this kind were the *unemployment centers,* which sought autonomous ways to resolve the problems created by layoffs. The *centers for community services* also operated as informal employment agencies. The most common organizations today, however, are the *committees of unemployed people* and the *independent (or temporary) workers' unions.* The main difference between these last two is that the workers' unions comply with certain legal formalities.

Organizations for Basic Consumption

These are organizations of families with very low incomes who work together to find ways to obtain food and improve their diet.

The most traditional are the *popular dining rooms,* generally linked to parishes and Christian communities. Another type of organization which has become very common since 1981 is the *community soup kitchen,* whose efforts to satisfy the need for food also involve an important element of social criticism. *Consumer collectives,* made up of families combining limited monetary resources to take advantage of discounts on wholesale purchases of foods, have also grown very fast in some parts of Santiago.

Other organizations for basic consumption are *community food warehouses, family kitchen gardens and small farms,* and *self-help groups.*

Organizations Concerned with Housing Problems

The focus of these grassroots organizations is housing, an issue of deep concern to people in poor areas.

This category includes *housing committees* and *committees of homeless people,* organized in traditional ways to press for concrete demands. The *pre-cooperative groups,* which work to further their own interests, also have access to social benefits associated with housing.

Between 1981 and 1983, the *debtors committees* (including committees of people with debts for water, electricity, and mortgage payments) were quite important. They tried, often successfully, to renegotiate the terms of payment of existing bills and debts still outstanding.

After the 1985 earthquake, there was a marked growth of committees of people whose homes had been damaged, the objectives of which were to resolve the problems caused by the earthquake.

Other Grassroots Service Organizations

It is debatable whether the following are really economic organizations, although they exist to resolve specific needs. This category includes health groups, alternative schools, groups organizing recreational activities, neighborhood cultural centers, etc.

A document published by UNICEF[2] suggests a way of classifying these organizations based on their potential for growth. This approach identifies the following three categories. First is subsistence organizations, whose products or services are dedicated entirely to satisfying the basic needs of their members. They do not have the capacity to produce surpluses, nor to replace the capital investment, which is therefore gradually used up. Second is organizations that develop without producing surpluses. This is a transitional category, although the organization itself may remain for a long period. Here capital is replaced and the number of members grows, but there are no plans for savings or fresh investments. Third is organizations that developed by generating surpluses and increasing their capital, whose initial capital is reproduced and increased through the production of goods or services. The organization thus operates as businesses.

These three classifications are an indication of the great differences among popular economic organizations. It would be a grave error for governmental or private institutions seeking to establish policies and take measures to assist this sector, to treat it as a homogeneous whole.

These are, moreover, "complex organizations tending to carry out integrated activities."[3] Whether or not this integration of activities is effective, basic needs are bound up not merely with economic aspects but also with cultural, socio-political, and ideological issues.

History of Popular Economic Organizations

Five stages in the development of popular economic organizations can be distinguished after 1973.[4] The first popular economic organizations appeared, in a very incipient form, shortly after the 1973 military coup. They were a response to the problem of unemployment by some union leaders who had been fired.

Next came a period of consolidation of institutions, which lasted from mid-1974 to mid-1977. It was marked by the setting up of productive workshops, unemployment centers, and popular dining rooms, to deal with unemployment and reduce the impact of the sharp fall in living standards on the poorest sectors of the population. At the same time, a number of support institutions were consolidated, providing a channel for resources and support for the development of OEPs. Chief among these institutions was an ecumenical body, the Commission for Solidarity and Development (COMSODE), which was controlled by the churches and religious groups of the Committee for Peace in Chile (Comite Pro-Paz) between 1974-75, and subsequently came under the responsibility of the Vicariate of Solidarity. COMSODE supported projects put forward by the grassroots organizations.

This was followed by a period of crisis in the original OEPs. It began in the second half of 1977 and continued for the whole of 1978, and brought to light deep-rooted problems in the way the organizations functioned. On the one hand, there was excessive dependence on external support; on the other, there was still a general view that the organizations were temporary mechanisms to deal with an emergency. This situation weakened cohesion between members.

Gradually, the social base was extended, and experiments with other forms of action and organization were undertaken. This period lasted until the beginning of 1981 and saw a reappraisal of methods of work, with emphasis on the need for training from support institutions. At the same time, new types of organization were tried out and developed, such as housing committees, committees of unemployed people, consumer committees, etc.

The present period is one of recovery, integration, and broadening the social base. The development of OEPs is now associated with the economic and political crisis through which Chile is passing. Economic activities are once again a priority, this time with a greater degree of realism about the present conditions. New types of organizations are now emerging, and pressing for concrete demands. In some cases, efforts are being made to integrate different organizations and create coordinating committees; there has been a rapid growth in the number of existing organizations.

Naturally, the division of a process as recent as this into distinct stages is influenced to a great extent by the particular perspective of the person making the divisions. Looking back, what seemed to be a separate period may turn out to have been a brief episode with little or no significance in the overall process. It is therefore appropriate to ask what remains at the end of this ebb and flow of development. Hardy and Razeto argue:

> These organizations have two distinctive characteristics, that are repeatedly revealed in practice, which allow one to think in terms of their maintaining and consolidating their work, independent of the external circumstances which may affect their future development.
>
> The first is the real capacity they have shown, even in the most adverse national economic and political conditions, to generate real benefits for their members which, although they may be precarious and may not be adequate to properly satisfy the needs for which they were created, are in fact considered important by the organizations' members.
>
> The second is their integral nature, which seems to be well-suited to the complex structure of integral needs found in poor communities. An indicator of this is that many of these organizations remain active even during long periods when their specific economic activities have been reduced or even suspended, but when their members find that they can satisfy other types of cultural, moral, political and even emotional needs, and this motivates the group to maintain its cohesion for much longer than one might have expected.[5]

In a qualitative assessment of the present period, the following aspects of the organizational process can be identified:[6] (1) a higher degree of participation by men and young people than had been seen in earlier periods; (2) growing participation by people with higher levels of education and training, who were also severely affected by the economic crisis; (3) a close relationship between economic and organizational aspects; (4) an increase in the number and range of support institutions, some of which now play very specialized roles; (5) an incipient tendency for organizations to function autonomously from the institutions that support them; and (6) creation of a space to discuss popular economic organizations within the debate on economic, social, and political issues.

The Sector

Since 1982, the Labor Economics Program has made periodic surveys of the popular economic organizations. As these organizations are widely dispersed and characterized by a high degree of informality, it is difficult to obtain figures on them and this survey does not pretend to be complete. The survey, moreover, only covers metropolitan Santiago and the neighboring province of San Antonio. OEPs exist in other major urban centers such as Arica, Antofagasta, Valparaíso, Talca, Concepción, Puerto Mont, and urban areas on the island of Chiloé.

The survey carried out in November, 1982 found almost 500 OEPs. In March, 1984, the number had risen to just over 700. This increase is not only due to the greater rigor with which data is collected but also reflects an effective quantitative growth. The workshops are predominantly producers of crafts, furniture, clothing, and baked goods, as well as laundries, locksmiths, and building workshops that do repairs and carpentry.

A number of methodological problems arise in estimating the number of people participating in these workshops. In some cases, only the head of household or another member of the family is involved; in others, the entire family participates. Bearing this limitation in mind, the total number of people participating either directly or indirectly in the 700 organizations identified by the survey made in March, 1984 was estimated at 120,000. In 1984, 44,994 people were directly involved in the support programs run by the Archbishopric of Santiago through its zonal administrative units (vicariates); thus the estimate based on the survey may be conservative.[7]

Information on the socio-economic situations of the members of these organizations is still very incomplete. A study by the College of Social Workers in 1983 showed that in two geographical areas of Santiago—squatter settlements known as Monseñor Silva Enriquez and Francisco Fresno—where significant efforts were made to promote OEPs, 49.1% of heads of household were either unemployed or enrolled in one of two government employment programs (Minimum Employment

TABLE 9.1

POPULAR ECONOMIC ORGANIZATIONS
IN METROPOLITAN SANTIAGO AND THE PROVINCE OF SAN ANTONIO

	November 1982	March 1984
Workshops	151	215
Committees of unemployed people	21	33
Independent workers' unions	8	21
Popular dining rooms	121	93
Community soup kitchens	34	41
Consumer collectives	57	113
Kitchen gardens	n/d	18
Pre-cooperative groups	27	18
Housing committees	5	51
Debtors' committees	12	n/d
Health groups	22	72
Other groups	31	33
Co-ordinating committees	5	12
TOTAL	494	702

n/d: no data available

Source: PET Survey

Plan (PEM), and Employment Program for Heads of Household or POJH, see Table 9.1).[8]

In the central zone of Santiago, where the Catholic Church has dedicated considerable work to organization, 26.1% of heads of household living in dilapidated shared accommodation (known by a variety of names such as *conventillo, cité, pasaje, pensión*) were in a situation of open unemployment. When other people living in the same accommodation who were not heads of household were included, the numbers rose to 51.6%.[9] Taking a selection of cases, the income generated by participants in OEPs ranged from US$15 to US$100 per person per month.[10] A study of the workshops in Conchalí, for example, showed that workshop income received by female heads of household constituted their families' main source of income.[11]

Purpose and Significance of Popular Economic Organizations

Three explanatory hypotheses have been put forward to identify the essential and inherent characteristics of popular economic organizations. These hypotheses have been designated minimum, intermediate, and maximum.

According to the minimum hypothesis, popular economic organizations are a conjunctional and transitory phenomenon produced by the concrete economic and political conditions in Chile today. The intermediate hypothesis also sees OEPs as conjunctional and transitory, and adds the view that when the present difficult conditions are surmounted, OEPs will develop into broader, more permanent grassroots organizations. Finally, the maximum hypothesis argues that this new type of organization not only produces changes relevant to the current situation but also represents a new structure for action.

Support for any one of these hypotheses is not merely an ideological question but also involves a personal view of Chile's economic and social prospects in the coming decades. Those who support the first hypothesis are nostalgic, and wish that the past history of the country could be recreated. Supporters of the intermediate hypothesis are optimistic about the popular sectors' capacity to adapt to new circumstances. Finally, the arguments of those who put forward the maximum hypothesis conceal a pessimistic view of the capacity of the political, economic, and social structures to satisfy the needs of the poorest sectors of the population.

Apart from the question of ideologies and psychological attitudes, "the problem still remains of how long the present crisis will continue to affect marginal sectors of the population, whatever the economic, social and political changes that one might reasonably expect to occur in the future."[12] To address this problem, the importance of the popular economic organizations must be examined.

The process of setting up a popular economic organization in itself implies a number of relevant factors. The value of the limited resources available in poor areas must be assessed in order to achieve the concrete objective of satisfying a basic need. The people involved must each be willing to contribute energy and creativity to carry out joint tasks. Most importantly, a mental attitude of self-help and of helping one another to satisfy these needs is required. None of these factors, however, has been properly considered in designing social policies.

> One cannot make a proper evaluation of these experiences—or of the projects which deliberately seek to support them—if one's reference points are the methods commonly used to assess the activities of a company operating in the modern sector of the economy.
>
> The economy of poverty is a universe in which all economic relations are dominated by the need to cover certain basic needs, these requirements being very closely linked with the daily reproduction of labor power. . . .[13]

We must, therefore, look further into the logic governing transactions, operations, and economic behaviors in an economy of poverty. Klenner and Zúñiga[14] have highlighted at least three important elements in this economic logic. First, the concepts of *equilibrium* and *optimum* are determined by amount of work done, rather than by maximization of profits. Second, in the management of OEPs, the organization's budget and the family budget tend to become confused. Finally, the economic significance of *time* is different than in the modern sector, which affects the processes of economic growth and accumulation.

Between the modern sector of the economy and the economy of poverty is a breakdown in communications, because these sectors operate according to contradictory rationales. In designing social policies, there has been a general failure to appreciate the value of resources contributed by the poor themselves. It becomes almost insuperably difficult to propose projects adapted to the logic of the economy of poverty.

Means of bridging this gap, however, are being put into practice. New approaches to education, training, technology, technical assistance, etc., are being developed by non-governmental organizations that support these grassroots organizations. The transferral of existing technology, education that is merely a transmission of information, and training not based on the concrete needs of the participants, are among the practices now being questioned.

The alternative approaches put forward in Chile have given rise, in recent years, to a qualitatively significant though numerically limited network of institutions which provide support for popular economic organizations.

Role of OEPs in Women's Advancement and Improving Children's Living Conditions

The present economic crisis has had a major impact on women and children in poor areas. For children, one effect of parental unemployment is that they have had to drop out of school before their physical and intellectual development is complete, in order to join the workforce. In the labor market, children find only occasional work with an extremely low level of productivity and a high degree of exploitation. In urban areas throughout the country children can be found working as street vendors, parking attendants, market porters, supermarket assistants, rubbish collectors, singers in buses, etc. More than half of the children between the ages of 10 and 14 who work are engaged in street selling.[15]

An even more generalized effect of parental unemployment is that the child's basic needs are not met.

> In particular restrictions on food consumption have taken a heavy toll on children, the effects of which are seen in phenomena such as low birth weight, limitations in the sphere of sensory co-ordination, vulnerability to infectious diseases and parasites, a lack of energy when faced with the normal load of school work, absenteeism and an increase in the likelihood of school abandonment.[16]

The concrete situation of a child is very closely linked to the family's income level and to the parents' income in particular. Although empirical evidence on this subject is still inadequate, it seems that in crisis conditions in poor areas the mother's income is more important than the father's in meeting the children's needs. The following testimony from one member of a craft workshop in Conchalí provides a good example of this.

> (My husband) works in the PEM, but he barely earns enough to pay for his own things. He's young, he's got his own expenses, and he can hardly cover them; I couldn't expect him to pay for things for the house as well. He helps me by just maintaining himself; what I earn doesn't cover everything either, but at least I can pay for the most important things, the essentials, like the food for the family.[17]

Their efforts to earn an income have led women to free themselves from domestic work. This has meant making sacrifices, but they have also made notable achievements. In the process of earning an income the women gain self-esteem, and their work is valued more highly by other members of their families, particularly their husbands.

In spite of the difficulties encountered by the Labor Economics Program in obtaining precise figures for the numbers of people participating in popular economic organizations, it is certain that at least two thirds of the participants are women. In productive workshops, approximately 80% are women. In poor areas, it seems to be women who need to work rather than men, and who find that the popular economic organizations provide a suitable structure in which to achieve their goals.

Work to Support Popular Economic Organizations

There are several main problem areas in the work of the popular economic organizations.

Management Attitudes

The logic underlying behavior in the economy of poverty, and therefore the logic of popular economic organizations, has had concrete effects on the way in which they operate. An analysis of operations from the perspective of the modern sector reveals the following common management problems: (1) lack of management ability to define objectives and organize resources; (2) difficulties in sharing work efficiently and fairly; (3) difficulties in resolving conflicts within the group; (4) generally inadequate methods for sharing profits; (5) lack or inadequate use of the principal administrative tools (accounting, budgeting, regulations, etc.); (6) tendency towards paternalism or authoritarianism on the part of leaders; and (7) failure to appreciate the importance of replacing capital, especially in younger organizations.

Technical assistance and training are fundamental to overcoming these problems. Although training and technical assistance should respond to needs put forward by the organizations themselves, training and technical assistance workers need to develop an acute sensitivity in order to detect these kinds of problems. The workers can then help the groups to recognize these problems themselves.

Experience shows that the main reasons for the failure of a popular economic organization are the following, in order of importance: (1) conflicts between workshop members and the incapacity to resolve conflicts without fundamentally affecting the organization; (2) failure to fulfill the members' expectations, especially in relation to income; (3) inability to establish stable prices and an even quality in goods and services offered; (4) serious errors in the administration of resources (failure to replace capital, use of resources for objectives different from those of the organization, significant imbalances between total sales and purchases, etc.); and (5) unanticipated events (loss of a rented or borrowed base of operations, fraud by clients, etc.). In examining these causes, it becomes clear that training and technical assistance are crucial to reducing risks.

Financing of Investments and Operations

An organization generally depends on three sources of financing: funds generated by the organization itself, contributions by members, and resources obtained from institutions, foundations, or the credit market.

Organizations generating their own funds function on a regular basis. Their operations involve the distribution of surpluses, and the replacement and expansion of the capital base. The level of funds generated internally is usually proportional to volume of operations and to capital invested in the organization. As the initial capital is likely to be small, the level of funds generated internally will also be low. The decision to reinvest these funds must be weighed against other possible uses, such as the members' own consumption needs.

Contributions by members have many forms other than monetary contributions. These include raw materials, tools, machinery, personal labor, etc. To obtain cash contributions, the organizations sometimes use novel methods such as holding raffles, folk evenings, etc. Many organizations have some difficulty in establishing the value of non-monetary contributions and incorporating them into overall resources.

The most important source of major funds is obviously external, in particular from institutions, foundations, and finance agencies. The conditions on which external financing is obtained are varied, ranging from direct donations to commercial loans. This issue has given rise to important debates among those concerned with promoting and supporting popular economic organizations.

Some argue that donations are just hand-outs, which encourage dependency and irresponsibility in the organizations receiving them. Others take the more extreme position that the only valid conditions are those prevailing in the commercial credit market. Loans given on more favorable terms are therefore no better than donations, and promote economic inefficiency in the organizations.

In fact, donations are generally conditional. That is, if an organization complies with specific requirements (such as the level of internal contributions, personal labor, etc.), it will receive contributions to support operations and development. Establishing the same conditions for financing as found in the commercial credit market, however, is directly contrary to the idea of designing social policies that are valid in an economy of poverty.

Commercialization of Products

Organizations producing goods and services face their greatest difficulty in the commercialization of products. This problem arises as soon as a decision on what to produce, and where, is made. Often the decision is based on what the members are able to produce, without taking market conditions into account. When the organization comes to define its market, there is seldom a clear idea of how to proceed.

These organizations orient their work towards any of four main markets: (1) an exceptional (or solidarity) market; (2) a market within the economy of poverty; (3) unstable insertion in the formal market; and (4) a formal market. If the organization is clear about which market it is aiming at, the decision about what to produce does not have such a decisive impact on the economic viability of the productive workshop; the workshop's participation in the market is absolutely marginal. The main problem is not the market itself, but how to present the goods.

The decisive factors in the economic viability of a productive organization are location, prices, and ability to maintain a certain level of quality. *Location* is relevant for workshops offering personal and domestic services (hairdressing, repair of domestic equipment, etc.) and those whose products are sold in the same place they are produced (bakeries, etc.). For workshops producing goods that are easy to transport, a particular location has little effect on the market.

Prices are determined to a great extent by the workshop's structure of costs. Here technical assistance, along with commercialization, is very important. Prices in worker-managed businesses can respond to the market more flexibly, by increasing and reducing costs, than can traditional businesses, although reduction of costs may conceal a high level of self-exploitation.

Finally, the ability to maintain *quality standards* is very difficult for productive organizations, and is the factor that most affects sales of both goods and services. It can, moreover, slow the development of a workshop. Training and technical assistance can contribute greatly to ensuring adequate quality controls.

For the majority of workshops in the main cities, the problem is not so much the market as the process of commercialization. Although new workshops have great difficulty in marketing their products and services, once they have entered the market they can maintain and develop their position. Attention muxt be paid, however, to aspects such as location, price, and quality.

An Experience in Training

The following account of training in marketing provided for women's productive workshops in June and July, 1985, illustrates some of the points made above.

Characteristics of the Workshops and Participants

The training involved thirteen women's workshops, each with between twelve and forty members. The workshops operated in the same area of central Santiago, which is characterized by aging, dilapidated housing. The participants were between 18 and 50 years old. Almost all of them were either married, separated, widows, or single mothers. Those who had had paid work in the past (approximately 40%) were unemployed when they joined the workshop. Their previous jobs had been as shop assistants, office workers, domestic workers, assistant nurses, etc.

The husbands of almost 20% of the married women were unemployed. The husbands who were working received wages of not more than US$70 per month. Many of the husbands worked in one of the government's employment programs (PEM or POJH), while the majority of the others were either street vendors, office messengers, or building workers.

At the time of the training, these workshops were relatively new. Their participants had little or no experience, the level of cohesion was fairly low, and many issues remained undefined. As training for production, they had made articles of various kinds (knitted goods, baby clothes, crafts, etc.), and sometimes sold these to people in their neighborhoods. During this earlier stage, they received some non-monetary help from the promotion and solidarity team of the Episcopal Vicariate of the Central Zone of Santiago.

Development of the Work

The training program in commercialization was requested by the head of the promotion and solidarity team at the Vicariate of the Central Zone. In defining the program, the precarious organizational structure of the groups became clear, as did the fact that commercialization is a fundamental problem for OEPs. It was also recognized that the training program should help the workshops in the process of deciding what to produce, and give guidance to workshops that were already producing products not economically viable given current market conditions.

Each workshop nominated a person to be responsible for sales, for whom the program was intended. Throughout the course, attendance never fell below nine people. The program was divided into five sessions, held once a week for 2 to 2 and 1/2 hours.

The aim of the first session was to ascertain how motivated the women were, in relation to the content of the course, and to stimulate increased enthusiasm. Creating a sense of confidence and the ability to deal with administrative issues (timing, venue, etc.) were also goals. The session started with a personal introduction by the instructor after which each participant introduced herself, which dispelled the initial tensions.

The instructor then asked each person to describe a personal experience of selling something, and what problems they found in selling. Only one of the women had had experience with selling over a long period of time in a street market. In relation to problems in selling, they mentioned issues such as: "I never know what price I should be charging for things," "If I try to sell something and people start bargaining, I end up giving it away," "I feel embarrassed when I try to sell something and people say no," "I don't know where to sell the things," "People have so little money that they don't want to buy," etc.

It became clear that the women had not thought further about selling their products than fairs and exhibitions in church premises, where people attending services could be attracted. This method is commonly used by the most unstable productive workshops, and falls in the category of exceptional (or solidarity) market. Only three or four events of this kind are held during the year, and each producer receives an average of US$40 on each occasion.

The second session started with a discussion, initiated by the instructor, on how to establish the price of a product. It was generally felt that the cost of producing each article should be calculated, a margin of profit added, and the result would be the sales price. As the debate developed, however, the women recognized that prices are ultimately determined by competition.

Then followed a discussion of the different components in the cost of a manufactured article and their importance in relation to price. The idea of replacing labor capital was introduced. Some costs, which tend not to be taken into account because not directly incorporated into the article, were also identified.

The discussion provided a basis for looking at the problem of bargaining. It became clear to each of the participants that the lowest price an article could be sold for is the amount that allows all costs to be covered, including the producers' minimum expectations of what should be received per unit of time worked.

At the third session, the discussion opened with each participant explaining why her workshop had chosen the area of production in which it was working. The responses demonstrated that market was never taken into account. The reasons included, for example, "One of the women in the group knew how to make this article, and she taught the rest of us," "We took a vote on it," "We produce this article because the materials involved are cheap," etc.

Furthermore, it came out that in certain cases a particular article was being produced even though the group was not happy about it. Others had simply imitated workshops in other geographical areas. Thus the best use of the skills, initiatives, and interests of the workshop members themselves was not being made.

The rest of the session was devoted to making a list of the products which could be made by the workshops. The feasibility of each was analyzed in terms of market potential, abilities of the women themselves, resources available, and technology required. This suggested other products not previously considered, such as foods (bakeries, production of meat pies, and fried snacks, etc.), and domestic services (cleaning apartments and offices, window cleaning, gardening, etc.).

The fourth session focused on the issue of quality and how to improve it. As an exercise, each participant made an analysis of the technical training needs of her own workshop, linking quality with technical training and technology. As the instructor had hoped, this finally made the women recognize the need to clearly identify potential markets and demands, and how these could be met.

It was also agreed that each participant would bring a sample of her workshop's product to the last session, and that these samples would be analyzed in detail, from the point of view of each issue discussed during the course of the program.

The entire fifth session was spent analyzing the products that each of the participants had brought. In each case, the group discussed price, cost, reasons for producing that particular article, market, quality, and the most appropriate channels of commercialization. By this session, the women had greatly increased their capacity for self-criticism in terms of the economic decisions made by their different workshops.

Results of the Experience

Obviously, a sales training program lasting only five sessions cannot bring about radical changes in a workshop's relationship to its market. Certain important changes can nevertheless be seen in the workshops that participated in this training program. Some groups took definite steps to redefine their product, this time thinking in terms of market. Other groups drew up technical training programs, with support institutions, to improve the quality of their products. In all groups, the program participants passed the information gained to other members. Finally, in almost all groups, improvements in the level of internal organization were made, especially in terms of taking responsibility for the tasks defined and continuity of production.

Interpretation and Conclusions

The emergence of popular economic organizations described briefly above is a new phenomenon in the economic and social history of Chile. This phenomenon needs to be understood in relation to recent economic, social, and political changes, but it undoubtedly has cultural roots going much further back in time. What follows is an analysis of some principal characteristics of this phenomenon, and some explanatory hypotheses.

Any explanation must begin with the idea of collective survival through mutual support expressed in the OEPs. The economic processes of an authoritarian economic model inspired by monetarist principles have resulted in high unemployment, a drop in personal and family income, and the exclusion of major sectors from the formal economy. The response of the poor has been to develop survival strategies, such as organizing to take collective action based on mutual support, rather than individual adaptations or personal or family-level responses to these problems.

The factors that explain this response in hypothetical terms are rooted in specific social, cultural, and economic processes. A tradition of organization among the poor has accompanied the process of democratization in Chilean society during the twentieth century. The groups most affected by the present crisis have had some experience or recollection of the value and use of organization in unions, poor communities, among young people, etc. The cultural ethos favors organization; organization facilitates the assistance and co-operation of development and solidarity institutions.

Organization also enables people to learn and share experiences in a social context hostile to popular initiatives. Despite its many problems and failures, organization makes it possible for individual resources to be combined. Fields of work can then be defined in terms of members' skills, which produces increasing returns—in fact, returns which are more than the mere sum of individual capacities.

Secondly, the great range of unsatisfied basic social needs has been generated by two process which reinforce one another. The first is the drop in real salaries and the massive increase in unemployment. The second is the reduction of real per capita social expenditure by the public sector.

The drastic change in fiscal policy, especially in the amounts involved and the methods of carrying out the remaining social expenditures, has reduced the coverage provided by public services. This can be seen in the spheres of health, housing, and social security. The emergence of the OEPs is therefore in response to the gaps created by the economic changes, particularly those resulting from the redefinition of fiscal policy and the state's role.

In the third place, the phenomenon of popular economic organizations is supported and encouraged by the teachings and actions of the Catholic Church and some Protestant churches on human, economic, and social rights. Solidarity, the intrinsic dignity of all human beings, the value of labor, and active promotion of all kinds of social organizations encouraged the creation of popular economic organizations. It was principally the Catholic Church that created "areas of liberty" in which OEPs could develop and institutions specializing in promotion and technical support could work. It would be hard to imagine or explain the development and proliferation of OEPs without the action of these institutions.

In the fourth place, the size of the informal sector of the Chilean economy and the severe problems that the nation will inherit from its experience of authoritarianism are major challenges for any strategy for democratic development. To give one example: will it be possible to find an active and productive role for the popular economic organizations in the work of rebuilding the economy and improving the living standards of the Chilean population? In responding to this challenge, the following issues, among others, must be taken into account.

How will the concept of an informal sector, whose central focus is poverty and the inability to satisfy needs, be replaced by an appreciation of this sector's contribution in terms of labor, creativity, and production?

How will a sphere for the organizational development of a chain of supplies, production, appropriate technology, design, and sales be formally established in the economy for the OEPs? This network should include institutions to advise on and encourage the development of financial, technological, and commercial relations, and should have stable, complementary links with other sectors of the economy.

How will levels of production, employment, and investment for the OEP sector be determined, within a global policy for the development of productive forces in the economy? In setting priorities in terms of exportation, import substitution, protection of employment-generating activities, and assigning resources by sector and region, the OEP sector's contribution must be taken into account.

How will economic and financial instruments for regulating the economy to the conditions found in the informal sector be adapted? Taxes, interest rates, import taxes, prices, credit supplies, poderes compradores, public contracts, etc., should be adapted, and the OEPs should benefit from positive discrimination. The key to giving OEPs effective protection and support is to combine certain advantages with the demands that quality standards be met, the community be provided with decent services, and the benefits generated be distributed fairly.

In conclusion, the phenomenon of OEPs transcends the present economic and political circumstances. They are the clearest demonstration of the potential for solidarity and creativity that exists among the poorest groups in the country, poor women in particular, who are seeking a space in which to make a responsible contribution to an alternative strategy for democratic development. Failure to take the OEPs into account in this national enterprise would be a serious economic error, as well as the political negation of the objectives and goals of democracy itself.

Notes

1. Luis Razeto, et al. *Las Organizaciones Económicas Populares.* Programa de Economía del Trabajo, Academia de Humanismo Cristiano, Santiago 1983.
2. Arno Klenner and Luis Zúñiga. *Generación de Ingresos y Vinculación a los Mercados en la Economía de la Pobreza.* UNICEF Area Office for Argentina, Chile and Uruguay, Santiago, September 1984.
3. Luis Razeto, et al. *op. cit.*
4. See: Luis Razeto, et al. *op. cit.* See Also: Arno Klenner, "Las Nuevas Organizaciones Económicas Populares" in *Mensaje.* No. 328, Santiago, May 1984.
5. Clarisa Hardy and Luis Razeto. *Los Nuevos Actores y Prácticas Populares: Desafío a la Concertación.* Materiales para Discusión, CED (Centro de Estudios de Desarrollo), Santiago, November 1984.
6. Luis Razeto. *Las Organizaciones Económicas Populares en la Nueva Coyunctura Económica.* Programa de Economía del Trabajo, Santiago, May 1984.
7. *Noveno Año de Labor.* 1984. Vicaría de la Solidaridad, Santiago, 1985.
8. From Hardy and Razeto. *op. cit.*
9. Roberto Urmeneta. *Las Viviendas Colectivas Deterioradas de la Zona Centro de Santiago. Condiciones de Vida y Empleo.* Documento de Trabajo No. 34, Programa de Economía del Trabajo, Academia de Humanismo Cristiano, Santiago, June 1984.
10. From data given in Klenner and Zúñiga. *op. cit.*
11. Clarisa Hardy. *Los Talleres Artesanales de Conchalí. La Organización, su Recorrido y sus Protagonistas.* Colección Experiencias Populares, Santiago, December 1984.
12. Arno Klenner. *op. cit.*
13. Klenner and Zúñiga. *op. cit.*
14. Ibid.
15. Vicaría de la Solidaridad. *op. cit.*
16. Klenner and Zúñiga. *op. cit.*
17. Hardy, C. *op. cit.*

10

Experiences in Social Action and the Design of Social Policies: Replica or Reproduction? The Case of the Learning Workshops

Jorge Chateau

Latin American Faculty of Social Sciences (FLACSO)

During the past ten years, a number of Chilean institutions (private, non-governmental, or informal) have developed a series of social action and education programs to assist the poor. These programs, found in both rural and urban areas, share a similar style and approach to their work that constitutes a specific method of carrying out social policy.[1]

The following characteristic features are particularly significant. The projects offer opportunities for popular participation; the predominant methodology is active and participative, in contrast to the technocratic approach found elsewhere. The style of work is based on the belief that the way things are done is as important as what is done; real conditions are the starting point, the value of local culture is recognized, a horizontal relationship between the participants and people coming in from outside is encouraged, and activities are based on groups and thus encourage social organization. Due to the above characteristics, this group of programs can be seen as contributing to build democracy.

The value of these activities as an expression of the creativity and capacities of social groups is clear. There are also lessons to be learned from such programs and experiences, in relation to designing social policies that will help to resolve the problems affecting the poor, and society as a whole.

It is time that some thought was given to the relevance of these projects and their potential value in defining social policies. As a way into this issue, it was decided to take the example of the "Learning Workshops," started in 1977 by the Interdisciplinary Program for Research in Education (PIIE), which is a part of the Academy of Christian

FIGURE 10.1

FORMULA OF NOMOLOGICAL DEDUCTIVE EXPLANATION

$$\frac{\begin{matrix} L_1, L_2 \ldots, L_m \\ C_1, C_2 \ldots, C_n \end{matrix}}{E}$$

Humanism. These workshops are still in existence at the time of this writing, and cover a significant sector of the population.

Given the importance of reviewing the experience of recent years in terms of the possibilities of putting new social policies into practice in the future, this chapter will focus on one specific aspect of this issue: the potential for replication of the experience described.[2]

The basic argument is that, if the question of replication is important, then it must be approached in a quite different manner than would be used in the context of a laboratory experiment. In order to reproduce a project, the experience involved must first be systematized. A good description of the project, its achievements and problems, is therefore necessary.

The issues for consideration will be presented in the following order: (1) the replication of social action projects; (2) a proposal for systematization; (3) a description of the Learning Workshops; (4) an attempt to systematize this experience; and (5) discussion of the problems involved in replication.

"Replication" in Social Action

In order to analyze the Learning Workshops project in terms of its potential for replication, a number of issues related to this subject must first be resolved, even if only schematically. The way in which the problem of replication is normally formulated is based on what is involved in replicating a scientific experiment. For the purposes of the present discussion, we will clarify the central features of this concept, taken principally from physics.

Figure 10.1 expresses a common and widely-accepted concept of "scientific explanation"[3] (termed nomological deductive explanation). What is shown as L_1, L_2, through to L_m, refers to general laws; C_1, C_2, through to C_n, represent propositions or particular events related to the conditions in which the phenomena covered by these general laws occur. E, the explanation, which is separated by a horizontal line from the first arguments, represents a conclusion that follows necessarily from the premises established by $L_1 \ldots L_m$, and $C_1 \ldots C_n$ respectively.

The logical structure of an explanation is no different from that of a scientific prediction. All that changes is the point in time from which we are looking at E. In an explanation, E has already happened; in a prediction, E will happen.

The validity of an explanation is put to the test by making predictions. The ability to predict successfully depends both on the way the laws are formulated and on whether the conditions in which the phenomena occur have been correctly specified. This process, rather than being a verification, represents an attempt to prove the explanation false.[4] Thus, if a hypothesis or explanation still stands after various tests, it is considered valid until there is proof to the contrary.

Ideally, the experimental design developed in the laboratory allows the validity of the explanation to be tested. In a laboratory, variables can be controlled and thus the conditions in which the phenomena occur can be specified. The possibility of a literal description both of the phenomena to be explained (E) and of the particular circumstances (C) is a necessary condition and basic supposition of any process of reasoning.[5]

Despite problems such as the so-called "personal equation," which refers, for example, to the differences in calculations of the length of time of a star's orbit registered at the Greenwich Observatory in 1976,[6] it is generally assumed that if the procedures are specified clearly and the people involved have the necessary training, it should be possible to establish literal descriptions in the field of the natural sciences.

This definition of prediction is nevertheless arguably valid only in the context of the laboratory, where variables can be rigorously controlled, and the conditions for the occurrence of the phenomenon can be specified. This type of control is not possible in the "real" world, and the *ceteris paribus* supposition is seriously undermined. In the "real" physical world, one cannot speak so much of prediction as of prognosis, which does not imply the same sense of logical necessity.[7] Clearly, the concept of prediction is the basis of replication, since it is assumed that in identical circumstances a similar phenomenon can be reproduced.

The subject under consideration here is the social world and, in particular, social interventions and the possibility of replicating them. The difficulties in making predictions about the physical world are multiplied when it comes to social questions. This is not just a quantitative problem, although there are more variables to take into account, but rather a qualitative issue.

It is instructive to refer to Weber, who pointed out that the major difference between the natural and the social sciences lies in the fact that the former can only be analyzed from the outside, while the latter can also be analyzed from within, by trying to understand what an action means to the different individuals or groups involved.[8] Starting from this idea, he proposes a plan of work for "comprehensive sociology," in which the concept of action, understood as behavior meaningful for the actor, plays a central role. From this view point, what is described by scientific research into social issues and everyday life is action rather than behavior; this implies some concept of motivation on the part of the subjects.

In Weber's famous example, we know that a woodcutter is cutting wood not by a description of his movements from the outside—he could be doing something else—but because we recognize the action as meaningful and ascribe motives and purpose to the actor.

This qualitative change in the perspective of the analysis presents serious problems in terms of establishing a literal description. What are involved are not simply external criteria, but also processes of attributing intentions and meanings. Within a single culture there should presumably be a certain homogeneity in the meanings attributed, since the perspectives of those involved will be similar. But this supposition is repeatedly put to the test, and, as is known from daily experience, does not always pass.

The problem lies in the intrinsic difficulty of specifying that one situation is the same as another (reasons why they are different can be cited *ad infinitum*). The grounds for making predictions and, consequently, replicating actions are therefore tenuous. If it is impossible in the physical world to make predictions and thus to replicate actions, except in laboratory experiments, in the social sphere it would seem impossible, even in an experimental context.[9]

We would suggest, after this brief examination of epistemological problems, that it is more appropriate to speak of the reproduction or recreation of social action projects or experiences, rather than their replication. The basis for reproduction is the possibility of making a good prognosis in the new circumstances, rather than the ability to make predictions. This is not merely a question of changing names, but means fully accepting the implications involved in moving from the idea of repetition to that of reproduction.

The difference between replication and reproduction can be illustrated by thinking of a car journey between two cities made for the second time. Assuming that it is the same car, the car will be older;

there may be a different amount of traffic; weather conditions may have changed; even the roadworks will be in different places. Going beyond physical factors to social ones, the first journey may have been a holiday and the second a business trip; the situation, moods, objectives, and attitudes will have changed.

This point is important in using pilot projects carried out by non-governmental organizations as the basis for designing new social policies. It is necessary to define what is central and what is secondary; to what extent external circumstances are similar or different; whether the goal is to reproduce the experience and all the consequences it involved, or rather to use some results in a different context and for different purposes.

In order to reproduce a project, a systematic analysis must be made. This subject is examined in the following section.

The Systematization of Experiences

This discussion is based on ideas developed in the course of a joint study in which CIDE and FLACSO have been engaged for over two years.[10] The study obtained information from interviews on more than 100 social action projects carried out in Chile, and made in-depth analyses of 15 of these interviews. The aim was to perfect a framework and develop a methodological approach which would facilitate the systematization of projects and allow comparative analyses to be made. This study was inspired by a similar study done in Mexico by a team from the Center for Economic and Social Studies on the Third World (Centro de Estudios Económicos y Sociales del Tercer Mundo—CEESTEM).[11]

In recent years, teams of workers and institutions carrying out social action projects have indicated a clear need to systematize their experiences. Systematization is taken to mean the ability to describe an experience in a way that is meaningful in at least two senses. First, it allows the experience to be organized so as to provide conclusions about its meaning for the different people involved. Second, systematization makes transcending the unique and everyday features of the experience possible, and thus allows its significance to be viewed in a broader social context. This involves review and discussion of the work in a contextual framework that transcends particular details and anecdotal evidence, and allows conclusions to be drawn about achievements and difficulties, with a view to improving action in the future.

While it is difficult to distinguish between systematization and evaluation, there are two important differences. Systematization tends to describe experiences; evaluation tends to express opinions about them.

Also, systematization is a necessary condition for making an evaluation. Systematization is thus a vital process in recreating or reproducing a project or social action. Only by going beyond the particular features of an experience and understanding its main principles and perspectives can what is central and what is secondary be identified, and a similar kind of intervention can then be suggested.

We will summarize the main points emerging from the joint study by CIDE and FLACSO referred to above. This is not proposed as the only way of systematizing, but rather as one method which is useful and appropriate. The perspective taken here is that of the people who designed and carried out the project. Although this implies a bias (it could be looked at from the participants' point of view), the objectives of the analysis make this approach necessary. A brief description of several categories and concepts will be useful in explaining the project's central propositions.

The first aspect to examine is the diagnosis of the conditions in which the project was implemented. This diagnosis was not necessarily explicit, nor did it have to be given this name. In stating the grounds of any project, however, a description of the situation in which the project will be implemented must be given.

Two levels of description can be distinguished. One is an examination of the general features of the situation. The other provides a precise characterization of the project's planned activities.

At both these levels two kinds of descriptive elements can be identified. The first are established facts, given without further explanation as they are taken to be obvious and self-evident, with general agreement as to their verity and significance. The second are interpretations, which require some kind of explanation, as they are not obvious to the people making the diagnosis.[12] These distinctions are more than academic. They are important in understanding the basic logic of the project in terms of how a specific, micro-social experience relates to social change in the longer term.

The relationship between the diagnosis of the global and of the specific situation can thus be analyzed. The interrelations between established facts and interpretations allow an understanding of the long-term wager which is part of any project. Certain reference points can eventually be established to assess whether this wager is rational and viable.

The study of the relationship between the objectives of the project and the projects' prospects for bringing about change in the longer-term is known as the strategic hypothesis.[13] This view of what a diagnosis involves emphasizes the work of a group seeking to characterize a situation in order to take action, not merely to collect data which will ultimately reflect an "objective" reality. This perspective is clearly relevant in identifying the conditions for reproducing an experience.

The second set of considerations is related to the project itself, to the specific way in which the project intervenes in the particular situation diagnosed. This is called the action hypothesis.[14] Its description includes problems to be dealt with and the strategic design of the project.

The processes to be implemented in solving problems can be differentiated in terms of whether they are central or support processes,[15] according to how crucial their role is in the strategy for action. These terms are used in place of the more common "sub-projects" or "methodologies" in order to put the different elements of a project into a preliminary order of importance and relevance. The overall design of the action to be implemented can thus be visualized. In this context, a description of the methodologies and specific procedures to be used can be given.

Using the elements described above, the principal features of a project or plan of action can be conceptualized. Thus the central aspects of what is being attempted are made clear, as well as how these are to be achieved. The different processes can also be specified.

Doing all this is some progress, but it is not sufficient to resolve the problem of how to reproduce an experience. It is necessary to know what happened when this strategy and plan were actually put into action. This brings up two issues.

The first is whether or not the project proposal is consistent with the strategy actually put into practice. The term consistent is not intended to have a moral connotation which would imply judgements about the failure to do what was promised. The point is rather to recognize that there is a difference between a project—something intended to be done—and the way it is actually implemented, its concrete, material expression. The difference is in how the intention was adapted to the circumstances in which it was carried out.

Recognition of the differences between what was planned and what was put into practice is vitally important in recreating the experience. There may have been errors that caused changes, and it may be possible to prevent such errors. The strategy finally implemented may have proved to be more appropriate than the original proposal, and therefore the necessary changes can be introduced in the recreation as well.

The second important considerations are the obstacles and facilitating factors encountered, and the errors and successes of the team in charge.[16] Obstacles and facilitating factors refer to aspects of the situation in which the project was carried out. Errors and successes have to do with the people who introduced and carried out the actions.

It is useful to know which obstacles and facilitating factors were foreseen from the start, and how they were to be taken advantage of or avoided. Secondly, those that appeared unexpectedly should be examined. In both cases, the outcomes must be assessed. The importance of assessing the successes and errors of a team in the actual implementation of the project clearly cannot be overestimated. This assessment will allow defects to be corrected and successes to be multiplied.

This account has been brief, in order to leave room to examine a concrete experience in terms of the possibilities and conditions for its reproduction. The meaning of the different concepts set out above should become clearer in describing this experience.

Any serious attempt to reproduce a project should at least take the following points into account. First, how similar or different the conditions of the original project are from the conditions in which it will be reproduced. A review of the original diagnosis and the obstacles and facilitating factors it identified, is extremely important in assessing the new conditions. Second is the strategy, procedures, and methods developed in the initial project. The clarification that occurs in systematizing the project can help to determine whether the same experience should be reproduced or only parts of it used, in a different context or for a new purpose. Third, errors and successes of the original experience should be reviewed, in order to either prevent or re-achieve them. It is also important to note alterations in the initial strategy, and examine what was actually done.

The Experience of the Learning Workshops

This section will give an account of the experience of the Learning Workshops,[17] using a narrative style in order to highlight the different stages.

Pilot Project

In 1977, a pilot project was started in the Parish of the Holy Cross (Parroquía de la Santa Cruz), in an area known as Los Nogales in Santiago. The aim was to develop a methodology and tools for working with children from poor urban areas who had learning difficulties and poor school performance.[18] This project was based on an agreement between PIIE (Interdisciplinary Program for Research on Education) and the parish, with the PIIE researcher Liliana Vaccaro taking responsibility for the work. The pilot stage lasted until 1979.

Central Ideas of the Pilot Project. The basis of the project's strategy was the idea of training people from the community to be group leaders and use specially-prepared materials to help the children overcome their learning difficulties.

The implementation of this project involved the choice of an area in which to work, selection of group leaders, the elaboration of a training program, production of educational materials for the children and the group leaders' training, the precise definition of procedures for work, and creation of a system to run the project which would allow responsibility for the project and its administration to be gradually transferred to the group leaders and other members of the community.

The Start of Activities and Their Development. Activities started in September 1977, when setting up the workshop was discussed by community organizations. From the beginning, the idea was well received by parish committees and groups linked with the Church. Teachers and local schools also became interested in the project.

At the beginning of 1978, the group leaders were chosen from names put forward by people associated with the parish; they were generally young people working in the Christian communities. In this pilot stage, the requirements were that these people should not have other jobs, since funds were available to provide a reasonable payment for the work; that the average income of their families should not be high; that they be residents of the area; and that they should have completed at least the sixth grade of primary education. The project started with five group leaders, and two more joined later.

While educational materials were being prepared, children were selected to participate in the workshops, on the basis of information provided by schoolteachers and other sources. In general, they were children between six and nine years old with learning difficulties, or who had repeated grades but did not have severe psychological problems.

The group leaders' training covered three stages. The first increased their awareness of the problems in development encountered by children from marginal areas. In the second stage, the theoretical tools and the materials to be used in the workshops were provided. The third stage involved systematic support for concrete activities with the children.

The workshops began to meet in September, 1978. Groups of no more than 20 children were created. These groups met three times a week with their group leader, and used the materials prepared for this work.

The methodology used was based on several key ideas, such as the concept of learning by doing, of starting from one's own life and experiences. Games play a very important part in these activities. The group leader's relationship with the children should be warm and personal, in order to encourage them to participate creatively in sessions. The group leader should also develop all aspects of the children's ability to express themselves (oral, physical, artistic, etc.) and encourage learning by means of group work and games.

Along with the workshops' programmed activities organized around subject units with specially prepared materials, extra-programmatic activities were also organized, such as outings and exhibitions. Methods of monitoring the work through the group leaders, families, and schools were designed to assess the progress made by the children.

The materials were structured as subject units, which included suggestions for the group leader and work sheets for the children's homework. The subject units looked at issues related to the children's own experience, such as "our friends in the workshop," and "our neighborhood." Each subject unit was to be covered in approximately six sessions.

Achievements During the Pilot Stage. A total of 204 children participated in this pilot stage. The success of the workshops was demonstrated by a follow-up study which showed that over 70% of the children had overcome their learning difficulties and been promoted to the next grade. It was also found that the degree of progress was linked to how long the child attended the workshop.

Overall, the pilot experience was positive. It succeeded in providing the children with an effective means to deal with their learning difficulties. The underlying hypothesis of the strategy, that local people with no professional or specialized training could collaborate effectively in overcoming children's learning difficulties, was proved. It was shown, moreover, that these people could progressively take responsibility for the work and make a success of it.

On top of this, a set of materials was developed, and experience gained in preparing monitors. Finally, the project began to receive recognition. Requests for collaboration from PIIE in carrying out similar work in other sectors were made.

Second Stage

This was the project's consolidation stage, and lasted from 1980–1982. The project was expanded from one parish to involve the four parishes which together form the deanship of Estación Central. The strategy used in the work was basically the same, although a number of alterations, other than changes in the numbers of workshops and children participating, were made.

These changes can be divided into four main categories: (1) provision of and improvements in educational materials; (2) introduction of new work methods, as a result of the employment of voluntary group leaders; (3) progressive and effective implementation of programs of work with the children's families and with members of the community; and (4) emphasis on transferring responsibility for the workshop to group leaders and members of the community. Each of these changes will be examined briefly below.

The Materials. The first materials were produced in 1978. After an evaluation by the team, some modifications were decided on. Among other things, each unit had a large number of exercise sheets, but no central theme linked the different activities with each other.

A second version was produced in 1979. This divided the materials into eleven units of six sessions, each unit with one central theme. The children were divided into two age groups, to facilitate dealing with their different kinds of problems.

The team's evaluation of this second version indicated that, despite the improvements, there were still a number of weaknesses. Too many activities were suggested, which contributed to decreased participation. Less was learned when teaching aids other than work sheets (such as games) were used. When the prepared materials suggested activities for each session, these activities tended not to be flexible, thus not allowing the group leader to adapt the work to the dynamic of the group.

In 1980, a new, more definitive version was produced. This set was also divided into six units, with a variable number of sessions. The activities presented were linked together by a common idea, leaving the group leader free to decide how to organize them, but providing him/her with support materials, such as games. The new version was based on a more active approach (using songs, games, etc.), and the exercise sheets as such were eliminated. The group leader was instead given suggestions on preparing his/her own exercise sheets.

Emphasis is put on reading and writing rather than mathematics. There are fourteen workbooks which the children can use outside the sessions but with supervision from the group leaders. These workbooks were also tested with different groups.

Different Approaches to the Work. Although this stage was designed for the four parishes of the deanship of Estación Central, shortly after it started the PIIE team received proposals for its implementation in South Pudahuel, North Pudahuel, and San Felipe. It was decided to start new workshops in these areas, although there were not adequate material resources to run these workshops in the same way as in Estación Central.

It was not, for example, possible to pay the group leaders and they therefore had to participate on a voluntary basis. Consequently, they could not be expected to show the same degree of dedication as the group leaders in Estación Central. It was also to be expected that some of them would drop out.

Given these new circumstances, it was decided that the workshops would have only one session a week, but would continue for more months of the year. In some cases, two people were made responsible for a workshop, in case some group leaders dropped out.

In keeping with the principle that responsibility for the workshops should be transferred to the community and given that the PIIE team could not dedicate the same amount of time to the new areas, it was decided that as many responsibilities as possible should be handed over to the group leaders. Their training was based on a shorter, more intensive program, and the same leaders' training activities prepared for the project in Estación Central were often used.

The situation created by these new work experiences was very interesting, since it offered the posibility to study and evaluate the results and achievements of the project under different conditions and in different forms.

Work with the Community and the Families. While one of the basic principles of the project is that members of the community can collaborate in overcoming children's learning difficulties, in the first stage no clear strategy was developed to put this into practice. In this second period, work was carried out directly with the community, not just with Christian groups, to encourage active support from local organizations for the workshops. This took place when the workshops were publicized, and in the organization of various joint activities.

The work with the children's families assumed greater significance. Initially, family participation was limited to providing information for a diagnosis and assessment of the child's progress. Gradually, and as a result of the group leaders' experience, it became clear that more collaboration from the families was necessary to make the workshops function better and to give the children more effective help in dealing with their problems. Consequently, special activities were designed, such as meetings and talks, and periodic visits to the home.

Operation of the Project. From the start of the pilot stage, control and responsibility for running the project were intended to be transferred to the group leaders and the community. The technical team's role was to evolve from managing the project to being advisors, and then to act as a resource for dealing with technical issues. The idea was that the project should be appropriated by the sectors it served.

In the second stage this goal was expressed more clearly by both the team and the group leaders. The decision to extend the work of the PIIE team to new areas made it necessary to adopt methods of administration in which the group leaders and area representatives would assume greater responsibilities. This process of transferring control did not occur without a measure of conflict. There was a difference of opinion between group leaders and the PIIE team members about the degree of autonomy appropriate at each point.

In fact, the differences with some group leaders in Estación Central became so acute that three parishes decided to continue the workshops independently of the PIIE team. It is interesting to note that the parishes were able to continue the work successfully. This is an indication both of the validity of the overall design of the project, and more specifically of its strategy for the transfer of control.

Achievements During the Second Stage. A total of 87 workshops were organized, involving the participation of 1,447 children. The work in Pudahuel and San Felipe accounts for 27 of these workshops, and 324 children.

Participation in the workshops gave the children real assistance in overcoming their learning difficulties. The data obtained by the 1982 evaluation showed that over 70% of the children participating had been promoted to the next grade at school.

The evaluation indicated that at the end of this second stage the fundamental elements of the program were: (1) the concept that it is possible for people in poor areas to resolve their own problems—in this case, learning difficulties encountered by some children in the formal school system; (2) a strategy for putting this concept into practice, composed of a method for selecting and training group leaders, a methodology of work with the children, and emphasis on the need for support from the children's families and the community; (3) a set of educational materials, organized into subject units, as the principal tool used by group leaders in their activities in the workshops, as well as a set of fourteen workbooks for the children to work through on their own; and (4) a model for the organization of work and distribution of responsibilities which makes it possible for group leaders and local coordinators to gradually take over running the work with a minimum of technical assistance.[19]

In addition to this assessment, the evaluation raised a number of issues, such as the need to study the effects of the different forms in which the workshops operated (three times a week, or once a week for a longer period), the consequences of working with paid leaders or volunteers, and the possibilities of making the materials more flexible in order to use them in different regions of the country. Also emphasized was that the team's concern for research aspects and for future evaluation had had a positive impact on the development of the project.

The Period from 1983 to 1984

The team in charge of the project referred to this third stage as the expansion stage. Once the stages of experimentation and consolidation had been completed and a program with a clear strategy and methodology was established, steps were taken to extend the coverage of the program. During this period the PIIE team worked in Copiapó (Tierra Amarilla, Paipote, Chañaral, and Copiapó), Valparaíso, North Pudahuel, South Pudahuel, Curanilahue, Lota, and Penco. The work in Estación Central also continued, although in three sectors there was little contact with PIIE.

To give some idea of the scale of this work, in this period 143 workshops were organized (63 in 1983; 80 in 1984), and a total of 2,366 children enrolled (1,045 in 1983; 1,321 in 1984). One hundred and twenty-nine group leaders were involved in 1983, and 168 in 1984; many of them participating for the first time (102 in 1983; 92 in 1984). During the same period, 993 children were assisted by the program in Estación Central.

In new areas, the work was initiated in different ways. In some cases it started after requests from parish priests or Church workers in the area, who had heard about the program and its achievements; in others, PIIE approached Church authorities directly. In each case, the methods of work chosen were adapted to the situation and characteristics of the individual sector.

Thus there were cases in which the parish priest managed to get some funding, so the group leaders and coordinators could be paid; in other cases, people participated on a voluntary basis. This meant that the frequency of weekly meetings and the number of months they continued was different in each workshop. The coordinators and group leaders in each area chose the materials to be used with the children. The group leaders were much younger than in the earlier stages; the advantages and problems created by this change have yet to be assessed.

PIIE's role was mainly to give advice and train group leaders. This training involved passing on experience from group leaders who had worked the previous year, and who participated in the training sessions for new leaders. PIIE also prepared new educational materials for the group leaders' training; at present these texts are being revised, so that they can be adapted to the different conditions of children's lives in different parts of the country.

A major part of the program's administration was handed over to the group leaders and local coordinators from the start. This was done not only because it was one of the main objectives of the program but also because the method of operation had been consolidated. Also, the physical size of the region covered made it impossible for a small team to take responsibility for running the program in each area.

The people involved and the PIIE team members reported that, as in the earlier stages, the workshops were successful in helping the children to learn and get back to their proper levels in the formal education system. Unfortunately, at the time of the evaluation in 1984, the statistics had still not been prepared.

The evaluation did indicate, however, that this expansion had been successful, and suggested that the materials be adapted for use in other regions of the country. Furthermore, recognizing the limitations of a small team being in charge of work on such a wide scale, efforts were made to study the influence of the different ways the workshop was organized on the children's learning, and what happened after the workshops finished. For this follow-up analysis, the team had only samples to work with.

Proposal for Systematizing the Learning Workshops

Given that the aim of this analysis is to give a clearer, more precise idea of the project's basic design, one period and the specific way chosen to work with the children will be described. The pilot phase was principally dedicated to identifying a method of work, with greater emphasis on research and experimentation than on action, and the aim here is to identify the fundamental aspects of the model of action outlined, so this analysis will focus on the point at which the experience was consolidated. The description here will be brief and schematic, since the principal details were given in the previous section.

Diagnosis of the Situation

Documents produced by the team in charge of the project give a detailed account of the situation of children in poor areas and their relations with the school system. The basic elements of the diagnosis can be organized in the following manner, using the model presented earlier.

The established facts are that in recent years there has been a significant deterioration in the living conditions of poor people. Opportunities available in the school system are unequal; rich children have greater opportunities than poor children. This inequality is aggravated by the deterioration in living conditions. Children from poor areas have high drop-out rates and repetition of grades, in comparison with children from higher socio-economic levels, which is another consequence of unequal opportunities. In recent years, local church bodies have sought to tackle this problem.

The following interpretations can be made. It is extremely difficult for people in poor areas to find individual solutions to their children's learning difficulties through specialized help (from educational psychologists, for example). The school system, because of the way it works, tends to locate the source of learning difficulties in the children themselves rather than in the system's method of operation. The system labels these children "problem children," and the families often accept this classification. Families of children with learning difficulties can be involved in activities designed to overcome these difficulties, and people in poor neighborhoods are able to organize to resolve their own problems; in this case, their children's learning difficulties.

Project Design (Hypothesis for Action)

The problem which the project seeks to resolve, the aspect of the situation which it hopes to influence and affect, is the learning difficulties experienced by poor children.

The central process around which the different methodologies and procedures are organized is the active participation of the community in dealing with children's learning difficulties. This involves the selection and training of group leaders to take responsibility for the work. The entire management of the project will eventually be transferred to these leaders, as well as the preparation of educational materials to be used by them and the children.

The support processes include working with the children's families to encourage them to help in dealing with these problems; working with the community as a whole to encourage participation in some workshop activities, such as publicity, and support for specific events; participation by the local church and parishes, such as allowing their premises to be used for the workshops; and, wherever possible, assistance from teachers and/or schools in suggesting names of children who might take part in the workshops, and in the monitoring process by reporting on progress.

The Long-Term Perspective (Strategic Hypothesis)

While the main concern of this project is to overcome the learning difficulties of children from poor areas, it clearly has a wider interest, related to the potential for communities to participate in resolving their own problems. In this sense, the project's fundamental perspective and aims are to encourage democratization and participation. The project's model does not relate to the issue of learning alone but also to something more general, which can be applied universally.

How the Project Was Put into Practice

In the previous section, an account of the project's different stages was given. The project developed on the basis of a pilot phase that was implemented in the subsequent stages of consolidation and expansion. There have been changes, some of them significant, but the basic design remains. In fact, the changes were alterations in procedure or scale, such as adaptation of educational materials, definition of the area of work with the families, clarification of ways of collaborating with the community, etc.

Some things, identified by the person responsible for the project as points of tension, still need to be clarified through a more detailed study. These include the advantages and disadvantages of having paid leaders rather than volunteers, the level of intensity of the work with the children, and that the new group leaders are much younger than the previous ones.

Obstacles, Facilitating Factors, Errors, Successes

Before analyzing these points, it is important to emphasize that the project and its work are considered highly successful. The description of obstacles, facilitating factors, errors, and successes must be seen in this context. The analysis will be made in general terms, in terms of aspects that affect the overall design of the project, not its details.

The greatest obstacle was the deterioration in living standards of people in poor sectors, which created at least two problems in relation to this project. First was the family's difficulty in dealing with the child's problems, since the greater part of family efforts were dedicated to ensuring survival. Second was the exaggerated expectations for projects of this kind; people often hope that problems of subsistence will also be resolved, although this is quite beyond the possibilities of the project. Another obstacle was the increase in social divisions as a result of the deepening segregation and isolation which hampered the possibilities of cooperation between people in poor neighborhoods and technical or intellectual workers willing to collaborate in finding solutions to specific problems.

More minor obstacles included the confusion created by the fact that the program was part of the activities taking place in the parish, because it is a non-religious activity; the diverse interests and expectations of the group leaders created certain problems in defining a common line of action; people's fear of repression as a consequence of participating in grassroots organizations; and scarcity of human and material resources needed to cope with the full complexity of this work.

The following facilitating factors should be highlighted. The support of the Church, especially certain parishes, meant, among other things, that there was access to the infrastructure needed (meeting places, for example) to hold the workshops sessions. The parish youth organizations, whose members were interested in participating in preventative community work, made it easy to find group leaders. The PIIE institution had the past experience, human resources, and the willingness to undertake a project of this kind. Finally, the fact that there is a real need for programs of this kind in poor neighborhoods.

Many of the errors made in the development of the project were subsequently corrected. Several of them, however, are worth noting.

They include the failure to clearly comprehend the difficulties involved in a project based on collaboration between poor communities and technical workers or intellectuals, in the context of a highly segregated society; the failure to foresee the problems inherent in transferring responsibility for management and administration, and the decision to delay this process in the pilot experiment; the failure to design an effective system to monitor the progress of the children, so that their subsequent position and performance in school could be assessed; the lack of importance given to research work related to expansion, which meant that doubts about different approaches have still not been resolved.

The following successes are noteworthy. A program of work was established, which people in poor communities could effectively, and very successfully, take control of. The project was accompanied by an ongoing process of discussion, research, and evaluation, which made it possible to overcome the problems that arose. Continual evaluations identified the errors that were made, and enabled corrections to be made in the course of the project. People in poor communities were incorporated into the project, and the transfer of responsibility to them clearly produced the results expected. The methodology and procedures designed (sessions, materials, style of work) were successful, as shown by the fact that the children were able to overcome their learning difficulties.

Conclusions

First, the experience of the learning workshops is extremely important in relation to the problem of how the idea of replication can be adapted for use in the field of social action. New workshops have been organized many times since the pilot stage in 1977–1979, and have functioned successfully. An examination of this process shows that these are not replicas in the strict sense in which this concept was defined.

Indeed, the conditions and situations found in the initial stage were not present in subsequent stages, nor was any effort made to reproduce them. On the contrary, the new circumstances were taken into account. Alterations and adaptations were made in order to achieve the desired results without changing the core of the project.

The case of the learning workshops is not special, but representative of what happens in social action projects. In seeking to repeat a project, the idea is not to repeat every aspect and detail, excluding all new influences. Instead, the new aspects should be incorporated in a creative fashion, new procedures drawn up or previous ones adapted, in order to obtain the desired results using the strategy which is being repeated.

It is certainly more useful to look at this question in terms of the reproduction of experience rather than the possibilities of replication. This approach makes it necessary to distinguish between the central and secondary aspects, the necessary and the contingent conditions, for the reproduction of a project. This distinction will help to avoid the errors that could lead to the creation of an inappropriate replica.

Second, referring specifically to the case of the workshops, there are elements that remain constant and others that vary.

Besides the existence of a central team, the *constants* are: an unchanging basic diagnosis of the learning problems of the children involved, and the capacity of people from poor communities to tackle and resolve their own problems, given adequate tools and the possibility of organizing; the desire to collaborate in overcoming the learning difficulties of children in poor areas; a central strategy to select and train people from the community as group leaders who will then take responsibility for the workshops, using educational materials prepared for this purpose; the institutional support of parishes and other Church bodies, which give access to the physical space for community organizations to meet, and have administrative facilities; an ongoing interest in studying the problems and achievements of the work in different areas.

These constants are the nucleus of the project. Precisely because they were maintained, the experience was reproduced. In each case variations were made, allowing the same project design to be put into practice in different circumstances. The most important variations were related to either the central process or the support process.

In the central process, variations were made in ways of organizing the management, in that the group leaders had different degrees of responsibility. Changes and adaptations were made in the educational materials as the project developed. Different systems of working with group leaders (paid workers vs. volunteers) were used, and had different consequences for the duration of the workshops and number of weekly sessions.

Variations in the support processes included redefinition of the work with the children's families; development of work with the community and grassroots organizations, in order to obtain support for the workshops and carry out joint actions; different degrees of contact with the schools in selecting children to participate in the workshops and monitoring their subsequent progress.

These variations reflect the innovative and creative aspects of reproducing the experience, which were a necessary response to the different circumstances in which the project was implemented.

Finally, in order to use this experience in defining social policies for education, which means reproducing the project on an even wider scale, the conditions required to reproduce it on such a scale must be established. In situations such as those in Chile and other Latin American countries with similar socio-economic systems, some of the conditions needed for the reproduction of this project do exist, but other conditions, also essential, do not.

It should not be difficult to find an infrastructure of meeting places, technical teams with training in this methodology of work, and the funding necessary to produce the educational materials. A smoother relationship with the formal education system should also be possible, making it easier to select and monitor the children participating. Other conditions, however, will be harder to find; their absence could have drastic consequences for the core design of the project, therefore making it impossible to reproduce it as a social policy.

The organized participation of poor communities in finding solutions to their problems, in the way presupposed by and which did occur in the workshops, is the condition least likely to be found elsewhere. This participation was achieved principally through the work of the group leaders who, without having had full technical training, nevertheless made a success of this project. This is a very significant point for both the diagnosis and the definition of the central process in the project.

Recognition must be given to the valuable human resource that exists in civil society. Poor people are creative, responsible, have a legitimate interest in participating in social life, and are capable of autonomously carrying out effective actions without being specialists in the field. The project's activities must be designed to facilitate the idea that social groups should organize to advance their own interests, so that these groups can freely and creatively take action to resolve their own problems. This requires a physical space in which people can express themselves freely and organize independently. It is unlikely that this space will be provided by an authoritarian regime, given the regime's lack of confidence in civilian society.

Notes

1. See García-Huidobro: Paper presented to Seminar on Social Development Policies. Catholic University, Santiago, 4–5 October 1983. The following paragraphs follow his line of argument very closely.

2. The relevance and importance of discussing the issue of replication became clear to me after a conversation with Professor R. Zúñiga of the University of Montreal on the subject of experiences of social action in Chile. On this issue, see Ricardo Zúñiga, *Logique de la recherche et logique de l'intervention* (manuscript in preparation). University of Montreal, 1985.

3. See, for example, Karl Hempel, "The logic of functional analysis" in Gross (ed), *Symposium on Sociological Theory.* New York 1955. Richard Rudner, *Philosophy of Social Science.* Englewood Cliffs.

4. Karl Popper, *The Poverty of Historicism.* New York (1959: 133).

5. A literal description is one that can be made out of context, and that is assumed to be a valid description of the events it describes. Thomas Wilson, "Conceptions of interaction and forms of sociological explanation," in *American Sociological Review,* August 1970.

6. See Neil Friedman, *The Social Nature of Psychological Research: The psychological experiment as a social Interaction.* New York, 1963, especially p. 3.

7. Richard Rudner, *Philosophy of Social Science.* Englewood Cliffs, 1966. Especially pp. 55 and 65.

8. Max Weber, "Objectivity in social science and social policy" in *The Methodology of Social Sciences.* New York, 1968.

9. An illustrative example of this is found in Moscovici's reformulation of Asch's classical experiment. See Norbert Lechner. *Poder y orden: La estrategía de la minoría consistente.* FLACSO, Santiago, 1977.

10. CIDE-FLACSO. *Apuntes sobre sistematización de experiencias.* Final report of seminar on the systematization of experiences in community education and social action. Talagante, 9–13 January, 1984. Sergio Martinic, *Algunas categorías de análisis para la sistematización.* CIDE-FLACSO. Santiago, mimeo. Doc. No. 3 presented at the Talagante seminar, 1984a. Sergio Martinic, *Educación y Cambio Social.* CIDE, Santiago. Doc. de Trabajo No. 7, 1984b. J. Edo. García-Huidobro and Carlos Piña, *Obstáculos, Facilitadores, Errores y Aciertos: comentarios a la marcha de los proyectos.* CIDE-FLACSO, Santiago. Doc. No. 2 presented at the seminar on systematization. Talagante, 1984. J. Edo. García-Huidobro and Sergio Martinic, *Instituciones y educación popular: El caso chileno.* Mimeo. CIDE, Santiago, 1984. Eduardo Pino, *Cómo se plantea el problema de la sistematización en equipos de educación popular y acción social.* CIDE-FLACSO. Doc. No. 1 presented at Talagante seminar, 1984.

Adriana Delpiano and Daniela Sánchez (eds.). *Educación Popular en Chile. Cien Experiencias.* CIDE-FLACSO, Santiago, 1984.

11. P. Latapí, et al., *La educación no formal en México: Un análisis de sus metodologías.* (preliminary version). Mimeo CEESTEM, México, 1982.

12. Martinic, op. cit. 8–9.

13. Martinic, ibid. 8–9.

14. Martinic, ibid. 10–13.

15. A process is referred to as "the set of actions and interactions which must be carried out by the team in charge and the project's beneficiaries in order to achieve the proposed objectives." Latapí, op. cit., 49. Given that various processes frequently occur together, one of these "is the central process which unites the rest, giving them their coherence, meaning and content." Latapí, ibid, 50.

16. These concepts are dealt with by Latapí, ibid.

17. The following documents provide fuller details: Liliana Vaccaro, "Reflexiones en torno a una experiencia de educación no formal," in *Anales de la Escuela de Educación.* Catholic University, Santiago, 1982. Liliana Vaccaro, *Evaluación de programas y proyectos de educación popular: Sugerencias de un modelo a partir de la experiencia de los talleres de aprendizaje* (preliminary version). Mimeo, 1983. Liliana Vaccaro and E. Schiefelbein, *Talleres de atención a niños con problemas de aprendizaje.* PIIE, mimeo. Santiago, 1981. J. Edo. García-Huidobro, *Exposición realizada en el seminario sobre políticas de desarrollo social.* Catholic University, Santiago, 4–5 October 1983. Informe de Evaluación: *Informe de evaluación del proyecto "Consolidación y extensión de experiencia piloto de formación colectiva,"* made by PIIE and the Estación Central Deanship. FLACSO, Santiago, Mimeo, 1982.

18. This discussion is very closely based on Informe de Evaluación. *Informe de evaluación del proyecto "Difusión y estrategias de transferencia de los talleres de aprendizaje a comunidades populares,"* made by PIIE. FLACSO, Santiago, Mimeo, 1984, and Informe de Evaluacion, 1982.

19. Evaluación, 1982: 17–18.

11

Self-Sufficiency and Ways to Strengthen Institutional Aspects of Social Projects in the Non-Governmental Sector

Luis Zúñiga

United Nations Children's Fund (UNICEF)

The ideas of social mobilization and community participation in processes of local development have become major reference points in much of the discussion of public policies in recent years. The many efforts to conceptualize these ideas and the increasingly natural way in which arguments about participation are being incorporated into projects and programs of action reflect this underlying concern. Naturally, the importance given to participation and to mechanisms of mobilization meant that the local level became the central focus in designing development programs and projects.

Private sector technical support agencies (non-governmental organizations) have also concentrated most of their efforts at the local level. These agencies, as well as encouraging development processes, have through their work indicated many alternative methods of action. Approaches to social planning focusing exclusively on the global level failed to take these alternatives into account.

As a result, the kind of relations established between non-governmental organizations and public sector areas concerned with social policy are relevant to how policies and programs are designed and put into action. Indeed, the issue of how agencies in civil society and the public sector might complement one another is a real problem for people who analyze social policy and for those who design and implement alternative policies, programs, and concrete projects.

This chapter will demonstrate that it is feasible for the work being done by NGOs and by the public sector to be complementary, and that this would be a substantial advance in the design and implementation of policies and programs which improve the quality of life in local communities. Equally, the emphasis placed on self-help and self-sufficiency by NGO projects can inadvertently serve to exacerbate the exclusion suffered by the poor when pressure for formal provisions is undermined and no attempt is made to strengthen the demands of poor sectors for institutional services.

The arguments set out here refer to the many non-governmental organizations in the Southern Cone countries of Latin America whose efforts focus on children's survival and development and on making major changes in the restrictive conditions in which women from poor areas carry out their daily activities. The tremendous moral value of the work that such organizations, whether big or small, engage in every day cannot be over-emphasized. The efforts of development agencies in the private sector are among the most eloquent expressions of solidarity and cooperation found today.

Organizations of Civil Society from the Perspective of Social Policy

The work of non-governmental organizations is uniquely significant in terms of overall social development. In this discussion, we refer to those agencies that transfer social technology resources to the community, initiate processes of participation designed to improve family living standards, and encourage local communities' capacity for organizing to resolve their own problems. These features need to be taken into account in establishing a framework of action that seeks realistic means to support non-governmental organizations' efforts in the field of social policy.

A variety of projects developed in Chile and Uruguay in recent years indicate how action within local communities can be combined with global policy objectives. This was done by organizations whose operations mobilized a whole system of interactions at the local level. As can be seen in Chile, these interactions were motivated by the implementation of solutions in which simplicity was supported by a degree of basic knowledge and applied research.

In societies where program design has basically been carried out at central decision-making levels, agencies are now appearing which accept the restrictions and particular characteristics of work at the local level. These agencies have implemented development projects very much colored by direct negotiations with local communities and families.

This kind of negotiation is based on mutual acceptance and increased confidence between the communities and the support agencies. Acceptance and confidence are of crucial importance in making joint analyses of problems and in discussing the solutions best adapted to local characteristics.

Along with the capacities to develop and transfer technological resources and engage in social negotiations with local communities, these agencies are willing to establish relations of cooperation and support with other groups in the NGO network. The sharing of experiences and the facility in setting up new organizations or creating parallel teams, produce a dynamic of work which, if not examined carefully, could lead to the assumption that many efforts are being duplicated.

In the Southern Cone countries, NGOs concerned with development have made significant progress in a number of fields normally within the sphere of public policy. An example would be the participation of women from poor sectors in developing programs for children. Particularly notable is the work in identifying methods of action to expand the coverage of pre-school care in areas of critical poverty by involving mothers and adolescents.

Not only do these approaches work, but they have also recently begun to receive serious examination by the public sector. In Chile, UNICEF is at present supporting a co-operative project in this field. This attention is already bringing an expansion in available provisions as national institutions adopt these approaches.

Efforts are also being made in the sphere of primary health care, and local communities are being mobilized to protect the health of children and families. There are also projects aimed at generating simple technologies for activities as varied as designing and building latrines, saving energy in food preparation, and recovering land that suffered a process of desertification, all of which are based on the mobilization of local communities.

Furthermore, in Chile, projects for income generation within the economy of poverty have made great progress. This is due to the work of NGOs which channelled the spirit of solidarity among the poor. Equally importantly, they provided technologies for running productive activities, for business administration, and for creating mechanisms to reduce the costs of purchasing essential goods.

In Uruguay, technical support organizations directed their efforts towards children's survival, growth, and development. Here also a serious attempt is being made to coordinate and combine the work of almost a hundred organizations. The level of technical sophistication and the complexity of business management achieved by some productive activities in Uruguay is well-known and documented.[1]

As the organizations of civil society concerned with development identify strategies for working at the local level and define appropriate methods of action, a new range of technical alternatives arises. The public sector needs to take these alternatives into account.

Experience shows that the design and implementation of alternative development programs and policies is a problem of options in which there may be varying levels of conflict. The prevailing relations between a government and specific political groups is sometimes mirrored by the relationship between the public sector and non-governmental organizations. This is a problematic area which requires serious efforts at negotiation; the success of such efforts is particularly important in spheres such as child survival and development, which require a basic degree of commitment from and agreement by all social sectors.

In summary, the experience of non-governmental organizations is a resource which should be taken into consideration in designing and implementing broad-scale social programs. Efforts to coordinate with the public sector would increase the NGOs' capacity to act at the local level. The public sector could demonstrate its interest in mutually complementary work by drawing up a body of regulations to facilitate the operations of the NGOs and provide backing for the exchange of information and the expansion of scales of action. This would of course have to be done without threatening the autonomy and basic characteristics of private agencies which offer technical support.

Demands for Formal Structures and Self-Sufficiency

The development organizations discussed here work with the poorest sectors of the population. They are very familiar with the situation of those who are bypassed by normal services, who are outside the sphere of formal economic transactions. Marginalization and exclusion are the typical circumstances of poverty, and as such are key reference points in designing alternative strategies for action.

The situation of being marginalized and excluded has compelled support agencies to find innovative, alternative solutions which use the resources available in poor communities. These solutions draw on approaches closely associated with the concepts of self-help and self-sufficiency. In terms of economic relations, areas of action governed by a rationale characteristic of the economy of poverty have been created.

From a social policy perspective, difficulties can arise if emphasis on working with the grassroots is set against the objectives of institution building and winning over the formal sector. The ones who suffer are the poor sectors who day by day assist in maintaining these institutions.

Short-term work must concentrate on providing for the basic needs of local communities, using methods agreed on by local people and support organizations. The implementation of mechanisms offering solutions in the short-term should also incorporate ongoing efforts to negotiate for facilities of an institutional nature. Some experiences with economic activities projects illustrate the possibility of working for short-term goals, at the same time as seeking a long-term role in the sphere of formal economic relationships. We will take economic activities aimed at promoting the development of poor women as an example.

Women have a right to share in the products they generate. This means winning an economic right; the daily role of women in sustaining the innumerable processes required to reproduce the labor force is the basis for this right.[2] When a non-governmental organization encourages specific economic projects, irrespective of the short-term benefits offered, it contributes to achieving this right. To give a concrete example, this right is defended when a revolving fund system is established, using the operational facilities provided by a government financial institution. When the technical support agency places the economic project in a highly protected and therefore insecure exceptional market, however, this is not an effective measure in asserting women's right to assume control over their contribution to social production.

In the process of regaining control over the formal sphere, projects involving economic activities may incorporate ongoing programs of contacts and negotiations, the design and introduction of credit systems, access to training in business administration, and technical assistance. In all these fields, respect and enthusiasm for grassroots initiatives should be expressed by transferring the best administration techniques and ongoing support to these projects, in the medium-term, in order to enable them to join the normal course of economic relations.[3]

Of course, fringe solutions are not the hallmark of the organizations we are concerned with here. There is a constant risk of these solutions being prioritized, however, because of the moral value often attributed to the principles of self-help and self-sufficiency. These principles, which appear so regularly on lists of objectives in non-governmental organization programs of action, need to be very precisely defined. Care must be taken to ensure that the programs agreed on between local communities and technical support agencies do not impede demands on the public sector or lessen the pressure on the formal sphere.

Nor should the commitment to approaches based on self-help and self-sufficiency be allowed to suggest to public sector agencies that NGO projects could be substituted for the state's obligation to transfer services or take the state's place in relation to local communities. It is important to bear in mind that the public sector belongs to the whole nation. An extreme version of the idea of self-sufficiency could be seen as telling the poorest sectors of society to give up all hope of gaining access to their patrimony, and to end efforts to negotiate for institutional support for locally generated solutions.[4]

The link between measures developed by local projects and resources available from public sector institutions is a key factor in resolving problems through the use of appropriate technologies. Projects carried out in local communities are educational interventions, which mobilize the capacities and resources of local communities to solve urgent problems. Local-level projects also allow the transfer of technical information and encourage the development of self-esteem, as well as increasing the ability of local communities to exert pressure and negotiate in order to obtain resources from the public sector.

The educational effect of the non-governmental organizations' work is that social demands are strengthened, and services offered at the institutional level are improved. This effect implies the possibility of introducing innovative approaches into social policy. Indeed, experimentation with innovative measures is one of the many contributions made by the programs and projects carried out by the non-governmental sector.

The possibility of influencing services at the institutional level is clearly not a simple question. Careful negotiations and the mobilization of political will are required in order to avoid risking important features of non-governmental organizations, such as autonomy, moral commitment to the local community, and characteristic scales of operation.

The work of documentation helps to demonstrate the viability of transferring small-scale experiments to a broader context. From a technical point of view, the central issue is showing that the initiatives are both feasible and effective. Thus the technical support agencies will be seen as not only valid but also necessary counterparts in putting genuine processes of development into action at the local level.

To sum up, in many countries in Latin America and in the Southern Cone in particular, there are a great many social development projects supported by non-governmental organizations. These projects are based on a real process of social engineering at the local level. Because they take into account the interests of both families and the local community, these agencies play a role which would be difficult for the administrative levels of the public sector to assume.

The ability of NGOs to set in motion development processes based on the objectives of self-help and self-sufficiency makes a valid contribution to social policy, especially when this development is associated with clear efforts to achieve a recovery of institutional resources, and with a demand for formal provisions.

If efforts in this direction are successful, there is a good chance that local development issues will be included in discussion of public policies. For the public sector, these issues will be a normal subject for debate and the allocation of resources. The local level will thus become an area that establishes norms and facilitates the development of actions.

Non-governmental organizations can thus contribute to improving services offered by institutions linked to the public sector. In particular, NGOs can make institutionalized and formal provisions more accessible to the poor. The improvement of institutional provisions and the strengthening of social demands are tasks which require that non-governmental organizations enter a broader field than that of small-scale, self-sustaining measures.

Inevitably, relations between the public sector and civil society will ultimately be determined by conflicts between those with political power and sectors of the political opposition. In such cases, although it will be more difficult to cooperate in technical questions, this cooperation should be attempted, except where political demands are the fundamental pivot of NGO activities. If marginalization and the search for alternative solutions are fundamental, there is no real point in attempting to establish connections between small scale measures and social policy on a global scale.

The mobilization of public sector institutions and resources by non-governmental organizations working at the local level is a basic means of working against the exclusion of the poorest groups. It is important to bear in mind that state and public sector institutions also belong to the poor, who fuel the daily operations of the formal sector of the economy. These are fundamental reasons for including, even in small-scale projects, elements which help strengthen demands for institutional provisions, and which improve the services offered by public bodies for the poorest sectors.

Notes

1. This has been the experience with the organization, "Manos de Uruguay."

2. Processes which range from food preparation, income generation in the non-formal sector, child rearing and its importance in the development of human resources, leadership roles within the family, etc., all activities which generate economic value and therefore contribute to social production.

3. This point is emphasized in A. Klenner and L. Zúñiga: *Generación de Ingresos y Vinculación a los Mercados en la Economía de la Pobreza.* UNICEF, Regional Program for the Participation of Women in Development, Santiago 1984.

4. For a discussion of the restrictive effects of the ideology of self-reliance, see R. Goodings, "Self-reliance versus the Welfare State," *Journal of Social Policy,* No. 14, Vol. 1 1985, pp. 25–47.

12

Toward an Evaluation of the NGO Experience in Chile: Implications for Social Policy and Future Investigation

Charles Downs and Giorgio Solimano

Center for Social Policy and Planning
in Developing Countries, Columbia University

In order to analyze the experience of the NGOs and understand the conditions necessary for that experience to serve as the basis for social policies directed toward the problems of poor children in Chile, we will first characterize these organizations and then objectively consider the nature, scale, and significance of the impact of their activities. We begin by highlighting the characteristics common to the preceding case studies.

As argued in the opening part of this book and shown in the preceding chapters, the non-governmental organizations involved in social policy in Chile are neither profit-seeking nor community-based organizations. They are organizations that work as intermediaries with organizations or individuals in one or more communities, providing non-governmental technical assistance. They also, as we have seen, carry out a wider range of functions and share other characteristics. They give priority to working with the popular sectors, a process which includes active popular or community participation in the various programs. Their activities are oriented toward needs clearly felt and defined by the population. They provide training to the population in order to develop the ability to analyze and respond to problems. They

A version of this chapter appeared in the April 1988 issue of *Community Development Journal*.

help to develop community organizations as a permanent mechanism for responding to problems of the popular sectors.

Within the wide range of NGOs, attention is focused on either providing assistance, stimulating participation, or developing organization. There are of course variations within each of these three perspectives, depending in part on whether a specific organization gives priority to service delivery, investigation, organizing, or training. All NGOs, however, respond to some immediate problems (if they did not do so, the local population would be likely to lose interest), and all three aspects are usually integrated in the dynamic of the work.

While the immediate effect is critically important for most participants, the overall impact of NGO programs is broader. NGO programs have led to the development of a significant group of professionals committed to working with community organizations to generate appropriate solutions for community problems. Another result is the strengthening of basic institutions of civil society, along with a broader awareness that these institutions are important, regardless of the political regime.

In this chapter, we present a preliminary appraisal of the NGO activities described above. We will focus on factors which constrain or facilitate them and on elements of conflict or complementarity which are already visible and can be expected to have greater effect. We will also indicate some prerequisites for a more thorough evaluation than we are presently able to carry out.

A systematic evaluation of each one of the NGO activities is a vitally necessary step for learning from those experiences, deciding which are useful models, and determining which could be expanded and carried out as broad social programs. Such an evaluation would require, among other things, evaluation of the projects themselves (i.e., comparing initial goals with actual impacts, considering obstacles and facilitating factors encountered, determining the efficiency with which organizational resources were used), and a comparison between the effects and effectiveness of NGO programs and those of other comparable programs. There is, however, a general lack of such project and program studies. It is important that the need for such evaluation be taken into consideration in the design of projects, so that they may be made in the future (e.g., by collecting appropriate baseline data and documenting changes in strategy).

All the programs considered here involved a direct relationship between local communities and organized non-governmental technical assistance groups. Does this mean that the programs are products of those groups? While in an immediate sense the answer may be affirmative, in a broader sense the existence of these programs is a result of the deep social and economic problems in contemporary Chile. The programs did not create those problems, but are a response, however incomplete, to them. In some cases, the technical assistance groups were instrumental in developing a counterpart community organization with which to work; in others, they were called in by existing community organizations.

Assuming that we have not excluded important categories of NGOs carrying out social programs, are the problems of the poor in Chile today limited (as if it were not enough!) to issues of health, education, employment, and technology, as reflected in the work of these NGOs? No, but of the NGOs with projects in areas of social policy for poor children, we have included a reasonably complete survey. Given the experiences presented above, we will focus especially on four areas: (1) characteristics of NGO social programs; (2) resources used; (3) methodology of work developed; and (4) relationship with government, particularly local government. We will also consider other, broader social impacts of NGO activities, as well as indicating what additional information we believe is necessary to take this discussion further.

Characteristics of NGO Social Programs

The first task is to determine which sectors of the population and which issues are either included in or not covered by the activities of the NGOs. Figures on the *population covered* are incomplete, but an answer can still be approximated. These programs are oriented predominantly towards poor families, and thus reach women and children most directly. The orientation is also primarily towards the urban populations of several cities, including the capital, although some programs (e.g., CIDE) are also quite extensive in rural areas. While it is very difficult to judge the numerical extent of this coverage, indications are that it is substantial. One estimate from Santiago is that more than 120,000 people have been involved in popular economic organizations (PET); one of the older organizations (CIDE) estimates that its popular education programs have involved more than 6,000 adults. These numbers are still only a small percentage of the total population, or of those in public schools, or unemployed, or affected by the National Health Service, for example, but they are significant in terms of the scale of effort, a partial response to serious problems, and provide the necessary experience to test the viability of such alternatives. It would be very useful to systematically collect more information on the number of people directly reached by NGO social programs.

What *issues* are covered by the programs of the NGOs? What issues are not covered, and why? As we saw above, the programs focus on issues of health (specifically prevention and public health education), education (preprimary and adult counseling), measures to reduce household expenditures without reducing consumption (garden plots, community kitchens, and improved energy efficiency), job training, and creation of employment.

A number of NGOs work in the area of *health promotion,* with special emphasis on health education and training the local population to provide primary health care. These NGOs also carry out programs to prevent certain risks, generally maternal-infant, through actions carried out by the community. They have not developed much of a role in areas such as environmental sanitation, which includes provision of fresh water and disposal of wastes, in part because such programs require a much greater investment of resources.

There has been significant development in the area of *popular education* during this period. It is now included as a component of most NGO projects, particularly those involving youth and young adults of both sexes. Experiments in pre-school education and training, carried out with the direct participation of women within their own communities, are a particularly significant source of innovative ideas for social policies directed toward impoverished children.

The use of *appropriate technologies,* especially for production and preparation of food, has received significant attention. These programs attempt to generate savings at the level of the family and provide an improved diet at a lower cost. These projects may involve study and revaluation of native plants (medicinal herbs), adaptation of traditional technologies (improved adobe insulation), or the design of new technologies (heat-retentive containers for energy efficient cooking), as well as programs for community training and innovation diffusion.

Several of the NGOs support the development of programs focusing on the *popular economy,* with an emphasis on training and workshops for the unemployed and creation of productive micro-enterprises. The result has been a particularly creative process, which has both responded to the needs of popular sectors and grown to include more participants. These programs are an effective way of simultaneously responding to needs for employment, income, consumption, and self-esteem. From modest beginnings, they have grown to include thousands of participants.

Finally, there are other organizations, not included in the preceding chapters, whose focus is nevertheless directly related to the theme of this volume. These others work with community groups to carry out projects involving investigation, training, technical assistance, and diffusion of innovation in such areas as agriculture and food production, the environment, housing and urban development, economic studies and planning, and cultural and artistic expression.

These programs share certain basic characteristics. The most important is the involvement of reasonably well-known technical responses, which enable individual or small group labor/self-help projects to have a measureable impact. This becomes clear in comparison to some obvious problem areas which have not given rise to significant local organizations. Some examples would be housing construction, or water and sanitation, which require either great amounts of material resources or a greater ability to obtain resources from the state, and cannot rely only on local self-help measures.

Thus the question of the relationship of NGO programs to state-sponsored social programs arises. Some NGO programs, particularly in health and nutrition, are largely remedial, taking up the slack where government programs have withdrawn or a worsening economic situation has had direct impact on health. At times this remedial role has been even more direct, as noted by a MISSIO representative who said that "half of our medication goes to fill government health system prescriptions, to make up for basic medication that the government system lacks." These programs respond, with private resources, to increased needs and to the withdrawal of public resources. They also mobilize local citizens, and health worker labor replaces paid labor resources lost through cutbacks in state programs and budgets. Such NGO programs tend to be replaced or absorbed by restored government activity oriented toward the poor or needy.

Other programs, particularly in adult and pre-school education, may be facing specific new problems that arise from the present crisis. Much of the material they deal with, however, is already in addition to what the state provided in the past, or to what is provided in other countries at similar levels of development. Some services may correspond to lack of government coverage, but others (especially those with a focus on quality) have often been developed by non-governmental organizations in other countries.

A third type of program focuses on strategies of economic survival based on reducing dependence on the market, by means of subsistence labor activities such as tending backyard garden plots. Whether or not this strategy is viable, given the option of regular employment which would make gardening either additional labor or labor done primarily by women and children without the necessary intensive technical direction, remains to be evaluated.

Finally, there is a fourth type of program which makes sense at any point. It consists of developing improved technological alternatives, such as energy-saving ovens, whose benefits clearly and quickly exceed costs. Here the problem is primarily one of directing appropriate research activities and promoting use of the products. This can be done through either formally public or private entities.

As the preceding discussion suggests, there is a need to analyze each specific program in order to determine effectiveness and viability both at present and given greater political and economic support. It is also important to consider distinct types of programs which may have similar dynamics—particularly as defined by their relationship to government programs and to economic conditions—and which thus may respond in similar ways to structural shifts. The above preliminary attempt to distinguish four types of programs presently exisiting with NGO support, as well as recognizing certain types of programs that have not been developed by NGOs, is an initial attempt in that direction, a first hypothesis for future testing.

Resources for NGO Social Programs

As noted above, we do not have sufficient information to evaluate how well resources are being used by the various NGO social programs. Hence we will only comment on the resources that are available, with particular attention to the limitations that may result from the need for additional resources for larger programs. It is important to remember that NGO resources are far less than those in the hands of the Chilean state, which under other political conditions could be redirected, at least partially, to social programs, without requiring dramatic increases in expenditures.

The development of NGO social programs is in part an unintended product of the political actions of the present Chilean regime. This fact is very relevant to the present discussion. First, the directors and much of the technical staff of the NGOs are either people who were expelled, for political reasons, from government or university employment, or else younger professionals who have not found employment—or do not wish to work—in the traditional public or private sectors, under the present conditions in Chile. This means that they are on the whole a highly skilled group, and probably working at lower than normal salaries in institutions much smaller and more organizationally simple than government agencies. These people are now working in situations where the largely administrative roles which they might otherwise have filled have become much more direct operational experiences. Having these professionals in active roles has made their respective organizations much more able to experiment, and to learn rapidly from this intense daily experience. While some may choose to continue in their jobs even when the option of returning to public sector employment is reopened, and although some NGO work could be continued from a university base, it does not seem reasonable (nor is it good public policy) to assume that most will do so.

Second, a significant portion of the funding for NGO staffs comes from development assistance agencies. These agencies may have chosen to fund NGOs in order to continue supporting projects in Chile without directly supporting or working through the present government. That attitude is likely to change with redemocratization, and the NGO sector is likely to lose many of those resources.

The preceding argument does not necessarily mean that fewer resources will be available for social programs. It is probable that NGOs have been a vehicle to draw in or maintain resources that would not otherwise have gone to Chile during these past years. But it is also true that the personnel involved in these programs, other participants, the potential gains, and many outside resources will continue to be available, even if not through the NGO sector. This is one more reason why it is important to consider the value and the possibility of the government taking over these programs, on the same or a larger scale. If NGO programs are of significant value but are not amenable to being run by the government, then action to selectively maintain the relevant programs should be considered. If the programs can be taken over by the government, then they can be carried out on a much larger scale with much greater resources and coverage as well.

Work Methodology of the NGOs

One of the most important features of NGO social programs, one which cannot be easily adopted by government organizations, is the participatory work methodology. This methodology is expressed by openness to participation and suggestions from the community, a willingness to adapt when judged appropriate, attempts to break down social barriers between NGO members and the community, and relatively egalitarian internal relations. While these features vary among the different NGOs and their programs, their priorities and practices all tend in the same direction.

Can these qualities be taken on by a government organization? If so, under what conditions? If not, are these features important enough to maintain non-governmental provisions?

First, this participatory orientation represents an ideological commitment for many of those involved, a commitment many have come to through their work. The three most important organizational roots of this ideology are: (1) popular education, which requires voluntary participation to be effective and provides a human experience which reinforces the participatory orientation; (2) that organizations involved be small, thus facilitating and requiring direct field involvement by the directors, and permitting specific elements of timing or content to be adapted relatively easily; and (3) many programs have recently been in early, innovative phases, where adaptation is quite necessary. As programs become more routine and consolidated, the required adaptations tend to be choices between defined alternatives, as exemplified by the programs of CIDE and CETAL.

Can programs with such a participatory work methodology be successfully implemented as government programs? This is partly an empirical question; to the extent that the need for innovation and responsiveness is a product of the experimental stages of a program, the results should generally be amenable to implementation through government agencies. Second, the answer depends on the degree of centralization of the government agency involved, since many programs require interactions that permit significant autonomy at the level of field offices. Reform of existing structures and creation of new ones may be required, but there is certainly precedent for this. Third, and perhaps most problematic of all, in order to be effective these programs require voluntary participation from community members. Voluntary participation cannot be created by a government, but rather arises from real community needs and a conviction that participation will result in positive benefits; such a conviction can only be sustained on a massive scale when programs provide real benefits.

According to the NGO protagonists, no bureaucracy can ever respond as they do. This argument, questionable in its absolute form, is valid in specific cases. They go on to argue that an authoritarian state cannot respond as an NGO can because the state could not respond, in good faith, to the demands that would arise from voluntary participation, and thus could neither generate nor sustain such participation. Also, because once participation began it could not be stopped, the dictatorship would not sponsor the necessarily voluntary participation that would unleash pressure for broader democratic participation. This aspect of the argument deserves more careful analysis.

While many forms of participation developed in recent years have become centers of opposition to the dictatorship, it is also the case that the government has sponsored some limited forms of participation. Furthermore, the incompatibility of participation with dictatorship is stated in terms that would apply equally well to many democratic regimes. The argument is clearly, in its simple form, not true, and thus deserves greater theoretical and empirical specification.

Other Significance and Impacts

It was suggested earlier that the actions of NGOs have strengthened civil society. This can be seen, first, in the increased ability of society to respond to social problems through local community organizations and without recourse to the state; and, second, in the development of an institutional sector of social experimentation and analysis which provides alternative criteria for evaluating the programs and decisions of the state. While the potential impact of these results is certainly very important, it still remains to be seen whether community organizations will continue to function in times of less dire emergency, and whether the NGOs will continue to be a practical alternative when state jobs are once again available.

Another important effect claimed by the NGOs is that their activities have provided the basis for a new, fuller concept of democracy. This change is related to the strengthening of civil society, as well as to the participatory work methodology and social programs. Again, the potential is significant, but the long term impact depends on the accuracy of the previous argument, and on the extent to which participation becomes an integral part of government programs.

The concepts of democracy and social change advanced by the principal political parties in the past were not very concerned with grassroots participation in decisions related to daily life and local social programs, but rather focused on large issues of national politics. The new model, then, both implies and requires a change in perspective by those political parties, and the assumption of a facilitating, rather than a directive and centralist, role. Again, this is an important change, but whether the political parties will transform themselves depends on the resolution of as yet incomplete political debates. It is, however, very significant that those debates are taking place, and that those who have been most involved in the activities discussed here are often the ones leading those debates.

Another significant impact of NGO activities is the training of a generation of professionals to use participatory and grassroots work methodologies. While the number of people thus affected should not be exaggerated, in a period of democratization they are likely to play a role greater than the proportion of their numbers.

Relationship to the Government

Perhaps one of the most important results of the analysis of the NGO experience in social programs is an increased sophistication regarding the nature and importance of their relationship to the government. There was an initial desire expressed by many in NGOs that "there should be no relation whatsoever," a position which is futile when the reality is quite different. The preceding analysis draws attention to the need to distinguish between the government and the public sector; to transform existing bureaucratic behavior in order to enable the public sector to take on some of the NGO programs (i.e., the necessary process of institutional and professional learning and adaptation). Also needed is an analysis of the varied dynamics of the many actors involved in the implementation of social programs with particular attention to the triangular set of relationships between local community, local government, and the relevant sectoral government ministry. The dynamics of this interrelationship have been given a potentially significant push by the municipalization of government services, especially in the areas of health and education. It is important to keep in mind that these changes are occuring within a political system characterized by arbitrary authoritarian action, and thus the extent to which the potential changes discussed in this section can be realized must be viewed cautiously.

Before going any further, there are two significant facts which will keep the discussion in perspective. First, it is not possible for a grassroots program not to have a relationship with the state. The relationship may be quite limited, involving only permission for use of some facility or for operating a clinic, or it may be with the local government or the local offices of a ministry, and it may range from opposition to cooperation, but it is always there. Second, the relationship between grassroots organizations and the government is, on the whole, of far more concern to the former than the latter. Curiously, the proper role of local government seems to be more of an issue for grassroots organizations than it is for local officials.

Present non-governmental experience is primarily at the local level, which can thus provide an appropriate setting for pilot programs to expand. The relation between grassroots organizations and the government is particularly complicated and conflictive, partly because of the NGOs' participatory style of work, anti-bureaucratic attitutes, and strong defense of autonomy from government. The frequent mutual suspicion with which they regard each others' motives only serves to further complicate the situation. There are, however, several lessons to be learned from the relationship.

While government = state = present regime are often loosely equated, it is very important to distinguish between the government and the public sector. The government provides political direction, which reflects and generally seeks to implement the ideology and programs of the regime. The public sector provides the technical direction and actual implementation of government programs. The former responds to an essentially political logic, while the latter responds primarily to bureaucratic and technical logics within political constraints. The government may exist over a considerable period of time but is essentially temporary, while the public sector is relatively more permanent. This distinction is supported by the various democratization processes of the last ten years as well as by the earlier processes of decolonization, which have had a great continuity in programs and personnel (below the topmost levels) from old to new regimes.

Experience has, on many occassions, shown that public sector employees are often far more willing to work with grassroots programs than are government officials. There are also many local officials willing to try programs that promise to benefit their communities and needy populations. This is, in part, an empirical observation that deserves further investigation.

In the long-term development of social policies, recognition of a certain autonomy of the public sector also implies the need to take advantage of whatever opportunities may arise to experiment and develop programs, at the same time as adapting the structure and personnel of the public sector. Cooperation between NGOs and public sector agencies normally requires some relationship with or official agreement from a government body. It is probably easier and more important in the long run, however, to work directly with the public sector in developing social programs and policies.

Furthermore, decentralization and municipalization (especially in the areas of education and health) have in principle begun to create a potentially more responsive public sector at the municipal level. The resulting conditions will allow for the development of a government decision-making center which will share the grassroots organizations' concern for comprehensive local development. This institutional change can only be fully realized when accompanied by democratic political changes. Nevertheless, it is very important to distinguish between the government and the public sector, and to take advantage of any opportunity to experiment and expand programs in conjunction with the public sector, especially at local levels.

In no country—certainly not present-day Chile—is the public sector as apolitical as the preceding comments might suggest, and it may be too early (or too naive) to speak of an independent public sector at the municipal level. The public sector obviously is not completely independent of the policies of the present regime, and is often dependent upon arbitrary decisions of local political leaders. Even the degree of autonomy, when it exists, is relatively weak. Nonetheless, at the level of local government there are institutions and individuals dedicated to public service in their own professional areas. While resources have been cut in recent years, administrative responsiveness has been improved by the process of municipalization.

If NGO programs are to be carried out on a larger scale, they will probably need to be adopted by government agencies. If public sector programs are to be improved by the experience of the NGOs, they will have to adopt significant parts of the NGO experience. The best way to effect this is through the rather arduous process of interaction, which is an important element in both "going to scale" and adapting the public sector more generally.

As suggested above, this interaction involves the three poles of local community, local government, and agency involved. Each actor must be analyzed in terms of its own dynamics and tensions (community–community organization; local government–staff–central government; local agency–staff–sectoral ministry). There is a tendency to address only the relation local agency–community (organization), but development of the institutional capacity for broader programs requires considering the full set of interactions.

There are important differences in the kind of work carried out by governmental and non-governmental organizations at the local level. Although grassroots social programs can be expanded to a national level, it is important to recognize that these programs do not provide as full a range of activities as a government must. Non-governmental organizations can choose the sectors and geographic areas in which to concentrate, while government must respond to all needs in all areas. Non-governmental organizations can focus on quality instead of coverage, while a democratic government in principle must respond equally to all its citizens. Non-governmental organizations can take more time to think and decide when to act, while a government must respond much more quickly or else suffer political repercussions. Finally, non-governmental organizations provide varied responses to different situations, with a minimum of bureaucratic redtape, while government—an institutional structure—tends to group situations according to similarities and to standardize its responses.

Experience shows that, especially at the local level, it is possible to develop at least mutual tolerance and sometimes cooperation between governmental and non-governmental organizations, although the real potentials and limitations of the relationship must be realistically regarded. The possibility of achieving cooperative relations depends very much on the responsibilities, maturity, and openness of the people involved, especially on the governmental side. This possibility has been structurally increased by the decentralization of important public functions, especially education and health. Among other changes, this decentralization has increased the importance of local officials—and their individual personalities—in establishing or limiting cooperation. It is also likely to result in a greater variety of local opportunities.

Decentralization does imply a greater possibility for varying programmatic responses according to local conditions, but it does not necessarily imply greater local authority or political autonomy. The experience of non-governmental grassroots social programs has led those involved to define development as a comprehensive and integral process, including health, education, housing, employment, and technology, based largely on local resources. It is worth noting that this conception of integrated development so often articulated by NGOs is not so much a reflection of their own direct experience as it is of the experiences of the local population and community organizations, who do not limit themselves to sectorally defined conditions but rather are concerned with the overall quality of life in their area; strong local governments have traditionally acted as institutional defenders of integrated development. Simultaneously with the development of a local public sector, the present experience is producing a group of advocates, outside of the government structure, who argue for greater local authority in decision-making and who are defining a model of a stronger, more democratic civil society, and a stronger, autonomous local government not previously known in Chile.

Conclusion

The widespread existence of non-governmental and grassroots organizations involved in social policy programs is a surprising and important aspect of contemporary Chilean reality. Their activities have provided a number of significant contributions. They are improvements in living conditions for those who directly benefit from their immediate work; technical advances in the specific areas of their work; development of participatory work methodologies; experimental programs which can be carried out on an expanded scale; training and experience for a generation of community members and technical personnel; contributions to the development of society as a whole, including a possible alternative model of democratic development; strengthening awareness, by political and professional sectors, of the significance of a broad non-governmental sector concerned with social policy, regardless of the type of political regime in power; and finally, strengthening civil society as a whole, in that non-governmental institutions have assumed specific responsibilities in the search for viable solutions to the problems and basic needs of poor families.

Among the many issues still open are the need to evaluate the real effectiveness of these initiatives and their potential for expansion; to determine the forms of outside support (technical, material, financial) necessary to enable local groups to act without being overwhelmed; and, given the great instability of non-governmental groups, to find a way to provide greater security and continuity for their grassroots projects, as well as for the non-governmental social sector in general. In addition, larger scale pilot programs are necessary in order to adapt appropriate initiatives into social policy. These pilot programs should be tried out at a sub-national level, perhaps using the network of relationships between local government and non-governmental organizations that already exists.

The overwhelming need for social policies to benefit the mass of Chilean citizens, the need to try out micro programs on an intermediate scale, and the structural possibilities which now exist at the municipal level make it critically important to be alert for and take advantage of opportunities for cooperation which respect the autonomy and interests of all actors. As one state employee said in a workshop, "non-governmental organizations should not leave it to the state to adapt and expand their programs, rather they should seek to reorient social policy and take part in redesigning it."

Grassroots organizations in Chile today provide many lessons for social policy both within and outside of Chile. They are moreover a source of tremendous hope for the future. Exacty how or when a return to democracy will occur cannot be predicted, nor are grassroots organizations likely to be the main factor in bringing it about. But they are developing the model for an alternative social and political organization of Chilean society, for a richer democracy with deeper roots that addresses a wider range of issues, and for a greatly increased role for the Chilean people in determining their own destiny. Whether the lessons will be learned or lost is, at least in part, a question of social policy.

About the Contributors

Manuel Baquedano: Engineer and sociologist, University of Louvain, Belgium, Coordinator of CETAL. Doctorate in Sociology of Development. Member of the Executive Committee of SATIS (Socially Appropriate Technology International Information Services—a world network of appropriate technology centers), and member responsible for the Committee Representing Latin America.

Patricio Cariola: S.J., M.Ed. (Harvard). Director of CIDE (Center for Research and Development in Education). Former president of the Federation of Institutes of Education (FIDE-Secundaria). Co-editor of *La Educación Particular en Chile: Antecedentes y Problemas,* 1971. Editor of *La Educación en América Latina,* 1981.

Antonia Cepeda: Graduate of the School of Geography, University of Chile, 1976. Degree in Nursery Education, Catholic University of Chile, 1984. Work involves providing advice for institutions and training for community agents in the spheres of early education and programs for children in education through recreation and the expression of emotions.

Jorge Chateau: Sociologist, researcher at FLACSO. Studied at the Catholic University of Chile and the University of California, Santa Barbara. In recent years he has been working on a FLACSO program concerned with the problems of evaluating and systematizing social action projects.

Rosario Correa: Degree in Psychology, Catholic University of Chile, 1971, with experience in the design, development, and evaluation of early education programs (involving professionals and community agents) and in the provision of advice and training. Works with grassroots groups concerned with educational activities and community mental health, in order to develop their abilities and help them to become autonomous.

Charles Downs: Assistant Professor of Urban Planning, and Director of the Center for Social Policy and Planning in Developing Countries, at Columbia University, New York. Specializes in the study of the relationship between community participation, planning, and development at the local level.

Antonio Infante: Physician specializing in Public Health. Has worked both in the National Health Service and in non-governmental organizations, attempting to introduce perspectives developed in both sectors into the field of primary health care. At present working as medical advisor to the National

Council for Assistance for Schooling and Scholarships (JUNAEB) and to the Alternative Program for Extending Mother and Child Health. Coordinator of the Primary Health Care Collective of the Chilean Medical College.

Arno Klenner: Economist; assistant director of the Labor Economics Program (PET).

Arodys Leppe: Chemical Engineer, Master in Applied Sciences, University of Montreal, Canada. Previously worked as a researcher at L'Ecole Polytechnique.

María Teresa Marshall Degree in Social Work. Coordinator of the Primary Health Care and Community Education Network of CEAAL.

Francisca Molina: Degree in Nursery Education, University of Chile, 1982. Field of work: direct care for pre-school children from poor communities; training in early education for community agents.

Adriana Muñoz: Degree in Primary Education, Teacher Training College No 2, Santiago, 1970. Degree in Educational Sciences, specializing in learning problems, Heredia National University, Costa Rica, 1976. Fields of work: formal primary education; training and support for community agents; early education; development of the expression of emotions.

Luz María Perez: Degree in Social Work. In charge of the Community Health Program at the Pirque Health Center.

Alfredo Rojas: State Professor, University of Chile, M.Sc. (DIE, IPN, Mexico). Author of Volume 2 of the series, *Necesidades Esenciales en México* (Educación), 1982.

Giorgio Solimano: Physician, and past Chief Professor of Public Health and Nutrition and Director of the Center for Social Policy and Planning in Developing Countries, Columbia University, New York. His interest and experience is principally in the field of planning, implementation, and evaluation of health and nutrition programs in Latin America and the Caribbean. He is presently Director of the Health and Social Policy Program of the Christian Humanism Academy University, Santiago, Chile.

Ximena Valdés: Degree in Social Work, Catholic University of Chile, 1970; Master in Social Work, University of Iowa, 1976. Member of the Social Work Collective, with experience in the design and implementation of preventative mental health programs for Spanish-speaking minority groups (Boston), and in the design and implementation of education and social development programs for poor communities.

Humberto Vega: Economist; Director of the Labor Economics Program (PET).

Blanca Velasco: Economist, Master in Economic Sciences, specializing in human resources, University of Paris VIII. Contributor to Seminar on "The work process" at L'Ecole Normale Superieure, Paris, led by Benjamin Coriat. At present working as a researcher at TEKHNE, with responsibility for productive projects using appropriate technology.

Carlos Vergara: Degree in Sociology, Catholic University of Chile; studied for a Masters degree in Social and Population Studies (CELADE-FLACSO) and for a Doctorate in Sociology at the University of Warwick, U.K. He has taught at the Catholic University of Valparaiso and the Catholic University of Chile, with studies on state agencies responsible for social planning. He was a Consultant for the United Nations Children's Fund, UNICEF. He is now a researcher with SUR Professionales, one of the principle centers of social science research in Chile.

Luis Zúñiga: Degree in Sociology, University of Chile; post-graduate studies at the University of Chicago. Has worked as a Consultant for UNESCO, CELADE, and UNICEF, and at the University of Chile and the Catholic University of Chile. Until 1987, he was employed by the United Nations Children's Fund, UNICEF. He is now a researcher with CIDE and a member of the Health and Social Policy Program of the Christian Humanism Academy University, Santiago, Chile.

About the Organizations

Consejo de Educación de Adultos de América Latina (CEAAL—Latin American Council for Adult Education). The Council is a grouping of individuals, organizations and institutions whose objective is to promote Community Education for Adults in Latin America and the Caribbean using all possible methods: literacy programs, primary education, training, and all kinds of educational activities or processes which seek to understand reality in order to act on it. CEAAL is the regional representative of the International Adult Education Council, whose headquarters are in Toronto, Canada, and is recognized by UNESCO as a consultative body.

CEAAL brings together community activists, educationalists, researchers, and social scientists working with adults at the community level, and promotes discussion and exchange of experiences among people involved in adult education, through a variety of programs coordinated by the General Secretariat.

Center for Social Policy and Planning in Developing Countries, Columbia University, New York. The Center exists to obtain, analyze and interpret information to evaluate the impact of social policies implemented in developing countries and in ethnic minority communities in the United States. It also provides an international forum for the interdisciplinary discussion of these policies.

The Center pursues these objectives by giving institutional support for applied research projects, and by promoting, among other activities, both meetings between researchers and specialists in social policies, and the development of a information center. The Center prioritizes work with relevant individuals and institutions in the developing countries and promotes research and the training of graduate students both at Columbia University and abroad. Center for Social Policy and Planning in Developing Countries, Columbia University, 420 W 118th St., New York, N.Y. 10027.

Centro de Educación y Tecnología (CET—Center for Education and Technology). The main purpose of this Foundation is to promote and implement initiatives to dignify the work process, and to promote development, solidarity, and community organization by finding, testing, publicizing, and introducing new technologies which are inexpensive, easy to understand and effective in resolving the basic needs of the poorest sectors of both rural and urban populations.

The activities are carried out as programs at the local level, implemented in urban, semi-rural, and rural communities in different regions of the country. At a national level, training seminars are organized for technical staff from other NGOs, to look at alternative agriculture and social development. This work takes place at CET's Experimentation and Demonstration Centers in different regions of Chile. At a Latin American level, the organization has held seminars for technical staff from non-governmental institutions in Paraguay, Brazil, and Peru.

Educational materials are published as a series called "We can do it" ("Somos Capaces"). Some titles produced so far are: "Intensive Family Kitchen Gardens," "Organic Vegetable Gardens in the Countryside," "Homegrown Vegetables in Your Diet," and "Do-it-yourself Using Wood and Clay" (all published in Spanish).

Centro de Estudios en Tecnologías Apropiadas para América Latina (CETAL—Center for Studies in Appropriate Technologies for Latin America). The organization's work has focused on developing, publicizing and studying socially appropriate technology (SAT). This involves research into, development of, and dissemination, through education, of SAT that can help to satisfy the basic needs of our nations. Its specific objectives are to provide grassroots economic organizations with technical assistance and training for members in SAT; to contribute to the search for socially appropriate technological solutions to help overcome concrete social problems found among sectors of the population with few resources; to help draw up policies for development and use of appropriate technologies which contribute to projects for democratic development in Chile and the rest of Latin America; and to contribute to the communication, spread, and sharing of SAT within the Third World.

CETAL defines itself as an autonomous, democratic, nonaligned organization that gives support to the worst-off sectors in Chile. The organization was created in 1979 and is based in Valparaíso, in the V Region.

Centro de Investigación y Desarrollo de la Educación (CIDE—Center for Research and Development in Education). CIDE is a private, non-profit foundation created in 1965. It is associated with the Company of Jesus, whose Superior nominates the organization's Council.

CIDE's most important areas of activity are educational research and the development of community education programs. In both spheres, the institution concentrates its activities on the poorest sectors of the population, studying the relationship between schools and poor communities, and introducing educational programs to assist these sectors.

In over 20 years of work with the poorest social sectors, CIDE has accumulated a mass of experience and a methodological background in issues related to the family, children, and marginalized young people in Chile.

CREAS. CREAS is an interdisciplinary team, formed in 1984, to promote and support organization and development of the autonomous capacities of people in poor communities to resolve their own needs. The name CREAS is based on the ideas of Creation, Education, and Social Mobilization.

CREAS approaches its work from a theoretical and methodological perspective which takes into account education, social work, and mental health. The team's lines of action include technical and organizational support for groups and organizations engaged in work related to early education and remedial education in the community; technical and organizational support for regional organizations in the autonomous management of activities and local development; programs and activities to develop the ability to express emotions; and the preparation of educational support materials for the activities being carried out.

La Facultad Latinoamericana de Ciencias Sociales (FLACSO—Latin American Faculty of Social Sciences). This is an autonomous international organization that operates at a regional level and is constituted by the countries of Latin America and the Caribbean. Its purpose is to promote teaching and research in the field of the social sciences.

FLACSO was created in Santiago, Chile in 1957. The institution is governed by an International Agreement registered in the Secretariat of the United Nations, in accordance with article 102 of the Charter of the United Nations. At present, FLACSO functions in Chile as an independent academic center and carries out its work on the basis of a formal agreement with the Academy of Christian Humanism. FLACSO is also a member of the Regional Organization whose statutes govern its operations.

El Programa de Economía del Trabajo (PET—Labor Economics Program). This organization is part of the Academy for Christian Humanism, and carries out research and provides services for grassroots organizations. Its main purpose is to contribute to develop and strengthen the labor movement in Chile, in all its activities and expressions, through a combination of training, research, advice, extension of activities, and communications.

The organization's special concerns are the fields of economic policy, union organizations, and grassroots economic organizations. In recent years, it has been carrying out research and providing support for economic initiatives being taken in poor urban areas (*poblaciones*), principally in Santiago.

Centro de Experimentación en Tecnología Apropiada (TEKHNE—Center for Experimentation in Appropriate Technology). TEKHNE is a non-governmental organization dedicated to encouraging, developing, and spreading knowledge about and the use of appropriate technology. It seeks to satisfy some fundamental human needs through research and training activities, which are seen as a contribution to a participative and integrative social development project.

The work is divided into two technical areas, and an area of administrative support. The lines of work within each of these areas are: (1) *Diet*—food preservation, nutrition, organic family vegetable gardens, medicinal herbs; and (2) *Engineering and Projects*—solar energy, wind and water power, dendroenergy, management of productive projects using appropriate technology. Each of these lines of work includes the design, development, and testing of proposals, whether they are tools for immediate use or prototypes produced to meet specific demands.

